Van Gogh's Women

Van Gogh's Women

HIS LOVE AFFAIRS AND JOURNEY INTO MADNESS

DEREK FELL

CARROLL & GRAF PUBLISHERS
NEW YORK

VAN GOGH'S WOMEN
HIS LOVE AFFAIRS AND JOURNEY INTO MADNESS

Carroll & Graf Publishers
An Imprint of Avalon Publishing Group Inc.
245 West 17th Street
11th Floor
New York, NY 10011

AVALON
publishing group incorporated

First Carroll & Graf edition 2004

Library of Congress Cataloging-in-Publication Data is available.

ISBN: 0-7867-1425-5

Printed in the United States of America
Interior design by Maria Torres
Distributed by Publishers Group West

In memory of my mother,
Mary Woodhouse Fell (1917-2001)

CONTENTS

ACKNOWLEDGMENTS

My investigation into Vincent van Gogh's relationships with women was a lonely endeavor, spent mostly in libraries, where I read for long hours through a massive amount of fact, speculation, and comment. I was fortunate, though, to also enjoy the benefit of numerous experts—art historians, artists, psychologists, theologians, and the research staff at the Van Gogh Foundation, Amsterdam (whose helpfulness should not be considered an endorsement of this book, however)—in dealing with the enormous number of contradictions and confusion about the artist's life.

I value the support of my wife, Carolyn, on whom I first tested my theories of Vincent's love, rejection, and suicide. She also accompanied me to Tahiti to help me research Vincent's influence on Gauguin's Tahitian paintings, since Gauguin went there within a year of Vincent's death, to fulfill a promise to Vincent that he would.

I owe a huge debt of gratitude to Lawrence A. Decker, Ph.D., Doctor of Psychology, who read my initial draft and provided expert guidance in light of his experience and training as a specialist in family counseling. Dr. Decker served as a consultant on this project whenever psychological questions needed verification. (Dr. Decker received his doctorate from Brigham Young University and a Post-Doctoral Fellowship from the Menninger Foundation. He was formerly a Senior Vice President at Medco and a consultant to U.S. Healthcare.)

A special thanks to Adeline Vincotte, interpreter at the Office of Tourism d'Auvers-sur-Oise, for providing access to the department's library and helping me tie together a number of loose ends concerning Vincent's last days; and to my literary agent, Albert Zuckerman, who first sparked the idea of this book during a brainstorming session following publication of my earlier book *Van Gogh's Gardens.*

Frances Fisher, an independent professional editor, was kind enough to read my initial draft and make many excellent suggestions for improvement. Terry Swaine, neurotherapist, contributed freely of his expertise. My editors at Carroll & Graf, Claiborne Hancock and Peter Skutches, also contributed greatly to the final result.

For a more detailed explanation of my indebtedness to Robert G. Harrison, of Montreal, for permission to use his copyrighted translation of Vincent's letters, see the "Copyrights" page. He also played devil's advocate during my research.

AUTHOR'S NOTE

In the text, I have chosen to refer to Vincent van Gogh as Vincent rather than van Gogh, as he said in a letter to his brother from Arles: "In future my name ought to be put in the catalog as I sign it on the canvas, Vincent, and not van Gogh."

The text refers to numerous works by Vincent, and though the most important of these are shown in a color insert in the middle of this book, others can be seen in books and on the Internet. *Vincent Van Gogh: The Complete Paintings* (Taschen), by Ingo F. Walther and Rainer Metzger, is the best book for this purpose, while *www.vangoghgallery.com* is the best Web site. This incredibly comprehensive Web site also contains an excellent translation of Vincent's letters, including those to his brother Theo, his youngest sister Wilhelmina (Wil), and his sister-in-law Johanna (Jo). Another Web site I found invaluable, for insights into Vincent's Replacement Child affliction, is *www.psychematters.com.* Under the title *The Ghost in the Mother: Strange Attractors and Impossible Mourning,* Edward Emery, Ph.D., presents fourteen pages of psychoanalytical information about ghosting of the mother and being haunted by an unmourned presence.

*"I cannot live without love,
without a woman."*

Vincent van Gogh

INTRODUCTION

A woman is not old as long as she loves and is loved.

—Letter to Theo, July 31, 1874,
from Vincent's lodgings in London

In the summer of 1890, an hour by train from the sweltering heat of Paris, the riverside village of Auvers-sur-Oise was a haven of gentle breezes, its cobbled streets cooled by the shade of weeping willows. Boathouse clubs fronted the river, where men in straw boaters and women in long gauzy white dresses lazily paddled its mirror-smooth surface. Along a ridge of wooded hills, farmworkers' quaint thatched cottages contrasted with the new, architect-designed weekend residences of affluent Parisians, many of them Tudor-style timbered structures with orange pantile roofs.

This is where the visionary painters Charles Daubigny, Honoré Daumier, and Camille Corot—precursors to the Impressionists—had lived and painted their romantic landscapes. The father of Impressionism, Camille Pissarro, still lived nearby in an apple orchard. A youthful Paul Cézanne had lived in the village and studied under Pissarro's tutelage. Claude Monet had only recently moved north to Giverny, where he established his house and garden.

In this painters' paradise, even the sound of gunfire was little cause for alarm, as farmers with shotguns frequently protected their grain fields from marauding crows. Also, the hunting of small game was common among the locals.

And so, when the shimmering afternoon air of the amber wheat fields above the village was shattered by a single gunshot, nobody paid any attention. Nor did anyone notice the wounded man who stumbled downhill and staggered along a narrow back alley to his room at a tavern on the main avenue.

The man was 37-year-old Vincent van Gogh. A bullet was lodged against the wall of his stomach, and he was slowly dying with a smile on his face. When his landlord, Arthur Ravoux, spotted the trail of blood leading upstairs and found the painter curled up in a ball on his bed, he summoned Vincent's doctor and brother. The life of a great artist, at the peak of his powers and on the verge of artistic recognition, was drawing to a close.

But why? What prompted this man—so enthralled with his surroundings, so pleased at last with the progress of his art and his mental health—to shoot himself? The enigma has endured for more than a century. Only now, by examining Vincent's relationships with the women in his turbulent life, is it possible to unravel the mystery.

Most people think of Vincent van Gogh as the brilliant but disturbed artist who sliced off his ear. A lunatic, we are inclined to believe. Certainly Vincent's life was filled with contradictions, and today art historians, theologians, and psychologists continue to explore the perplexity of his genius, which was wrought out of a life marked by melodrama, bizarre love affairs, and mental anguish.

Vincent was born in the vicarage at Groot Zundert, a farming community in southern Holland, on March 30, 1853. For Europe this was a time of significant social change; in France it was known as la Belle Epoque—to signal a golden age of cultural and industrial development. The recent invention of the steam engine had made ships independent of the wind; railroads dramatically shortened travel time on land; and electric lighting became available to millions. Large cities saw the building of grand hotels, department stores, and wide boulevards. The opportunities for wealth were immense; across Europe and North America, industrialization spawned an affluent middle class with disposable income and leisure time. But the working class remained poor and continued to struggle against meager wages, job insecurity, and the need to work long hours to feed their families.

Born to middle-class Dutch parents, Vincent was the eldest of his siblings, three sisters and two brothers. He was not the firstborn, however; an older brother had died at birth. Vincent's father, Theodorus, a Calvinist pastor, ran a strict, autocratic household in which the redheaded, freckle-faced Vincent fit uncomfortably. An intense, sullen child with low self-esteem, he was prone to temper tantrums. He walked around awkwardly, with his head bent low. A family servant described him as being aloof, ill-mannered, and having the disposition of an old man. Nepotism gained him his first job—as a clerk in an uncle's art gallery in The Hague. He then moved to the firm's London office as an art dealer and made a promising start there, until his love for his landlady's daughter, Eugenie Loyer, was rejected. When she revealed that she was secretly engaged to a previous boarder, "He tried everything to break this engagement," wrote his future sister-in-law, Johanna, "but he did not succeed." This was the first in a series of disastrous romantic relationships that further damaged his already diminished sense of self-worth. "With this first great sorrow, his character changed," Johanna wrote in a memoir. "When he came home for the holidays he was thin, silent, dejected—a different being . . . he grew more and more silent and depressed, and also more and more religious."

In a letter to an artist friend, Anthon van Rappard, a year after her rejection, he recalled: "It remains a wound which I carry with me; it lies deep and cannot be healed. After years it will be the same as the first day."

Vincent wrote at length to three women in his life: his youngest sister, Wil; his sister-in-law, Jo; and his mother, Anna. Significantly, he addressed not only his three female siblings and Jo as sisters, but he also addressed prostitutes in this same way, finding similarities in their work and his life as a struggling artist.

Volumes have been written about Vincent's relationship with Theo, whose considerable financial support enabled his older brother to pursue his art for more than a decade. Indeed, thousands of pages of correspondence between the two of them provide a remarkable chronicle of Vincent's thoughts and daily struggles in his arduous attempt to gain artistic recognition. No book, however, has yet focused on Vincent's relationships and correspondence with the women in his life. This is surprising, because these relationships, and the letters he wrote about them, shed light on some of the most puzzling and intriguing aspects of his life.

In his astonishing portraits and startling landscapes—some of them dazzling in their brilliance, others in gloomy shades and tones—the range and intensity of Vincent's emotions are dramatically manifest. The paint is applied with passion—in volcanic colors, ferocious swipes, daubs, and swirls that the force of his personality is evident. Painted into every canvas, consciously or subconsciously, is Vincent's personal symbolism, which bears poignant spiritual and psychological messages. In one of his last paintings, *Wheat Field with Crows* (July 1890), completed just days before he shot himself, dark clouds seem to reflect Vincent's overwhelming depression, while a flock of black crows suggests a foreboding of death.

In the following pages, the examination of Vincent's letters about the women in his life helps clear away much of the speculation surrounding his death. Vincent's heartfelt words not only express the hopes and disappointments in his relationships with women; they also illuminate the dark downward course of his journey into madness. In the letters, too, lie clues to the reason for Vincent's actions one beautiful summer afternoon, when a gunshot suddenly interrupted the songs of skylarks spiraling high overhead.

Chapter One

THE
REPLACEMENT CHILD

Etten, Holland, November–December 1881

The earliest known drawing by Vincent van Gogh was made in 1864 when he was not yet eleven years old. Vincent gave the drawing of a barn to his father for his forty-second birthday.

Amsterdam, both the industrial and cultural heart of Holland, is its largest, most progressive city. In 1877, after working for three months as a bookseller in Dordrecht, Vincent traveled to Amsterdam to study for a theological career. An uninhibited young person's city, Amsterdam was always thronged with students who found release from their grueling studies through nonstop parties, curbside flirting at outdoor cafés, and an exotic nightlife in dance halls. But the twenty-four-year-old Vincent condemned all this behavior as sinful. He kept his eyes downcast and his nose in the Bible. He also remained celibate, as his clergymen professors instructed.

A roommate, P. C. Görlitz, wrote this impression of Vincent at that time: "He was a singular man with a singular appearance into the bargain. He was well made and had reddish hair which stood up on end; his face was homey and covered in freckles, but changed and brightened wonderfully when charged with enthusiasm, which happened often enough. Van Gogh provoked laughter repeatedly by his attitude and behavior, for everything he did and thought and felt, and his way of living, was different from that of others of his age. And then his face always had an abstract expression, pondering, deeply serious, melancholy. But when he laughed, he did so heartily and with gusto, and his whole face brightened."

The bookstore owner, W. Braat, considered him a loner, "always a bit unsociable . . . whenever anyone looked at what he was doing he was either translating the Bible into several languages or making sketches . . . silly pen-and-ink drawings, a little tree with a lot of branches and side branches and twigs, nobody ever saw anything else in them."

Vincent's theological career was unsettled from the start. Because he considered ancient Greek and Latin dead languages that bore no relevance to missionary work, he refused to learn them, and thus he failed the university entrance exams required by a mission school in Laeken, Belgium. Another theological college, the School of Evangelization in Brussels, took a chance with the recalcitrant student and assigned him to an evangelical post in a remote coal-mining community located in the grim Borinage district of Belgium. Vincent found the plight of the miners disturbing. He himself descended into the mine and witnessed firsthand the miserable conditions under which they worked: often standing for hours in freezing waist-deep water, they labored at loosening the coal with their picks in the dim light of oil lamps. The coal dust not only was susceptible to explosion, it also invaded the miners' lungs and caused asphyxiation. Children of both sexes scurried like rabbits about the galleries, where they filled buckets with loose coal that was then tipped into dumpsters and pulled away by pit ponies. The miners worked long shifts and were poorly paid; if an accident or black lung rendered them unfit for work, they were simply dismissed and struck from the rolls.

When an explosion in the spring of 1879 buried many of the workers alive and injured others, Vincent worked himself to the point of exhaustion in order to help in tending the wounded and comforting the bereaved. When the miners decided to strike for better working conditions, he found himself embroiled once more in their cause. To show support for their struggle, Vincent gave his comfortable lodgings to a homeless person and moved to a hut without heat. He slept on straw, and he extended his compassion to insects that he rescued from the spiderwebs in his room and mice that he fed with dishes of milk. He refused to change his clothes or brush his teeth; he fasted and blackened his face with coal dust. It mattered little that Vincent willingly underwent such self-imposed sacrifices out of sympathy for his impoverished congregation; the miners complained that he was mad, and he was dismissed.

Still he hung on. He administered comfort and care without pay. Impressed by the manner in which the *London Illustrated News* documented social injustice with on-the-scene renderings by artists, Vincent sketched the miners at their labors. Early in 1880 he began to admire the work of French artist Jules Breton, whose paintings of peasants celebrated their humble lives and hard field labor. Breton's bucolic renderings of female peasants in rural landscapes bathed with atmospheric lighting became popular among American collectors in particular. Eager to meet Breton but unable to pay the train fare, Vincent walked sixty miles from his lodgings in Guesmes, Belgium, to Courrieres, a small village near Calais, France—a week's journey there and back. But when he arrived at Breton's studio, Vincent's courage failed him. Disappointed by the modest bourgeois appearance of Breton's newly built studio, he did not even knock on the door to introduce himself. He simply turned around and walked the sixty miles back home. Short of money, he slept in open fields or a hayloft; occasionally he bartered a sketch for a crust of bread. "He suffered so much fatigue that his health never really recovered," Jo wrote. There was one consolation: he found that the scenic journey had stimulated his creative energy and desire to express himself.

After two years with the miners, Vincent left the Borinage for Brussels, where he took up sketching with a new fervor and briefly attended formal art classes. He studied anatomy, drew from living models in the studio, and taught himself perspective by sketching local historic architecture. Meanwhile, the wretched time Vincent had spent in the Borinage had cooled his intense religious passion. A fire and brimstone mentality in the beginning, it began to change to a more reasonable view of spirituality. "I said to myself . . . I will take up my pencil . . . I will go on with my drawing. From that moment on everything has seemed transformed for me."

In the spring of 1881, concerned about his living expenses, Vincent returned to Holland and moved in with his parents at the vicarage in Etten. He yearned to become an artist, and, in exchange for continued financial support from his brother Theo, a successful art dealer in Paris, Vincent surrendered to him all rights to his art, in the hope that Theo could also sell his work.

Encouraged by his mother, whose favorite pastime was painting wildflowers, Vincent had sketched the countryside intermittently since the age of nine. The time that he had spent among the Belgian miners now awakened him to the similar hardships and poverty suffered by farming families and the elderly around Etten. Inspired by French artist Jean-François Millet's paintings of fieldworkers, he began documenting local peasant life. He sketched faces etched by labor and weather, humble thatched cottages, and the bleak, flat fenlands where peasant families barely eked out a living growing potatoes.

In the summer, Vincent's recently widowed first cousin, Kee Vos, visited the van Gogh family with her young son, Jan.

Occasionally she accompanied Vincent on his sketching excursions to the countryside. What on her part may have been a simple interest in Vincent's work, or mere companionship, misdirected him down a romantic path. She was still grieving the loss of her husband; so, when Vincent declared his love for her, she was more insulted than moved, and she saw in Vincent's declaration a pathetic desperation rather than true love. Kee firmly rejected him with the words "No, never never!" and returned immediately to Amsterdam to live with her father, Vincent's uncle, the Reverend Johannes Stricker.

Although the law in Holland has since changed, the marriage that Vincent wanted with Kee, a marriage between first cousins, was then against the law and against the teachings of the Bible, for it was tantamount to incest. Kee was also six years older than Vincent and considerably more mature. A dour, matronly woman, she dressed in mourning with a white lace cap on her head. She in fact bore a remarkable resemblance to Vincent's mother—and, like her, Kee too had lost a child at birth.

Vincent's thirty-five pages of letters in which he asserts and explores his love for Kee are so farcical in their expressions of profound despair and absurd optimism that they are worthy of Shakespeare at his most comical and romantic. As Shakespeare, in Sonnet 18, found a summer's day to be a reason for optimism in love, so Vincent saw a mild spell as a sign that Kee's mood was softening. He even quotes Shakespeare's *As You Like It* in a letter to Theo at this time: "And that 'no, never never' is not as sweet as spring air, but bitter, bitter as nipping winter frost. 'This is no flattery,' as Shakespeare would say."

Obstinately, Vincent clung to his belief that Kee was the woman he would cherish and remain faithful to for the rest of his life—the woman he epitomized in the phrase "She, and no other."

Before Kee was widowed, Vincent had visited her and her husband and small son in Amsterdam. He had admired the idyll of their cozy household, and he yearned for similar domestic comforts: Kee knitting by the hearth, her husband reading a newspaper after the evening meal, little Jan sleeping in an adjacent room. He wrote: "When one sees them sitting together in the evening . . . they are devoted to each other and one can readily see that where Love dwells the Lord commands his blessing."

When Kee's husband died, Vincent wanted desperately to restore to her the security and contentment that, in his mind, she had lost. Furthermore, he believed that he had found in Kee the only woman in the world capable of fulfilling his own desires for a domestic life. He wrote to Theo, linking his vision of domesticity to his art, "I want to go through the joys and sorrows of domestic life in order to paint it from my experience." Vincent's anguish over Kee's rejection is evident in the many letters he wrote to Theo as he strove to find a way back into her heart. He would present scenarios for conversations with Theo in which Vincent would anticipate his brother's objections to his reasoning and strike them down before they could be stated. Vincent also tried to manipulate his parents' views of his romantic plight by using Theo, whose opinions they valued, as a conduit; and he enlisted Wil as a spy to report any change in Kee's determination not to see him. He went so far as to justify his pursuit of Kee by comparing his ardor and devotion to romantic situations in literary works like Charlotte Brontë's *Jane Eyre,* a classic love story that, in his view, supported his patience and persistence.

The painful letters continued over a period of three months. The first one, from Etten, dated November 3, 1881, began:

Dear Theo,

There is something on my mind that I must tell you about. You may perhaps know something of it already and it will not be news to you. I wanted to let you know that I fell so much in love with Kee Vos this summer than I can find no other words for it than, "It is just as if Kee Vos were the closest person to me and I the closest person to Kee Vos." But when I told her this, she replied that . . . she could never return my feelings.

I was in a tremendous dilemma about what to do. Should I resign myself to her "no, never never," or . . . should I keep in good heart and not give up?

I chose the latter. And up to now I do not regret this approach, though I am still up against that "no, never never." [November 3, 1881.]

Vincent tied his ardor for Kee to the success of his artistic endeavors. His attachment to her, he believed, helped him keep depression at bay and thus accounted for a vast improvement in his work. Though one uncle suggested that he take Kee's rejection lightly, the rest of the family stood adamantly opposed to any attempt by Vincent to meet with her again. Vincent rationalized that the family objected only because they thought that if he and Kee did communicate, Kee might change her mind. He concluded, too, that the only reason his family disapproved of their union was because he was poor and didn't "earn at least a thousand guilders a year." Still, he asserted he was not trying to force the issue, as "forcing is senseless in love." Free discussion, on the other hand, seemed perfectly reasonable: "A year of keeping in touch with each other would be beneficial for her and for me," he wrote, "and yet the older people have really dug their heels in on this point."

Vincent vowed to do all that he could to bring himself closer to Kee, and to the possibility of at least an hour's discourse. It was his intention

> To go on loving her
> Until in the end she loves me.

In his anguish and frustration, he hoped that Theo was in love too: "I hope you are," he declared, "for believe me, even its little miseries have their value. One is sometimes in despair, there are moments when one seems to be in hell. . . ."

In a subsequent letter from Etten, Vincent asked Theo if he was astonished to learn that Vincent deemed his love to be serious and passionate enough not to be chilled even by "no, never nevers."

> I suppose far from astonishing you, this will seem very natural and reasonable. For love is something so positive, so strong, so real that it is as impossible for one who loves to take back that feeling as it is to take his own life. If you reply to this by saying, "But there are people who put an end to their own life," I simply answer, "I really do not think I am a man with such inclinations." [November 7, 1881.]

He then compared Kee's rejection to a block of ice that his heart would have to thaw: "If I try to make it thaw and disappear, who can object to that? What physical science has taught them that ice cannot be thawed is a puzzle to me." Strengthened by his metaphor, Vincent spurned his family's attempts to cool his ardor: "They occupy themselves with trying to wrench the ice from my breast; unconsciously they throw *more cold water* on my ardent love than they are aware." Yet, he insisted, "no amount of cold water" could cool his love, not even encouragements to

Kee that she cease her mourning, improve her appearance, and accept another, richer, suitor. Nor would he respond with anything but anger to the suggestion that he and Kee remain no more than "brother and sister," so that he might pursue a more socially acceptable relationship.

Vincent's parents accused him of weakness, passion, and stupidity. In the same letter to Theo, Vincent defended himself against their charges. He also made an extremely revealing admission:

> Let this my weakness be my strength. I will be dependent on "her, and no other"; even if I could, I should not want to be independent of *her.* But she has loved another and her thoughts are always in the past; and her conscience seems to bother her even at the thought of a possible new love. But there is a saying, and you know it, "one must have loved, then unloved, then loved again."
>
> I saw that she was always thinking of the past and buried herself in it with devotion. Then I thought, Though I respect the feeling and though that deep grief of hers touches and moves me, yet I think there is some fatalism in it.
>
> So it must not weaken my heart, but I must be resolute and firm, like a steel blade. [November 7, 1881.]

The word *mother* might be substituted for all references to Kee in this passage, as Lawrence Decker, Ph.D., clinical psychologist, points out to illustrate Vincent's perception of Kee as a mother substitute. *"I will be dependent on her and no other"* recalls Vincent's psychological history of living with an emotionally remote mother. *"But she loved another and her thoughts are always in the past"* could apply as much to his mother's chronic mourning over a dead child as to Kee's widowly bereavement.

"I saw that she was always thinking of the past and buried herself in it with devotion" reads like a subconscious evocation of his mother's pious withdrawal into the past, while *"That deep grief of hers touches and moves me, yet I think there is a fatalism in it"* echoes his mother's long grieving over her dead infant son. These allusions provide the first clear clue to the deep hurt Vincent experienced in his mother's grief over the death of her firstborn child—a boy she had named Vincent—and to the profundity of pain he felt as a "replacement child," to use the term preferred by psychologists. Indeed, he was even named after the dead child. Vincent constantly craved to be loved for himself, yet he bore his dead brother's name—a circumstance that did not enable him to ease his mother's mourning or to gain her love for himself. Vincent must have suffered early from a feeling of abandonment that few of us could ever imagine, and his extreme sensitivity to emotional rejection appears to have exacerbated the innate personality disorders that would eventually drive him to the depths of despair.

Vincent described his childhood as "gloomy and cold and sterile." He wrote that his mother did not love him enough; that Theo was the one who comforted her and the one she found worthy to be comforted by her.

Anne Stiles Wylie, writing about Vincent's infancy in the bulletin of the Van Gogh Museum in 1975, explained that the psychological factors put in motion by this so-called Replacement Child Syndrome can assume a variety of dynamic positions. "The mother's guilt may be displaced on the new baby, or he may assume the melancholy into which a mother's mourning is often transformed," states Wylie. "From his first hours the new baby may be challenged to live up to unrealistic standards of behavior and success: dirtying his diapers is hardly part of a mother's fantasy of how the dead child would have pleased her had he lived." Whatever the weight of Vincent's psychological burden, Wylie concludes that the first Vincent's grave was a daily symbolic reminder to his namesake of the special forces that had shaped, and would continue to shape, his destiny.

Dr. Decker summarizes the problem at Vincent's core as follows: "The tragedy of Vincent is that he was shrouded under the force this dead brother exerted on him, and not free to become his own person. In fact, he was in an impossible situation, for whenever he tried to be himself, he would betray the perfect image of his deceased brother, for whom he was nominated by his mother to replace. Poor Vincent felt condemned to be some approximation of himself and not the object of his mother's true affection. Vincent could never be good enough in his own right, and would always sense that something was wrong with him that couldn't be identified. There was an impossible longing to know himself, which could never happen because he was carrying around the ghost of his brother. He was condemned to be the longed-for other."

Decker identifies a second major problem for Vincent: "His early life set up an impossible longing for the kind of unconditional and boundless love that only a mother could provide. He would forever be incapable of awakening the part of his mother who was lost in a mournful swoon over her beloved stillborn child. He could never repair the damage. He would always be the exiled third, the endless witness to others' successes. He would always choose impossible love objects, and idolize them."

A third problem for Vincent, according to Decker, was born of his impossible longing for unconditional love. "Rejected over and over again, Vincent tried to come to grips with the anger he felt whenever threatened with abandonment. He was sensitized to this, of course, by not having a chance to be nurtured unconditionally by his mother. His acts of violence were all in response to threatened rejection, and were the internalization of aggression felt towards those who threatened him. He roasted his hand over a flame, cut off his ear, and shot himself in the stomach, all following anger at the rejection he received from people he loved."

Edward Emery, Ph.D., training and supervising analyst at Westchester Institute for Training in Psychoanalysis and Psychotherapy, in a paper entitled *The Ghost of the Mother: Strange Attractors and Impossible Mourning,* wrote that "ghosting" by the mother—treating a second child as a replacement—damages the replacement child by burdening it with the mother's *impossible mourning,* her refusal to let go of the loss of the first child, and *impossible longing,* her desire that the second child replace her loss. Vincent's mother, Anna, became pregnant with him barely three months after delivering a stillborn child, her first, and Vincent was born exactly one year after her dead baby. She saw Vincent as the second coming, the incarnation of the dead child she idolized and preserved in her subconscious.

Anna probably became disappointed in Vincent around the time he turned two, when his demands as a normal, healthy child would have spoiled her fantasy of Vincent as the embodiment of her perfectly imagined firstborn. As Vincent failed to ease the pain of her loss, she descended deeper into depression and left young Vincent confused about his identity. Abandoned by his mother as she withdrew from him into melancholia, Vincent could neither redeem her nor esteem himself. He could only sense his failure to assuage her impossible mourning and to fulfill her impossible longing. His rejection by his mother appears to have engendered his lifelong quest for the perfect, nurturing love that he ardently desired.

During his infatuation with Kee, "He became irritable and nervous," Jo writes. "His relations with his parents became strained, and in December, after a violent altercation with his father, he left suddenly for The Hague." Van Rappard, who befriended Vincent in Brussels, also noted Vincent's tendencies toward violence when he wrote: "Vincent used to flare up so often and was so irritable, but he still deserved friendship and admiration for his noble mind and high artistic qualities."

Dr. Emery, reporting on studies into the dynamics of replacement-child relationships, also observes that a replacement child will often yearn for an impossible perfect love—one of intense, uncontrollable passion—and will usually respond with violence whenever perceptions of neglect or emotional rejection occur.

Adding to Vincent's boyhood confusion and emotional pain was the distressing fact that the dead Vincent was lying in a graveyard adjacent to the family's rectory garden, so that daily the living Vincent could see the gravestone inscribed with his name and birthdate—a sight that could only further foster his confusion over his personal identity and his preoccupation with death. Perhaps more damaging, though, was the agonizing ritual of mourning that Vincent's mother had established: every Sunday she took young Vincent by the hand to visit her dead child's grave, which she decorated with flowers. The gravestone became a constant reminder to Vincent of what he wasn't—the perfect Vincent—and may even have fostered the perception that his mother considered him dead. Could anything have been more dreadful for a developing child to endure?

"To be haunted is to be caught up in a web of exclusionary images," according to Emery. This condition, with its sense of isolationism so characteristic of Vincent's plight, might well have prompted the sort of sentiments he expressed in a letter to Theo three years after his infatuation with Kee: "Involuntarily, I have become more or less a kind of suspect person in the family, at least somebody they do not trust, so how could I in any way be of use to anyone? Therefore, above all, I think the best and most reasonable thing for me to do is to go away and keep at a convenient distance, so that I cease to exist for you at all." Vincent's conclusion here probably mirrors his childhood perception of himself, for he had always felt different from his siblings and other children. Incomplete, ultrasensitive to teasing and criticism, he preferred to be alone and became increasingly more introverted. While other children played together, he stood apart. Or he took long, solitary walks in the countryside, where he read and sketched. His sister Elizabeth described him as being intensely serious and uncommunicative: "Not only were his little sisters and brothers like strangers to him, he was a stranger to himself."

Vincent would never hold that "stranger" in high esteem—he constantly put himself down as a misfit in later life—but he did accord the "nobody" some redemption, as he wrote in a letter to Theo explaining his artistic goal:

> What am I in most people's eyes? A nonentity, or an eccentric and disagreeable man—somebody who has no position in life and never will have, in short the lowest of the low. Very well, even if this were true, then I should want my work to show what is in the heart of an eccentric and such a nobody. [July 21, 1882.]

Responding to suggestions that he should get a paying job while trying to make a living as an artist, Vincent wrote to Theo: "I should be very glad if you could see me something more than an idle fellow. Because there are two kinds of idleness, which are a great contrast to each other. There is the man who is idle from laziness and from lack of character, from the baseness of his nature. If you like, you may take me for such a one." Vincent, however, rejects such a perception of himself and offered, instead, a darker self-analysis: "On the other hand there is the idle man who is idle in spite of himself, who is inwardly consumed by a great longing for action but does nothing, because it is impossible for him to do anything, because he seems to be imprisoned in a cage.... Such a man does not always know what he could do, but instinctively feels, I am good for something.... There is something inside me. What can it be?"

As Vincent became more isolated from society, he began to pour all his energy into painting. Like his mother, he painted flowers in an attempt, in Decker's view, to soothe her pain. Yet he continually failed to gain his mother's approval and win her love. What is apparent in his letter to Theo is that painting enabled him to quell the pain of rejection and advance toward self-acceptance, as it provided him the means of expression: "This is my ambition, which is, in spite of everything, founded less on anger than on love, more on serenity than on passion. It is true that I am often in the greatest misery, but still there is a calm pure harmony and music inside me." In art Vincent found sanity, but he also sought sanity in love. That quest led to his extreme attachment to Kee. She represented serenity, harmony, music, and calm: a motherly kind of love on which he could be dependent. "I will be dependent on her and no other," he wrote of the solace he hoped to find in an engagement to her. However unrealistic his love for Kee may seem, the bottomless well of emotional need from which it sprang was very real.

The life of an artist can be a lonely one. Shouldering an

easel and lugging palettes and boxes of paints, the solitary Vincent wandered through the countryside in search of subjects for his canvases. So he would naturally be pleased when Kee voluntarily accompanied him on his sketching and painting forays. One can imagine her quietly sewing or knitting while Vincent sat at his easel and her son hunted for birds' nests in the hedgerows. The image of the three of them sitting comfortably together and harmoniously pursuing their individual interests might have inspired Vincent to imagine himself married to her. His desire to win her love, despite her continued mourning for her husband, could have been fueled by a subconscious wish to see her released from the memory of her husband in the same way he always wanted to free his mother from the ghost of her firstborn. The pain Vincent felt over Kee's rejection appears to echo the pain caused by his mother's misdirected love. Behind Vincent's perceived need for Kee lay the neediness of a child starved of maternal love, a child crying out to be loved for himself and equating the want of that love with death.

Vincent's entire love life was characterized by this subconscious yearning for a mother substitute. He was drawn to older women, and his desire to be their savior was involuntary: he had been conditioned for the role from childhood. In particular, Vincent responded to women who, like his mother, seemed to need a ghost expunged from their lives—the memory of a dead husband, for instance, in the case of Kee.

Although Vincent wrote that Kee's "no, never never" was at first "as terrible a blow as a death sentence," he remained confident about the positive effect she would have on his art; he had no doubt whatever that his progress as a painter was linked to his love for Kee: "I think that nothing awakens us to the reality

of life so much as true love. . . . For indeed when a man falls seriously in love, it is the discovery of a new hemisphere."

Days later, Vincent wrote to Theo again. Before pouring out
his mounting agony over Kee's rejection, he expressed his disappointment in Theo for writing a letter to their parents in
which he seemed to take their side. Vincent then went on to
chide his brother for being a man of business, with no intimate,
tender feelings for a woman in his life:

> Though you have gone pretty far in the world without a "she, and no
> other," though you stand firmly in your shoes without a "she, and no
> other," though you know how to bring off business deals without a
> "she, and no other," though you are a man of will power, energy and
> character without a "she, and no other," though you have knowledge
> of men and experience without a "she, and no other," though you have
> high spirits, buoyancy and courage without a "she, and no other,"
> though you dare to take sides and hate halting between two opinions
> . . . yet you will get further in the world, stand more firmly in your
> shoes, be a man of more will power, energy and character, obtain
> more knowledge of men and experience, have higher spirits, more
> buoyancy and courage, take sides more decidedly, be more averse to
> halting between two opinions, to wavering, oscillation etc., than you
> have until now as soon as you have somebody, to whom "she, and no
> other" then applies. In short, you will be more yourself *with* an hon-
> estly meant and deeply felt "she, and no other" than *without* the same.
> [November 9-10, 1881.]

Vincent's repetition of the phrase "she, and no other" here provides a significant clue to his ideal conception of love. At first
the repetition seems to be merely a rhetorical means of rein-
forcing his belief in monogamous love and lifelong fidelity, but

Dr. Decker believes the emphasis on *"no other"* further suggests Vincent's imagination of a perfect love between himself and Kee *without the ghost of her husband,* like the love he desired between himself and his mother *without the ghost of her firstborn.*

Having lectured Theo on the need for a wife free of hindrances, he hammered home the need for a home of comfortable domesticity. Vincent acknowledged the solace of having parents to go home to, but he asserted: "There is a resting place better, more necessary, more indispensable than our home with our parents, however good, however necessary, however indispensable it may be—and that is our own hearth and home with our respective 'she, and no other.'" Then he issued Theo a challenge: "There you are, O man of business, closing profitable deals, your biggest deal—your own home with your own 'she, and no other.'"

> In my opinion this is the point you would do well to bear in mind, the stimulant which more than any other "tonic" will keep alive your courage, strength, energy and love of life, and renew them more and more every day. . . . Do not forget you are twenty-six, and in "the season of renewal." Close the biggest deal of your life! Renew yourself radically by . . . looking at girls more seriously and attentively, and be very careful to find out if *your* "she, and no other" is not among them. [November 9, 1881.]

Vincent continued in a more shocking vein. Asserting Kee's rejection to be the result of some internal abnormality, he likened himself to a surgeon operating on her:

> That very thing convinces me that there was some fatal disease . . .
> of burying herself too much in the past; now a crisis of indignation

follows, but the surgeon laughs up his sleeve and says, "Touché!" This is just between ourselves, however, Theo—she must not know that I laughed up my sleeve over the result of the knife's thrust. Toward her I am of course more or less repentant: "Did I hurt you? Oh, how brusque and rough I was! How could I be so?" That is my attitude toward her. [November 9, 1881.]

It is astounding that Vincent should take such pleasure in the idea of metaphorically cutting Kee open with a surgeon's knife in order to save her, especially in view of the fact that many years later, at a moment of rejection, he would use a razor to threaten his friend Paul Gauguin, then turn the blade on himself. Although Vincent expresses elation in the success of his "surgery" on Kee, he is cautionary, for her cancer—"the fatal evil of burying herself in the past"—may grow back again. He wrote:

I should like to shout with glee; but I must not show it, and must attack her again in some other way. But how to approach her, how to come near her? I must do it someday quite unexpectedly and take her unawares. For if I do not stick with it, then the fatal evil of burying herself in the past will come back with sevenfold strength, and yet to love more is such a good thing, and worth all the efforts of one's soul. [November 9, 1881.]

It would appear that in Vincent's psyche, Kee shared her evil disease with Vincent's mother, who also buried herself in the past and who withdrew from her son—in essence, rejecting him to withdraw into an exclusionary world of grief and loss. Vincent believed that by helping the widowed Kee overcome her mourning, he would not only save her from the same fate as his mother but also spare himself her rejection and thus make himself more complete. Significantly, in his next sentence his thoughts shifted to his mother, whom he bitterly criticized. A word from her on his behalf, he believed, might have made Kee more amenable, but his mother's refusal to get involved "cut off every opportunity for me." Instead, his mother offered him a face full of pity and comforting words. He told Theo how she prayed that he might receive strength for resignation, and how he wished that rather than a beautiful prayer, she had given him the chance to have an intimate conversation with her.

A few days later—still in the month of November—Vincent mailed a fourth letter to Theo, in which he confided his intention to visit Kee in Amsterdam and swore Theo to secrecy. Projecting onto Kee's father the fearful specter of his own father, he imagined the Reverend Stricker as a monster, as a man who could assume unheard-of, quite gigantic proportions. Whatever the danger Vincent perceived, though, he stood determined and ready to confront this formidable figure.

All fathers of girls possess a "key to the front door," wrote Vincent. He described the key as a very terrible weapon, with which fathers could open and shut the front door like Saints Peter and Paul guarding the gates of heaven. But he rationalized that while the Reverend Stricker could lock the door to his house, doing so would not necessarily lock the door to his daughter's heart. "Only God and love alone can open or shut a woman's heart," he told Theo. Stricker was not the last obstinate father with a "key to the front door" that Vincent would encounter.

However he rationalized it, Vincent had essentially been locked out of Kee's heart. His profound anguish over this impasse continued to produce intense feelings of frustration and self-analysis, and in yet another November letter he again equated lack of love with death: "Without love, a man cannot survive." Then he recalled the emotional toll of another occasion when his love was rejected—by Eugenie Loyer, the beautiful nineteen-year-old daughter of his landlady in London. At the time, Vincent had been twenty.

> What kind of love was it that I felt when I was twenty? It is difficult to define—my physical passions were very weak then, perhaps because of a few years of great poverty and hard work. But my intellectual passions were strong, meaning that without asking anything in return, without wanting any pity, I wanted only to give, but not to receive. Foolish, wrong, exaggerated, proud, rash—for in love one must not only give, but also take; and, reversing it, one must not only take but also give. Whoever deviates either to the right or left falls, there is no help for it. So I fell, but it was a wonder I ever got up again. What helped me recover my balance more than anything else was reading practical books on physical and moral diseases. I got a deeper insight into my own heart and also into that of others. Gradually I began to love my fellow men again, myself included, and more and more my heart and soul—which for a time had been withered, blighted and stricken through all kinds of deep misery—revived. And the more I turned to reality, and mingled with people, the more I felt new life reviving in me, until at last I met *her*. [November 12, 1881.]

Revived though he was by his love for Kee, Vincent concluded that it would be wrong to continue to pursue her in the face of her refusals; he had made that mistake once before. Alluding to his failure with Eugenie, he told Theo: "I gave up on a girl and she married another, and I went away, far from her, but kept her in my thoughts always. Fatal."

A few months before he declared his love for Eugenie, in October 1873, Vincent wrote to a married couple, Carolien and

Willem van Stockum, whom he had befriended in The Hague. In the letter, Vincent described his ideal love interest, paraphrasing a romantic passage from a book by Jules Michelet entitled *Amour et la Femme:*

> From here I see a lady, I see her walk pensively in a not very large garden, bereft of its flowers, early in the season, but sheltered, as you see them behind our cliffs in France or the dunes of Holland. The exotic shrubs have already been put back into the conservatory. The fallen leaves reveal a number of statues. An artistic luxury which contrasts a little with the lady's very simple, modest, dignified dress, of which the black (or gray) silk is almost perceptibly brightened by a lilac ribbon.
>
> But haven't I already seen her in the museums of Amsterdam or The Hague? She reminds me of a lady by Philippe de Champaigne *(Woman in Mourning)* who took my heart, so candid, so honest, sufficiently intelligent, yet simple, without the cunning to extricate herself from the ruses of the world. This woman has remained in my mind for twenty years, persistently coming back to me, making me say: "But what was she called? What happened to her? Did she know some happiness? And how did she cope with life?" [October 1873.]

Vincent was obsessed with this image of an intelligent woman in mourning. Kee certainly fit the description. So did Eugenie Loyer, in an oblique way. Without even a period of courtship, Vincent built up a fantasy of a love relationship with Eugenie, and he was crushed when his declaration of love was rejected. Though Eugenie was not a widow, her mother was and fit the description of the woman in black perfectly. Photographs of Eugenie show her to be a beautiful, elegant young woman, not at all his idealized vision of the perfect woman, compared to her mother, whom he also loved.

The following statement from a letter Vincent wrote to Theo at the time would appear to support this claim: "There is no old woman as long as she loves and is loved." A theater production that played in London and New York, *Vincent in Brixton,* was in fact based on Vincent's love for the mother. Considering Vincent's penchant for older women, and the fact that he made such a profound statement about older women at the age of twenty, a stronger love between Vincent and Eugenie's widowed mother seems plausible. However, Vincent claimed that his love interest was a girl who had married another, which would point to her daughter Eugenie.

Vincent was happy with the Loyers. They treated him with kindness, they offered him the solace of a peaceful household, and he undoubtedly enjoyed sitting before the hearth with the mother and daughter in the evening, with Mrs. Loyer fussing over him, engaging him in intelligent conversation, with Eugenie perhaps knitting or reading quietly beside the fire, but always attentive to her mother's comfort.

In a letter to his sister Anna, dated January 6, 1874, written following Eugenie's rejection and shortly before he left the Loyer household, Vincent reveals that he loved *both* women. Anna wanted to work in England, and he urged her to visit the Loyers to see for herself that they bore him no grudge, that they were a respectable family and not a household that Vincent's father considered "full of secrets." Vincent said "I'll say nothing more than that I never heard or dreamed of anything like the love between her and her mother," and he cautioned Anna not to put the wrong meaning on his affections for both women, "to read nothing more than that he valued them as friends." He obviously envied their close relationship and the emotional support they afforded each other, an element that was still missing from his own life. Subconsciously, it seems, his love for Eugenie's mother was more important to him than his love for Eugenie, and so Eugenie's rejection was a crushing disappointment because it thwarted Vincent's desire for Michelet's woman in black. It was undoubtedly this lost hope for an idealistic mother substitute in the person of Mrs. Loyer that damaged his personality the most, and made him all the more introverted and argumentative with customers at the London branch of the art dealers, Goupil & Company.

By the time Vincent left the Loyers, in June 1874, Vincent thought he had found his identity and purpose in religion. Vincent's religious mania reached its peak during a brief period in Paris, from October until December 1874, when he was transferred to Goupil's main showroom. He memorized vast portions of the Bible and befriended a younger fellow employee, an eighteen-year-old Englishman with the Dickensian name of Harry Gladwell. Up to this point, Vincent's friendships tended to be pairs: the Tersteegs (his "second family" in The Hague), the Loyers, the van Stockums, and others. The son of a London art dealer, Gladwell roomed in the same building as Vincent in Montmartre. They became inseparable and spent hours reading poetry and portions of the Bible to each other. Eventually they roomed together. It was from Gladwell that Vincent picked up a host of quaint English expressions, such as "old boy" and "old girl," which he frequently used as terms of endearment in letters to Theo and Anna. He enjoyed dressing the part of a conservative English gentleman and wore a top hat to go to work. Dismissed from Goupil's for lack of motivation, distraction by religion, and absenteeism without permission, he returned to England, where he took a teaching position at a religious school near London. To Theo he wrote: "When I was standing in the pulpit, I felt like somebody who, emerging from a dark cave underground, comes back to the friendlier daylight. It is a delightful thought that in the future, wherever I go, I shall preach the Gospel in one's heart. May the Lord give it to me."

Five years later, though, the gospel in twenty-eight-year-old Vincent's heart was love, and its focus was Kee. If Kee never returned his love, Vincent told Theo, he would probably remain forever a bachelor; and if he learned that she loved another man, he would cease his pursuit. If she should take a man she did not love for his money, then he would plead guilty to short-sightedness and acknowledge his stupidity in mistaking a forgery for a masterpiece. Certainly, he did not think himself to be mistaken or Kee to be anything less than genuine, and, as he confided to Theo, he felt an irresistible urge to see Kee's face again and to speak to her once more, even before her parents' upcoming silver wedding anniversary. If he did not see her soon, he stated, he might have to do something that could cause himself harm. Vincent was not more specific, but his words sounded a sinister warning.

He pleaded with Theo for funds: "I want money for the trip to Amsterdam; if I have but just enough, I will go." In return, he promised to send Theo lots of drawings of landscapes, and of whatever other subjects he might want. He also admitted to Theo that he had lost his temper with his parents because of their unbending opposition to his desire to renew his relationship with Kee, to whom he felt bound forever. Reiterating the depth of his feeling for her, he imagined Kee and himself as two parts of the same being:

Theo, I love her—her, and no other—her, forever . . . and Theo, although as yet nothing seems to be resolved, there is a feeling of something like redemption within me and it is as if she and I had stopped being two, and were united for all eternity. [November 18, 1881.]

Vincent regarded his parents as a powerful entity aligned against him, but he did not want to be contentious, as he felt they were getting old and clung to prejudices and old-fashioned ideas he did not share. He thought it ridiculous, for instance, that his father disapproved of his reading material—especially books by French writers such as Jules Michelet and Victor Hugo—on the grounds that they encouraged immorality. Though he had asked his father many times to read French novels, even just a few pages, to prove to him that they were not immoral, his father obstinately refused. Then, too, Vincent was living with his parents; and while he acknowledged, and appreciated, that they provided well for him, he also declared that food and drink were not enough to sustain a man—he longed for something more, for something nobler and higher to sustain his soul: for what he absolutely could not live without—his beloved Kee. His parents were clearly not sympathetic to his moods and desires, and he worried about the possibility of being evicted from their house: "Though they think me a weak character, a man of butter . . . nothing in the world will make me give up this love. No delaying from day to day, from week to week, no *silent* waiting. The lark cannot be silent as long as he has a voice. What is to be done now?"

Although Vincent had received no communication from Kee since her initial rejection, he imagined that she might have had a change of heart:

> I think she is beginning to understand that I am neither a thief nor a
> criminal, but, on the contrary, am inwardly more quiet and sensible
> than I appear outwardly. In the beginning she did not understand
> this—at first she really had an unfavorable impression of me—but now,
> I do not know why, while the sky becomes clouded and overcast with
> quarrels and curses, a light rises on her side. [November 18, 1881.]

Vincent's tragic lack of self-esteem is evident in the closing to
his letter: "Without her I am nothing," he wrote in his parting
lines, "but with her there is a chance. To live, to work, and to love
are really one."

The next day, November 19, a woeful Vincent wrote again to
Theo and confirmed his commitment to Kee. After thanking
Theo for sending him money for the trip to Amsterdam, he laid
out the plan for his visit. He wanted to be sure, of course, that
Kee would be at home when he arrived, and so, he confided to
Theo, he had drawn his younger sister, Wil, into his scheme: She
would be on the lookout and would warn him if Kee had travel
plans. Of Wil, he wrote: "Oh, Theo, there is so much depth in her
character, but one does not see it at once. She, you and I, we all
have an outer bark of lightheartedness, but inside is a trunk of
firmer wood, and hers is of a fine grain! Well, we shall see how
things go."

Vincent then offered counsel to Theo on matters of the
heart. He recommended that Theo read *L'Amour et la Femme* by
Michelet, *Our Neighbors* by Harriet Beecher Stowe, and *Jane
Eyre* by Charlotte Brontë, among other romance novels. "Those
people can tell you more and better things than I can," he
advised. Vincent viewed these writers as the vanguards of modern civilization and, for him, their message was clear. From
them he gleaned a lesson in staying focused: of limiting oneself

to one profession and one's love to one woman only. He determined that he should make his profession a modern one and that he should create in his wife a free modern soul, so she might be delivered from the terrible prejudices that for centuries had chained women.

Finally, he reaffirmed his determination to win Kee's heart—"Though I fall ninety-nine times, the hundredth time I shall stand"—and decried the need to prove to his family a means of livelihood first: "What artist has not struggled and toiled, and what other way is there but struggling and toiling to gain a foothold?"

Four days later, on November 23, Vincent wrote to Theo again, this time discussing his destructive childhood relationship with his father. He recalled how he had often wanted to question his father's authority and express his own personality, only to be beaten down by his father's autocratic domination.

In Vincent's obsession with Kee, every scar on his personality, every consequence of his troubled childhood came pouring out onto the page. And still he believed that if only his mother or father would put their arms around him, sit down with him, and *listen* to his cries, all his problems would be set right. But no matter how hard he tried, even in adulthood, it never happened. Yet Vincent did not consider his father an enemy, but a friend, one who would be even more his friend if he were less afraid of being "infected" with French "errors." He bemoaned: "Father thinks my opinion entirely wrong, considers it forbidden, and systematically rejects it."

Vincent then described himself as being in a state of terrible suspense over the outcome of a registered letter he had sent to Kee's father in an attempt to gain his sympathy.

Despite the overwhelming evidence to the contrary, Vincent at this point still believed he would soon win Kee's heart. When he did, Vincent told his brother, all the time he devoted to his correspondence with Theo would be devoted to Kee instead. That Vincent decided he could not continue writing these very long letters indefinitely must have come as some relief to Theo, who was repeatedly being assaulted by Vincent's desperation over Kee. Theo may indeed have winced every time he read another "no, never never" or a "she, and no other"; yet it becomes increasingly clear that the no, never nevers throughout Vincent's life led him into despair—the no, never nevers of his unbending father; the no, never nevers of a mother who refused to come to terms with her grief; the no, never nevers of his land-lady's daughter; and later in life the no, never nevers of other women and friends like the painter Paul Gauguin, to whom he formed an especially strong emotional attachment.

Vincent regretted that he was still entirely in the dark about what was going on inside the Stricker household in Amsterdam: "I mean, I don't *know* anything, but only *feel*." But how can one feel things at a distance? he wondered. He wrote that he could not explain it, but only by falling in love was it possible to hear voices in the distance and surmise the reality of things from a fragment of information—as one guesses there is a fire from see-ing the smoke. Vincent was building up incredibly unrealistic expectations.

He asked Theo: "Do you think Kee knows how terribly she unintentionally thwarts me? Well, she will have to make up for it afterward!!! That means I count on her joining in many artistic campaigns with me, you see." He rationalized that "a married artist with his wife spends less and is more productive than an unmarried one with a mistress. . . . You do pay the mistress anyhow," he pointed out, "and those ladies laugh at you behind your back."

As he had in a letter to Theo the previous week, Vincent again alluded to the necessity of perhaps doing something sinister at his uncle and aunt's silver anniversary celebration: "Will they expel me on or shortly after the silver wedding party? God forbid."

Vincent does not reveal what he might do that would prompt the Strickers to expel him from the anniversary festivities, but the agony he continued to feel in the aftermath of Kee's rejection was unquestionably driving him to drastic measures.

"I am in the greatest suspense," he concluded.

Chapter Two

A KNIGHT IN SHINING ARMOR

THE HAGUE, HOLLAND, DECEMBER 1881–NOVEMBER 1883

View from Vincent's lodgings when he lived in The Hague with the prostitute, Sien, and her two illigitimate children. The image shows a carpenter's yard, done in pencil, pen, and brush work.

For my part, I can only marry once,
and how can I do better than marry her?
It is the only way to help her....

—Letter to Theo,
after Vincent announced his intention to marry

By December, the unusual warm spell had ended. So had Vincent's hopes with Kee. His next letter to Theo was sent from new lodgings in The Hague. An uncharacteristically short note, it said only that he had gone to Amsterdam and had a confrontation with Kee's father.

Vincent reported at greater length on this visit several days later, but even then he did not divulge to Theo all the disturbing and dramatic details of his encounter with the Reverend Stricker, who refused to permit Vincent an audience with his daughter.

Vincent began his confessional with a plea to Theo: "I am afraid you sometimes throw a book aside because it is too realistic. Have pity and patience with this letter and read it through, though you may think it a bit much." After noting that recollections of his trip to Amsterdam and then The Hague still aroused in him conflicting and confusing emotions that had yet to be resolved, he proceeded with his narrative.

Vincent found the Reverend Stricker's house in the center of Amsterdam, fronting on the Keizersgracht Canal, and rang the bell. The family was still at dinner. He was invited in, but when he entered the dining room Kee was not there. Although the family claimed that Kee was out, he was certain they had taken her plate from the table, and he suspected that she was hiding upstairs. He thought they all played the scene rather like a farce.

The parents engaged Vincent in conversation about an art exhibition in town. As they finished dinner, his uncle then announced that he had just been about to mail a reply to Vincent's registered letter; but since Vincent was now there, he would read it aloud. Vincent, however, interrupted him: "Where is Kee?" he asked again. The answer unsettled him, for he was told that she had left the house as soon as she learned who was at the front door. He could not believe it was in her nature to avoid him so coldly. Vincent endured the reading of his uncle's letter, which sounded like a sermon and bore no substance except for the request that Vincent end all correspondence and put the matter behind him. To try to close the issue, the Rev. Stricker advised Vincent: "To your 'she and no other' her answer is 'Certainly not you!' Your persistence is disgusting." The word "disgusting" shocked Vincent. Exasperated, he then placed the palm of his right hand over the flame of an oil lamp and declared that he wished to see Kee only for as long as he could bear the heat from the lamp. His uncle had the presence of mind to blow out the flame, but not before Vincent had badly burned his hand.

Although this incident would not be mentioned by Vincent to Theo until a month later in a letter, and again, years later, in a letter to artist Emile Bernard, recourse to self-mutilation in order to prove his love for Kee certainly appears to be the most salient and vivid detail of his encounter with her father. It suggests, too, that the emotional pain of rejection was so intense that Vincent could alleviate or deflect it only by inflicting upon himself correspondingly intense physical pain. Nor was this an isolated incident: in subsequent years, Vincent would react in similarly extreme fashion to cope with rejection.

Vincent's uncle announced angrily that no further discussion was possible. Once the thwarted Vincent had calmed down, his uncle and aunt offered him a bed for the night. He thanked them politely but refused: since Kee was apparently not there, he said, he preferred to go to an inn. The Strickers insisted upon helping their nephew find comfortable lodgings at a reasonable price, and even accompanied him through the dark, muddy streets to an inn. Vincent recalled that he found something humane in their behavior.

Vincent bandaged his hand and attempted another talk with his uncle. But he did not get even a glimpse of Kee. Indeed, the parents considered the matter settled, and Vincent felt only more lonely and forlorn. Exhausted, depressed, he made one final attempt to persuade his uncle to view his suit differently. On Sunday morning he confronted him for the third and last time, but to no avail. His uncle mumbled something inaudible about a woman's passions as he rushed off to church. He left Vincent stunned, feeling as though he had been standing in punishment too long against a cold, whitewashed church wall.

Vincent had been in Amsterdam two days. He then traveled to nearby Haarlem, where he spent a few pleasant hours with Wil. That evening he caught a train to The Hague to visit friends.

When he arrived in The Hague, Vincent still felt chilled to the depths of his soul: "I did not want to be stunned by that feeling. Then I thought, I should like to be with a woman for a change—I cannot live without love, without a woman. I wouldn't give two cents for life if there were not something infinite, something deep, something real." That Vincent had vowed forever to be faithful to Kee, and now found himself assailed by lust for another woman, initially seemed to him to be contrary to all logic. "And my answer to that," wrote Vincent, his emotions superseding logic, as he told Theo, was "That damned wall is too cold for me; I need a woman, I cannot, I may not, I will not live without love. I am only a man, and a man with passions; I must go to a woman, otherwise I shall freeze or turn to stone—or, in short, I shall have let events browbeat me."

Thus began the battle that raged within Vincent, his emotions at war with his romantic ideals. Whatever hold he imagined Kee had over him, he realized that he, like many men, could not live too long without a woman—and concluded that he must find a new one. He reported to Theo:

And, my goodness, I didn't have to look all that far. I found a woman, by no means young, by no means beautiful, nothing special, if you like. But perhaps you are somewhat curious. She was fairly tall and strongly built; she did not have the hands of a lady like Kee, but the hands of a woman who does a great deal of work; but she was not coarse or common, and had something very feminine about her. She reminded me of some quaint figure by Chardin or Frere, or perhaps Jan Steen. Well, what the French call *une ouvrière* [a prostitute]. She had had many cares, you could see, and life had been hard for her. Oh, nothing refined, nothing out of the ordinary, nothing unusual. Any woman at every age, if she loves and is a good woman, can give a man, not the infinity of a moment, but a moment of infinity.

Theo, for me that slight fadedness, that something over which life has passed, has infinite charm. Ah! For me I even saw in her something of Feyen-Perrin or Perugino. You see, I am not quite as innocent as a greenhorn, much less a baby in a cradle.

It is not the first time I was unable to resist that feeling of affection, aye, affection, that special affection and love for those women who are so damned and condemned and despised by the clergymen from the lofty heights of the pulpit. I do not damn them, I do not condemn them, I do not despise them.

See here, I am almost thirty years old, and do you really think that I have never felt the need of love? Kee is even older than I am, and she has also known love in the past; but she is all the dearer to me for it. She is not inexperienced, but neither am I. If she wants to hold on to that old love and have nothing to do with a new love, that is her affair; and if she insists on doing that and cold-shoulders me, I shan't stifle my energy and all my mental powers on her account. No, I refuse to do that. I love her, but I will not allow myself to become frozen and my mind crippled because of her. And the spur, the spark we need, that is love, and not mystical love either. [December 21, 1881.]

In the wake of his experience at the Stricker household, Vincent came to another milestone rationalization—this one regarding his love of religion—in a letter to Theo:

Then, not at once, but very soon, I felt that love die within me; a void, an infinite void came in instead. You know, I believe in God, and I did not doubt the power of love, but then I felt something like *My God, my God, why hast Thou forsaken me?* and everything became a blank. I thought have I been deceiving myself? Oh, God, there is no God! That cold terrible reception in Amsterdam was too much for me, my eyes were opened at last. [May 14, 1882.]

The once ardently religious Vincent began questioning his faith and its concomitant morality. The fact that he had paid the woman money for her services demanded some reflection on his part, but he found it only commendable that she did not provide him merely with the hour he had paid for. Instead, seeing that he was distraught and lonely, she took him to her home and spent the entire night with him. "That woman has not cheated me," he insisted. And in her defense he continued:

Oh, he who takes all such women as cheats is so wrong and has so little understanding. That woman was very good to me, very good, very
dear, very kind—in a way I shall not even tell my brother Theo,
because I strongly suspect that my brother Theo has had a similar
experience. So much the better for him.

Did we spend much money together? No, because I didn't have
much, and I said to her, Look here, you and I don't have to make ourselves drunk to feel something for each other; you had best put what
I can spare in your pocket. And I wish I could have spared more, for
she was worth it. [December 21, 1881.]

Some of that worth lay in conversation, certainly, for they
talked about everything—her life, her cares, her misery—and indeed,
Vincent told his brother, he had a more interesting conversation
with this ouvrière than he ever could have had with Kee. He confessed these things to Theo, he said, not to wallow in sentimentality,
but rather to clear his mind and bolster his emotional health so that
he could improve his work. Henceforth, he would strive to banish
Kee from his thoughts so as to combat his distress and melancholia
about their thwarted relationship. Further, he scoffed at the
thought of those clergymen who might call him a sinner for the way
he chose to find some release from his emotional torment: "Bah!
What dreadful nonsense that is. Is it a *sin* to love, to need love, not to
be able to live without love? I think a life without love is a sinful and
immoral condition." If he repented anything, he said, it was the
seclusion he had sought in his younger days when the Church's
teachings closed him off from life. He had since thought better of it:

When you wake up in the morning and find you are not alone, but
can see a fellow creature there in the half light, it makes the
world look so much more friendly. Much more welcoming than the

> devotional journals and whitewashed church walls, beloved by
> clergymen. [December 21, 1881.]

This rebellion against conventional church morality is voiced with similar passion in a later letter to Theo: "Oh, I am no friend of the present Christianity, though Jesus was sublime . . . I have taken revenge since—how? By worshipping the love which they, the theologians, call *sin,* by respecting a whore . . . and not respecting many would-be respectable pious ladies."

In an amazing word picture, Vincent described for Theo the woman's modest room, which became for him an enchanted love nest shared by two downtrodden fellow creatures:

> She lived in a modest, simple little room; the plain wallpaper lent it a quiet gray tone, yet warm like a picture by Chardin, a wooden floor with a mat and a piece of old dark-red carpet, an ordinary kitchen stove, a chest of drawers, a large perfectly simple bed—in short, a real working woman's home. The next day she had to work at the wash-tub. Fair enough, I could have found her no more charming in a purple camisole and a black skirt than I did now in a dress of brown or reddish-gray. And she was no longer young, perhaps the same age as Kee, and she had a child—yes, life had left its mark, and her youth was gone. Gone? There are no old women. Ah, and she was strong and healthy—and yet not coarse, not common.
>
> Are those who care so very much for distinction always able to spot the distinguished? Good heavens, people search high and low for what is right under their noses, and I do, too, now and then. [December 21, 1881.]

Defending his actions, eliciting the salutary effects of his night in the ouvrière's bed, Vincent continued:

I am glad I acted as I did, because I can think of no earthly reason to keep me from my work or cause me to lose my good humor. When I think of Kee, I still say "she, and no other"; but it isn't since yesterday that I have been taking a warm interest in those women whom the clergy condemn, despise and damn, indeed my love for them is even older than that for Kee. Many times when I walked the streets all alone, with time hanging heavily on my hands, half sick and down in the dumps, with no money in my pocket, I would look at them and envy the men who would go with one, and I felt that those poor girls were my sisters, in respect of circumstances and experience in life. And, you see, it is an old feeling of mine, and goes deep. Even as a boy I would often look up with infinite sympathy, indeed with respect, at a woman's face past its prime, inscribed as it were with the words: here life and reality have left their mark. [December 21, 1881.]

In light of the positive aspects of his experience with this humble working woman—the cleansing of his mind, the restoration of his good spirit, the spur to his creativity—Vincent again analyzed his feelings for Kee, the ouvrière's respectable middle-class counterpart, and projected onto her, significantly, an image of his mother, a woman imprisoned by grief and piety:

But my feeling for Kee is quite new and something quite different. Without realizing it, she is in a kind of prison, she too is poor and cannot do as she pleases, she feels a kind of resignation; and it is my belief that the clergymen and pious ladies often make a greater impression on her than on me ... they no longer have any hold on me. But she is devoted to them and would be unable to bear it if the system of resignation, and sin and God and I know not what else, proved to be vain. [December 21, 1881.]

While Vincent condemned the influence of clergymen upon women's lives, he nonetheless preserved his belief in a God that he perceived in the mysteries of human experience, in acts of love and charity for his fellow beings:

> For me that God of the clergymen is as dead as a doornail. But does that make me an atheist? The clergymen consider me one but you see I love, and how could I feel love if I were not alive myself, or others were not alive, and if we are alive, there is something wondrous in that. Now call that God or human nature or whatever you like, but there is a certain something I cannot define systematically, although it is very much alive and real, and you see for me that something is God, or as good as God. [December 21, 1881.]

Though Vincent no longer believed in God as an almighty being sitting high on a throne in judgment over all humanity, he did believe in the spiritual concept of Godliness—a spiritual condition that respected all human life and all of nature, no matter how unbeautiful—and he respected Jesus for his teachings of humility and humanity.

Vincent concluded his letter to Theo with the affirmation that he loved Kee for a thousand reasons, but that he was now a realist and held a perspective quite different from hers. Thus, while he would not give her up entirely, until such time that she might have a change of heart and let go her piety he would devote himself to his art and business. Nor would he deny the pleasures he had found with another woman, for they afforded him warmth and comfort and emotional well-being. He finished in a jubilant mood, with thoughts only of paint, watercolors, canvases, and finding a studio.

"Boy, if I could only find a studio!"

* * *

Vincent moved to The Hague to take instruction in painting from a relative, Anton "Jet" Mauve, a member of a group of painters known as The Hague School, which produced romantic depictions of the nearby sandy coast and inland waterways. Though the work of The Hague School bore similarities to the Impressionists, it was too brooding and dark to classify as truly Impressionistic. One of Vincent's most celebrated works of this second period in The Hague is titled *Beach at Scheveningen in Stormy Weather,* showing two fishing boats returning to shore in a surging surf under a threatening sky, a path leading down to the beach through sand dunes. The heavy, impasto brush strokes are impregnated with blowing sand, the wind was so violent.

Vincent's former business colleague in The Hague, H. G. Tersteeg, tried to help Vincent by loaning him studies of saleable art that Vincent might learn from. Vincent had worked briefly under Tersteeg when he was employed as a clerk in an art gallery in 1869, before Vincent was promoted and transferred to the company's London office. Tersteeg was then a handsome young man, intelligent, and at only twenty-four years of age he was appointed manager of The Hague art gallery. Vincent admired his gentlemanly charm and happy marriage. He and his wife had a baby daughter, Betsy; Vincent so much envied their domestic life and the loving attention they devoted to the child, that he had made of the Tersteegs his second family during his first stay in The Hague. He retained such warm and intense feelings for the Tersteegs that several years later, in 1873, while working in London, he had filled a sketchbook with drawings of the baby as he remembered her and had sent it to her mother as a gift.

In January 1882, still smarting from Kee's refusal to see him
but buoyed by the compassion of the woman who had recently
restored his pride, Vincent took pity on another prostitute: Sien
(her Christian name was Clasina Hoornik). She was a homeless
woman three years older than he and in an advanced state of
pregnancy when Vincent invited her to live with him. One can
imagine Theo's mortification at receiving the following:

> Which is the more cultured, more sensitive, more manly: to desert a
> woman or concern oneself with one who has been deserted?
>
> Last winter I met a pregnant woman, deserted by the man
> whose child she was carrying. A pregnant woman who walked the
> streets in winter—she had her bread to earn, you'll know how. [May
> 3-12, 1882.]

Rather than forsake her, Vincent had taken Sien for a model and
he had been working with her all winter. Unable to pay her for
this work, he was playing the part of a savior by ensuring that
she and her child did not go hungry or want for a warm, safe
place to live. He explained:

> When first I met this woman, she caught my eye because she looked
> ill. I made her take baths and as many restoratives as I could man-
> age, and she has become healthier. I went with her to Leyden, where
> there is a maternity hospital in which she will be confined. Small
> wonder she wasn't well, the child was in the wrong position, that is,
> the child had to be turned around by forceps. But there is a good
> chance she will pull through. [May 3-12, 1882.]

Vincent couched his actions in terms of decency and humanity,
for what decent man would not have done the same in similar

circumstances? Charity came simply and naturally to Vincent, and Sien responded positively to his care and compliments. He praised her for being a good painter's model and she "attached to me like a tame dove." Thus had Vincent set the stage for another of his shocking revelations: he planned to marry Sien, he told Theo, and for precisely the same reasons he'd wanted to marry Kee—to save the woman from herself and her "old ways" by being her knight in shining armor. "For my part, I can only marry once, and how can I do better than marry her? It is the only way to help her; otherwise misery would force her back into her old ways, which leads to an abyss. She has no money but she is helping me earn money with my work."

Vincent was pleased with her recovery from illness, telling Theo:

> I am quite astonished to see her become much brighter and more cheerful every day; she is so changed that she is quite different from the pale, sick woman I met this winter.... Perhaps I can understand her better than anyone else because she has a few peculiarities which would have been repulsive to many others. First, her speech is very ugly and is the result of her illness; then there is her temper caused by a nervous disposition, so that she has fits of anger which would be unbearable to most people.
>
> I understand these things, they don't bother me.... On her side she understands my own temper, and it is sort of a tacit understanding between us not to find fault with each other. [May 4-12, 1882.]

Psychologists find that many men who are drawn to women in distress suffer from low self-esteem. They therefore believe that by acting the savior, often with self-sacrifice to the extreme, they will prove themselves to be worthy of the infinite love they crave. Unfortunately, these vulnerable men frequently find themselves in dysfunctional relationships with women who have been so severely abused that the anguish from their poisoning traumas runs too deep for any man to ease. It is entirely possible that such was the case with Sien, and that no amount of care and loving would have endeared him to her over the long term, that no amount of sacrifice could have fulfilled her endless need.

Theo desperately tried to persuade Vincent to end the relationship, if for no other reason than the devastating effect it would have on their parents should they find out. But the more Theo tried to interfere, the more adamant Vincent became. Through Sien, love had been reborn in him. He further justified his desire for marriage to her as an experience that would improve his art:

> I want to go through the joys and sorrows of domestic life in order to paint it from my own experience. When I came back from Amsterdam, I felt that my love—so true, so honest and strong—had literally been *killed*. But after death there is resurrection. . . . Then I found Sien. There was no time to hesitate or defer. I had to act. If I do not marry her it would have been kinder of me to have left her alone. [May 14, 1882.]

Initially, Vincent seemed to enjoy genuine happiness with Sien. He reveled in camping with her among the sand dunes, finding stimulating subjects to paint. Like the ouvrière before her, Sien aroused Vincent's true sympathy. His instinct was to defend and protect her, as he revealed in a letter to Emile Bernard:

The whore . . . has more of my sympathy than my compassion. Being a creature exiled, outcast from society, like you and me who are artists, she is certainly our friend and sister. And in this condition of being an outcast she finds—just as we ourselves do—an independence which is not without its advantages after all. . . . So let's beware of assuming an erroneous attitude by believing that we can do her a service by means of social rehabilitation which for that matter is hardly practicable and would be fatal to her. [August 4, 1888.]

Like Kee and like his mother, Sien was cast as a woman bound by old ways and imprisoned in the past, a woman in need of help. Conditioned by the past, by the events of his painful childhood, again Vincent cast himself as the savior knight. In a letter to Theo, he reasoned:

A woman, no matter how good and noble she may be by nature, if she has no means, and is not protected by her own family, in present-day society runs a great and immediate danger of being drowned in the pool of prostitution. What is more natural than to protect such a woman? Our life is so dependent on our relations with women—and the opposite, of course, is also true—that it seems to me one must never think lightly of them. [April 11, 1883.]

However good and noble Sien may have been by nature, she had grown into a thin, pale, sickly-looking woman with mistrustful dark eyes, a raspy voice, and a sharp tongue. In Vincent's eyes, though, she was "beautiful." In a letter to Rappard, Vincent acknowledged her physical shortcomings but again rose loftily to her defense:

Oh, there is gossip enough, because I am always in her company, but why should that bother me?—I never had such a good assistant as this "ugly" faded woman. In my eyes she is beautiful, and I find in her exactly what I want; her life has been rough, and sorrow and adversity have put their marks on her.

When the earth is not plowed you can get no harvest from it. She has been plowed—and so I find more in her than in a crowd of unplowed ones. [May 28, 1882.]

Vincent's sketches of Sien for the most part depict intimate domestic moments. In one, Sien, in a casual white shirt and ankle-length white petticoat, is sitting quietly by the hearth smoking a cigar. She also appears in several unflattering studies, some of which show her in deep despair. Indeed, Vincent's most dynamic images of Sien do not disguise the ugly aspects of her appearance; they are beautiful in his eyes, and he explains why over and over in letters to Theo. Of his favorite "ugly" image of Sien, entitled *Sorrow*, he wrote: "I want to do drawings that touch some people. *Sorrow* is only a beginning." The sketch shows a thin, malnourished Sien in the nude, her body hunched forward, her arms around her legs, her face buried between her knees, her ratty black hair streaming down her back like that of a witch, her sagging breasts shriveled from dehydration and portraying intense privation. "I want to express something of the struggle for life in that pale, slender woman's figure," he explained in another letter to Theo. Vincent's inspiration for this remarkable sketch was a clump of gnarled, twisted tree roots that had been exposed during a storm among the dunes. The beauty in the tangled mass of sinuous forms—and in the roots still struggling for life—helped Vincent realize the dramatic potential of Sien's emaciated figure.

Whatever other pleasures or virtues Vincent found in this domestic arrangement, when Vincent's father and mother discovered his relationship with Sien, they were, as Theo predicted, more than upset. Profoundly concerned about their eldest son's welfare, they threatened not only to have him separated from Sien, but also to have him declared insane and confined to an asylum. They even had legal papers drawn up for him to be institutionalized. The thought terrified Vincent, and he appealed for Theo to reason with his parents:

> *I ask for one thing: to let me love and care for my poor, weak, ill-used little wife as well as my poverty permits, without their trying to separate, worry or hurt us.* Nobody cared for her or wanted her, she was alone and forsaken like a worthless rag, and I have taken her up and have given her all the love, all the tenderness, all the care that was in me; she has felt this and she has revived. [June 2-3, 1882.]

Fortunately, Theo was able to prevail on his parents not to have Vincent declared legally insane and confined to an asylum, but Vincent harbored the hurt for years for their considering such a drastic measure.

Prostitution carried a terrible stigma in the devoutly Protestant Holland of the 1880s, and Vincent soon found himself shunned by his friends and ostracized by members of The Hague School. Johanna explained the situation precisely in her translation of Vincent's letters: "This unfortunate liaison deprived him of sympathy of all in The Hague who took an interest in him. Neither Mauve nor Tersteeg could approve of taking upon himself the cares of a family—and such a family!—while he was financially dependent on his younger brother. Acquaintances and relatives were shocked to see him walking about with such a slovenly woman; nobody cared to associate with him any longer, and his home life was such that nobody came to visit him."

Nobody, that is, but Theo. When Theo went to visit Vincent to see the situation for himself, he found the family living in squalor. Jo wrote: "He found the household neglected, everything in bad condition and Vincent deeply in debt. He realized Sien was not able to live an ordered life, and she herself had realized that things could not continue because Vincent required too much money for his painting to leave enough for the support of her and the children. But to the last Vincent defended her and excused her faults with the sublime words: 'She has never seen *good, how can* she be good?'"

This was an age, after all, when young women of respectable families were expected to live in a chaste environment from birth until their marriage. Vincent in his espousal of his own chivalrous morality had forgone respectability, to be sure, and he had done so at some risk to his health. Prostitutes' lives were fraught with dangers, not least of them the virulent venereal diseases that had reached epidemic proportions in Europe. Before the birth of Sien's baby, Vincent was admitted to a hospital after he had been diagnosed with gonorrhea, which he had contracted from Sien. The treatment, excruciatingly painful, required a catheter to scrape pus and infection from inside his penis. He swore Theo to secrecy over his condition because he did not want his parents to be alarmed.

Within two weeks, Sien too was hospitalized. Despite a difficult labor that required five physicians in attendance, she delivered a healthy baby boy on June 30, and Vincent felt greatly relieved. He thanked Theo for providing financial assistance: "Without your help Sien probably would not be among the living."

Vincent enjoyed exerting a genial influence on Sien's two children. And a heart-warming portrait of Sien's four-year-old daughter shows her kneeling in front of her baby brother's cradle. Many moments of tender domesticity were expressed in his letters to Theo:

> At this moment the woman and the children are sitting with me. When I think of last year there is a great difference. The woman is stronger and stouter, and has lost much of her agitated air; the baby is the prettiest, healthiest, merriest little fellow you can imagine; and the poor little girl—you see from the drawings that her former deep misery has not been wiped out, and I often feel anxious about her, but still she is quite different from last year. Then she was in a very bad state; now she is already looking more childlike. [January 13, 1883.]

As Sien and her children slept, Vincent wrote the following description of the early-morning view from his window to Theo:

> So you must picture me sitting in my attic window as early as four o'clock in the morning, studying the meadows and the carpenter's yard with my perspective frame just as they are lighting the fires to make coffee in the yard and the first worker comes strolling in. A flock of white pigeons comes soaring over the red tile roofs between the smoking black chimney stacks. Beyond it all lies an infinity of delicate, soft green, miles and miles of flat meadow; and a gray sky, as calm, as peaceful as a Corot or Van Goyen.
>
> That view over the ridges of the gutters with grass growing in them, very early in the morning, and those first signs of life and awakening—the flying birds, the smoking chimneys, the small figure strolling along far below—that is the subject of my watercolor. I hope you will like it. [July 23, 1882.]

Yet, for all the optimism about art and love that Vincent had been able to sustain in spite of disease, disapproval, and ostracism, within six months his relationship with Sien had deteriorated so badly that he wrote to Theo: "I feel rather worried. There seems to be something the matter with the woman." He elaborated:

> Michelet rightly says: *"Une femme est une malade"* (a wife is a sickness). They vary, Theo, they vary like the weather. Now he who has eyes to see it finds something beautiful and good in *every* kind of weather; he finds the snow and the burning sun beautiful, the storm and the calm, the cold and the heat, he loves every season and cannot spare one day of the year, and in his heart he is contented and resigned to things being as they are. But even if one feels this way about the weather and the changing seasons, and the same way about the changing feminine nature—believing at heart that there is a reason in its enigma too . . . even if one could feel this way about it, still our own character and opinion are not always and at every moment in harmony and sympathy with those of the woman to whom we are united; and one personally feels anxiety, dissatisfaction, or doubt, notwithstanding the courage, faith, and serenity one may have. [May 9 or 10, 1883.]

Vincent felt helpless. The doctor who had attended Sien at her confinement told him it would take years before she completely recovered her health. Until then, her nervous system would remain very sensitive. Vincent deplored any thought of her falling back into prostitution: "That worries me continually and seriously. Her temper is at times so bad that it is almost unbearable, even for me—violent, mischievous. I can tell you, I am sometimes in despair."

The following months brought no improvement. Vincent discovered that Sien was consorting with other men and engaging in prostitution; his worst fear had become a reality. Drawing some comfort from the infant's first birthday, he described him for Theo as "a sociable little chap." But in another letter he confessed:

> Things are looking dark just now. If it were for me alone! But there is also the thought of the woman and the children, poor creatures whom one would keep safe, and feels responsible for. With them I cannot speak about it, but for myself it became too much today. Work is the only remedy. If that does not help, one breaks down. [July 22, 1883.]

Vincent began to feel out of touch with humanity. His work suffered from the strain of the relationship. "I am harassed, brother. Life is impossible here," he wrote, and finally—for the sake of his art—he summoned the courage to walk out of Sien's life. It was not an easy parting. As he knew he could not save Sien, he fretted mostly about the fate of the children, especially the little boy who had grown very attached to him.

The relationship between Vincent and Sien manifested many of the pitfalls of codependency, with Vincent initially responding to and taking pleasure in fulfilling her whims and wishes, but eventually feeling abused and manipulated. He wrote to Theo: "When I met this woman I was attracted to her because she looked ill. I made her take baths, and as much nourishing food as I could afford, and she has become much stronger." But however much Vincent did for Sien, he could not do enough. Vincent was fortunate, however. Codependents often find it impossible to wrest themselves from a destructive relationship.

Vincent, though, found the strength to leave both Sien and The Hague for the sake of his art, and he set out to pursue his artistic career in another part of Holland.

Writing to Theo, Vincent offered this bit of painfully gleaned wisdom: "Love is as frail as a spider's web; and grows to be as strong as a cable. But only on condition of faithfulness."

Chapter Three

FALSE
ACCUSATIONS

Neunen, Holland, December 1883–1885

A preliminary version of *The Potato Eaters*, 1883, composed while Vincent lived in Neunen.

A peasant girl, in her patched and dusty blue skirt and bodice which have
acquired the most delicate shades from the weather, wind and sun,
is better-looking—in my opinion—than a lady.
But if she dons a lady's clothes, then her charm is gone.

—Letter to Theo, April 30, 1885,
explaining why Vincent sends him portraits of a young peasant woman

After leaving Sien, Vincent moved as far away as his money would allow, to Drenthe, near the German border, but he soon found it a disappointing place. For two months he sketched and painted its brooding, marshy landscape and local peasantry. Then the loneliness became intolerable, and he moved in again with his parents, who had been transferred to a new congregation at Nuenen, in the south of Holland.

The vicarage at Nuenen was a simple two-story stone building that fronted the main street. A large garden at the back was enclosed by a high stone wall. Paths and hedges divided the space into flowerbeds, vegetable plots, and a small orchard. There was a duck pond with a boat dock, there were pollarded willow trees and oaks. The laundry room became Vincent's studio. The top floor of the house afforded him a splendid view across a heath to a church tower in the distance. The parsonage garden became a favorite motif of his paintings, which record it in the colors of all four seasons. Dark images portray the gloom of winter, but autumn views show avenues of trees and lines of pollarded willows glowing with russet colors. He painted produce from the garden—richly textured savoy cabbages, clusters of plump brown onions, baskets of ripe apples, bowls of succulent pears, and harvests of wholesome potatoes freshly dug from the soil. Vincent liked nests.

He collected them from nooks and crannies in the garden, and he painted them. The textures he was able to capture on canvas delighted him. The weavers' thatched cottages in the neighborhood especially caught his attention. For him, they stood as a metaphor for a nest, and a nest represented the hearth and home he longed to make his own.

He felt uncomfortable sharing the same house with his parents, telling Theo:

> They share the same dread of taking me in the house as they would about taking a big rough dog. He would run into the room with wet paws—and he is so rough. He will be in everyone's way. *And he barks so loud.* In short, he is a foul beast. . . . Also this house is too good for me, and Father and Mother and the family are so terribly genteel (not sensitive underneath, however), and, and—there are clergymen—a lot of clergymen.
>
> The dog feels that if they keep him, it will only mean putting up with him and tolerating him *in this house.* So he will try to find another kennel. The dog is, in fact, Father's son, and has been left rather too much in the streets, where he could not but become rougher and rougher; but as Father already forgot this years ago, and in reality has never meditated *deeply* on the meaning of the tie between father and son, one need not mention that.
>
> And then—the dog might bite—he might become rabid, and the constable would have to come to shoot him. [December 15, 1883.]

An especially abrasive issue among the family was Vincent's refusal to take a paying job while pursuing his artistic endeavor. But none of the artists he admired had been "spare-time artists," and so he felt it essential to devote all his creative energy to his art. At one point he felt so frustrated at Theo's inability to sell his work, he complained vehemently: "A *wife* you cannot give me, a *child* you cannot give me, work you cannot give me. Money, yes. But what good is it to me if I must do without the rest!"

As restorative as Vincent found the garden and surrounding countryside at Nuenen, he still bore a heavy burden of guilt for having left Sien and her young children. In fact, he was on the point of reconciling with her when, in the fall of 1884, he met Margaretha (Margot) Carolina Begemann, a shy woman whom he observed following him, probably in the hope that he would notice her. She turned out to be a neighbor. Twelve years Vincent's senior, Margot lived with her mother and three homely sisters, all of whom were single. Vincent was well aware of the intense rivalry among the sisters to be the first to marry, and he could easily have seen Margot as yet another woman in distress. Vincent's sister-in-law Jo described Margot as "neither beautiful nor gifted, but she had an active mind and a kind heart. She often visited the poor with Vincent; they walked much together, and on her part at least the friendship soon changed to love." In light of the surviving photographs of Margot, Jo's opinion that Margot was not beautiful seems harsh. Margot has pleasant features, a peaches-and-cream complexion framed by bouncy hair twisted into luxuriant curls. Vincent and Margot began a tenderhearted, and—according to Vincent—celibate relationship. When Margot confessed her love for Vincent, they decided to marry. Margot's mother and sisters, however, thoroughly disapproved of Vincent as a suitor, and violent arguments ensued between Margot and her sisters. Nor were Vincent's parents pleased. They withheld their blessing, as they thought Vincent should have a job other than painting before he took a wife.

In a letter to Theo, Vincent described a walk he took one morning with Margot across the heath. He sensed that she was upset by all the controversy surrounding their engagement, especially her family's objections that she was too old to marry Vincent and that he would never be faithful to her. They undoubtedly considered him to be slovenly and dirty, as he thoughtlessly tramped into their house in muddy boots after his painting forays dressed in herdsman's smocks and a tattered straw hat. They may also have been aware of his scandalous relationship with Sien, as well as his unseemly infatuation with Kee. As Vincent and Margot were walking through a field that morning, she furtively sipped a vial of strychnine and suddenly collapsed at his feet in convulsions. At first Vincent thought she was suffering a nervous breakdown; then he demanded to know if she had taken poison. She screamed, "Yes!" Forcing her to put her fingers down her throat, he tried to make her vomit, but with only partial success. Alarmed, he gathered her up in his arms and carried her home and called a doctor.

Vincent was mortified. "I am in a melancholy mood, and all these things have combined to upset me in such a way that there are many days when I am almost paralyzed," he wrote to Theo. "I cannot eat, I cannot sleep." Nor could he control his rages. Verbally and sometimes physically, he struck out at people who annoyed him. During a loud and violent argument about the incident, Vincent struck his father in the face.

Both Theo and his father were suspicious. It was rumored that Margot was pregnant, but Vincent swore he had "not taken advantage of her." Margot was sent away to Utrecht to see another doctor, and traces of a mild opiate were found in her stomach in addition to the poison. When asked by his father and Theo how it got there, Vincent replied that she must have taken it without his knowledge. The accusations of pregnancy and drugs preyed on his mind, and Vincent threatened to cut off all communication with Theo if he did not stop questioning him about his involve-ment in Margot's suicide attempt. "I went through an affair with Father—I decline to start all over again with Father No. 2," he declared.

Although Margot frequently accompanied Vincent on his painting expeditions and to local hospitals to comfort the poor and elderly, he never painted her. Nor did he sketch her. Neither did he write anything about her to Theo until her suicide attempt. Robert Harrison, a translator of Vincent's letters, believes she was too compliant in her affections for him to war-rant any comment in letters, while Kee's rejection had to be reversed and Sien's relationship had to be justified. Also, it's probable that Margot had not been "plowed enough" for Vincent's artistic sensitivity. Not enough struggle or grief or abuse showed in her features. She was, in fact, the epitome of women he had said he held no respect for—"a respectable pious lady," the daughter of a clergyman with a good education. Vincent blamed the narrow-minded churchgoers with whom Margot associated for suffocating her development. "It is a pity I did not meet her ten years before," wrote Vincent to Theo. "Now she gives me the impression of a Cremona violin which has been spoiled by bad, bungling repairs. And the condition she was in when I met her proved to be rather too damaged. But originally it was a rare specimen of great value."

When Vincent learned that Margot would not return soon from Utrecht, because her recovery might take a long time, he felt confused and bewildered. Margot's three sisters showed up at the vicarage one day and physically attacked Vincent. Although he had saved Margot's life by making her vomit up some of the poison and getting her to a doctor's care so quickly, he wrestled with guilt at the thought of almost causing her death, as his engagement to her had aroused such contentiousness with her sisters. He consulted the doctor who had treated her, to determine whether he should abandon the idea of marriage. "I wanted his advice as to what I must or must not do, for the sake of the patient's health and future," Vincent wrote Theo. "Whether to continue our relationship or break it off. . . . The doctor said she is too weak to marry, at least for the moment." On the doctor's advice, he abandoned his plan to marry Margot. Still, he maintained fond memories of her. Twice he mentioned her in subsequent letters to Wil. He not only asked to be remembered to Margot, but also requested that she be given a painting as a gift.

For all their difficulties with each other, Vincent's father anguished over his son's unhappiness and melancholy moods. "He seems to be becoming more and more estranged from us," he wrote to Theo. And he continued to wish Vincent success in his painting endeavors. Nonetheless, many of the problems in their relationship remained unresolved when, on March 26, 1885, just nine months after Margot's attempted suicide, Vincent's father, returning home from a meditative stroll across the heath, suffered a severe stroke and fell dead at the doorstep. He was sixty-three years old. As a result, Vincent's mother would have to vacate the vicarage within one year: an eventuality that raised fears among the children—particularly the eldest sister, Anna—about what they might do.

Vincent's grief over his father's death was profound, in spite of their long series of misunderstandings, and he could not bear the recriminations of his family. In bitter arguments, Anna accused him of contributing to their father's death. Distressingly, his mother reiterated her opinion that he should seek mental treatment for his confrontational attitude and dark moods. So, a few weeks after his father's death, Vincent moved out of the vicarage and took lodgings on the edge of town, next to the Catholic church, within an easier walk of woodland and heath.

There, among the weavers, Vincent focused again on his art. More than the weavers' thatched cottages now commanded his attention. He wrote Theo that he spent from morning to night with the weavers themselves, who sat at massive wooden looms. These were so big they could fill an entire room. Vincent's paintings of the weavers working at their looms are sinister; he described the workers and their looms as "spectral," and the weavers themselves as "spooks." These black apparitions of men are encased in a massive wooden structure of uprights and crossbeams. "Seen through Vincent's gloomy monochrome, the weaver's apparatus becomes a cage, a prison or a mechanical spider enclosing its prey," wrote art historian Bradley Collins, and in Vincent's subconscious it's possible that these gruesome paintings symbolized the ghost inside his ribcage.

Intrigued, too, by the way the weavers entwined colors to create paisley and tartan patterns, Vincent formulated new ideas about the relationships among colors. Thereafter, he kept in a lacquered box several balls of wool in contrasting colors—red and green, orange and blue, yellow and violet—as a remembrance of his affection for the hardworking weavers, and also to reinforce his theories about the harmonies produced by contrasting colors. Michel-Eugène Chevreul, a Paris chemist, had published the world's first chromatic wheel in 1839, showing the scientific relationship between colors. Chevreul split the wheel into hot colors (for example, yellow, red, orange) and cool colors (green, blue, violet). In his book about the chromatic laws, Chevreul explained that colors opposite each other on the color wheel made the best contrasts (such as yellow and violet). Vincent agreed with Chevreul, but he went further to formulate color combinations not obvious from a study of the chromatic wheel. For example: black and white, black and orange, black and gold, silver and red. Moreover, he associated specific color combinations with particular seasons—black and white for silhouettes of branches against snowy fields, pink and green for the pink orchard blossoms and green shoots of spring, orange and blue for summer with its fields of ripe wheat and sunny skies. "Autumn is the contrast of yellow leaves with violet tones," he wrote to Theo.

Vincent also wrote Theo a detailed explanation of his "rules of colors," stating:

> The ancients admitted only three primary colors: yellow, red and blue, and the modern painters do not admit any others. In fact, these three colors are the only indissoluble and irreducible ones. Everybody knows that sunlight is made up of a series of seven colors, which Sir Isaac Newton called primitive—violet, indigo, blue, green, yellow, orange and red; but it is clear that the appellation "primitive" cannot be applied to three of these colors, which are composite, for orange is gotten by mixing red and yellow; green, by mixing yellow and blue; and violet, by mixing blue and red. As to indigo, it cannot be counted among the primitive colors, for it is only a variety of blue. So in accordance with antiquity it must be acknowledged that there are only three colors that are truly elementary in nature, and which, when they are mixed two at a time, produce three more composite colors which may be called secondary, to wit: orange, green and violet. These rudiments, developed by modern scientists, have led to the conjecture of certain laws that form an illuminating theory of colors, a theory which Eugène Delacroix commanded scientifically and

thoroughly, after grasping it instinctively. If one combines two of the primary colors, for instance yellow and red, in order to produce a secondary color—orange—this secondary color will attain maximum brilliancy when it is put close to the third primary color not used in the mixture. In the same way, if one combines red and blue in order to produce violet, this secondary color, violet, will be intensified by the immediate proximity of yellow. And finally, if one combines yellow and blue in order to produce green, this green will be intensified by the immediate proximity of red. Each of the three primary colors is rightly called complementary with regard to the corresponding secondary color. Thus blue is the complementary color of orange; yellow, the complementary color of violet; and red, the complementary color of green. Conversely, each of the combined colors is the complementary color of the primitive one not used in the mixture. The mutual intensification is what is called the law of simultaneous contrast.

When the complementary colors are produced in equal strength, that is to say in the same degree of vividness and brightness, their juxtaposition will intensify them each to such a violent intensity that the human eye can hardly bear the sight of it.

And due to a singular phenomenon, *the same colors which strengthen each other in juxtaposition will destroy each other when they are mixed.* So if one mixes blue and orange in equal quantities, the orange will be as little orange as the blue is blue; the mixture destroys the two tints, and there emerges an *absolutely colorless gray.*

But if one mixes two complementary colors in unequal proportions, they only partially destroy each other, and one gets a *broken tone,* which will be a variety of gray. This being so, new contrasts may be born of the juxtaposition of two complementary colors, one of which is pure and the other broken. As the fight is unequal, one of the two colors gains the victory, and the intensity of the dominant color does not preclude the harmony of the two.

Now, if one brings together similar colors in a pure state but in different degrees of intensity, one gets another effect, in which there will be a contrast through the difference in intensity and at the same time harmony through the similarity of the colors. Finally, if two similar colors are placed next to each other, the one in a pure state, the other broken, for instance pure blue and gray-blue, another kind of contrast will result, which will be toned down by the analogy. So it is clear that there are various means, divergent among themselves, but equally infallible, by which to intensify, to maintain, to weaken or to neutralize a color's effect, and this by its reaction to the contiguous tones—by its touching what is not itself.

In order to intensify and harmonize the effect of his colors, Delacroix used the contrast of the complementary and the concord of the analogous colors at the same time; or in other terms, the repetition of a vivid tint by the same broken tone. [April 13-17, 1885.]

During this period Vincent completed what he considered his finest painting, *The Potato Eaters,* which shows a family of peasants, the de Groots, at an evening meal. Potatoes served as a symbol for Vincent of his love of the earth and connection to the soil. He told Theo: "I have tried to emphasize that those people, eating their potatoes in the lamplight, have dug the earth with those very hands they put in the dish, and so it speaks of *manual labor,* and how they have honestly earned their food." When Vincent lived in London, his fascination for soil and gardening shines through in a letter written to Theo: "I am busy gardening and have sown a little garden full of poppies, sweet peas and mignonette. Now we must wait and see what becomes of it." In a subsequent letter from London he described weeding a row of potatoes that later in the season would be plucked from the soil like nuggets of gold. Significantly, the color gold is the predominant color in *The Potato Eaters*. Gold tones are used to represent lamplight reflected in the faces of the family, in contrast to the black shadowy interior of their humble home.

First and foremost, *The Potato Eaters* represents a rebellion against the traditional teachings of the academy, which Vincent described as a mistress "who freezes you, who petrifies you, who sucks your blood." Art historian Bradley Collins sees it as Vincent's celebration of the "coarse and ugly," and discusses its poignant symbolism in his book *Van Gogh and Gauguin*. Describing the work as an homage to Rembrandt's *Supper at Emmaus* in the Louvre, Collins sees the mysterious child in the foreground as Christ revealing Himself to the apostles. "The solemnity of the figures and the ponderousness of their gestures also make the scene readable as a *Last Supper*. The older man in particular seems to hold his coffee cup so reverentially that he he seems to offer it up as the body and blood of Christ. Vincent himself cues the viewer to his religious allusions by placing a small print of the Crucifixion behind the young man."

Psychoanalyst Dr. Albert Lubin of Stanford University also interpreted what he saw as religious imagery in *The Potato Eaters*. Collins states that Lubin "found in the spectral, haloed child an unconscious representation of the first Vincent. Just as the first Vincent would have become an angelic figure in the minds of the van Gogh family, so the child stands silhouetted by a holy light. And just as the stillborn first Vincent never came to possess either a concrete identity or particular features, so the little girl faces away from the viewer. Lubin, moreover, considers her position within the picture as a visual metaphor of Vincent's displacement by his namesake. He sees the young man, who sits on a chair bearing Vincent's signature, as the artist's symbolic counterpart. The older woman on the left represents Vincent's mother Anna, preoccupied by her grief. A strangely protruding partition blocks her off from the rest of the group, and she fails to meet the young man's imploring glance. She also stares downward and inexplicably points towards the earth as if fixing on the young Vincent's grave."

The group in the painting includes an attractive young woman named Stien; she is wearing a wide, white bonnet. At that time she was seventeen, doe-eyed, with thick dark hair and wide, sensuous lips. Vincent used her often as a model, and indeed felt compelled to explain to Theo the reason for a flurry of portraits of Stien: "A peasant girl, in her patched and dusty blue skirt and bodice which have acquired the most delicate shades from the weather, wind and sun, is better looking—in my opinion—than a lady. But if she dons a lady's clothes, then her charm is gone."

One day, while quietly working in his studio, Vincent heard a knock at the door. He opened it to two Roman Catholic priests from the parish, who had come to him with a sinister warning: Vincent must not to get too familiar with people below his social rank, they told him, and they threatened to excommunicate any parishioner who agreed to pose for him. Soon afterward, Vincent learned that Stien was pregnant. It was presumed by everyone in the parish that he was the father. But Vincent's relationship with Stien had been purely platonic, and the real culprit was one of the priests' parishioners.

"A girl I had frequently painted was having a baby," Vincent told Theo, "and they suspected me, though I had nothing to do with it. But I heard what had really happened from the girl herself, namely that a member of the priest's congregation at Nuenen had played a particularly ugly part in the affair, and so they could not get at me, at least not on that occasion."

Vincent remained good friends with Stien's family, but when he refused to reveal the father's true identity, the scandal turned the rest of the community against him. He did not care about public rejection, and when groups gathered to see what he was painting and pestered him with questions, he would remain mute. "What's the use of making yourself so disagreeable?" Theo had asked. Vincent replied: "Sometimes it cannot be avoided . . . when they hinder me in my work I sometimes do not see any other way than an eye for an eye."

Again, Vincent's work offered a sort of redemption. His accomplishment with *The Potato Eaters* had boosted his confidence as a painter, enough for him to decide to move to Antwerp in order to study at the Academie des Beaux Arts in search of further artistic development. He was also happy to distance himself from the scandal and rumor surrounding Margot and Stien. This would not be the last time, however, that he was falsely accused of sexual misconduct.

Chapter Four

MONTMARTRE: EXOTIC DELIGHTS

PARIS, FRANCE, MARCH 1886–FEBRUARY 1888

Two self-portraits and several details, using a pencil and pen while Vincet was living in Paris, 1886.

For my part,
I still continue to have the most impossible and highly unsuitable love affairs,
from which as a rule I come away with little more than shame and disgrace.

—Letter to Wil, responding to her concerns about being in a rut

At the Academy in Antwerp, Vincent found himself at the center of controversy over the definitions of artistic merit and technique. Vincent, of course, considered the Academy's teachings not only banal, but stifling of artistic creativity. *Frozen, petrifying,* and *bloodsucking* were words he used to characterize the teachings of the Acadamy to his friend van Rappard.

A student in Vincent's drawing class, Victor Hageman, wrote this recollection of the thirty-one-year-old Vincent: "I remember quite well that weather-beaten, nervous, restless man who crashed like a bombshell into the Antwerp Academy, upsetting the director, the drawing master and the pupils." He described the outlandish attire Vincent wore to class—his loose flannel smock, the sort worn by Flemish herdsmen, and his woodsman's hat—and he remarked especially on the wooden board from a discarded packing case that served as Vincent's palette.

Karel Verlat, the director of the Academy, was a perfectionist and a traditionalist whose aim was to preserve the integrity of classical painting with its patriotic and biblical themes. During one class, he instructed the pupils to paint two wrestlers, and with a rapidity that stupefied his fellow students, Vincent began applying paint to the canvas so thickly that it was literally dripping onto the floor. Verlat looked at the work, then studied its eccentric creator. He became enraged. His cheeks flushed purple, he declared: "I will not correct such putrefaction!" Thus was Vincent immediately dispatched to a beginner's class.

Vincent stayed six weeks at the Academy. He drew furiously with a visibly emotional effort to grasp the vigor of his subjects. He made sketches of everything in the room—the students, the tutor, the furniture, his view of the street through a window—although he sometimes forgot to draw the object set before the class to copy.

Vincent soon realized that he was headed up a blind alley at the Academy and, in March 1886, he moved to Paris, for a while taking art courses at the studio of Fernand Corman, where he met other avant-garde painters, in particular Emile Bernard and Henri de Toulouse-Lautrec. He shared rooms with Theo in Montmartre, and immediately he was seduced: "There is much to see here," he wrote of his arrival. "In Antwerp I did not even know who the Impressionists were; now I have seen them, and though *not* being one of the club yet, I have much admired certain Impressionist pictures—Degas' nude figure—Claude Monet's landscape."

Impressionism was a style of artistic expression that rebelled against the long-held belief that artistic merit should be judged by how lifelike a painter could capture a subject. For example, the Impressionists defined form in their paintings by using variations of reflected light. Influenced by the watercolors of J. M. W. Turner, the English painter, they eschewed sharply outlined shapes, and applied oil paints to the canvas with comma-shaped, flickering brush strokes. They used complementary colors in juxtapositions that enabled them to create images that could be extremely bright or intensely atmospheric, like drifting mist, falling rain or snow, and the movement of wind. Two recent inventions aided the Impressionists in their creative expression: the invention of the snapshot camera, which prompted artists to seek more than an exact likeness in their work; and the invention of oil paints in tubes, by John G. Rand, an American portrait painter living in England, so that artists could more easily paint outside—*en plein air*—and at the same time study the play of the changing light from moment to moment upon a scene. Monet's view of a harbor on a misty morning, entitled *Impression, Sunrise,* spawned the name "Impressionism," and perhaps he explained this new concept of painting best when he declared to a journalist: "I paint what I see, I paint what I remember and I paint what I feel." It was the desire among Impressionists to paint what they *felt*—what they saw with their inner eye—that was key to their innovative technique, which at first encountered a great deal of public ridicule. Numerous artists saw Impressionism as the ultimate mode of artistic expression, and for them nothing could replace it in visual excitement. Although Vincent embraced Impressionism while in Montmartre, he considered it only a stepping-stone to even more stimulating forms of expression.

The steep hills of Montmartre overlook the sprawling city of Paris. But when Vincent lived there, the butte of Montmartre was still undeveloped. Named for three Christians who were martyred there in the third century, Montmartre had by 1886 long surrendered its lower slopes to the city's encroaching, heavily populated urban sprawl; but the crest was crowned with windmills that had once ground orris root, a fixative used in perfumes, and was planted with gardens that grew fresh vegetables for the Paris markets. By Vincent's day the windmills had been converted into restaurants, cabaret clubs, and dance halls, which attracted throngs of young people and became a favorite place for artists to meet.

Driven by the rebellious work he saw at Impressionist exhibitions, Vincent painted the remnants of market gardens, the outdoor cafés, and the colorful locals. Montmartre had more eccentrics than anywhere else in Europe, and Vincent mingled with the best. Thirsty for knowledge, for perspectives, for technique, he soaked up new ideas of artistic expression. He met talented painters, both successful and struggling, not only through Theo—who represented many of them—but also at Pere Tanguy's art supply store. The proprietor, Julien Tanguy, extended credit to struggling artists and exhibited the works of painters who he thought were underrated, including Vincent, in his storefront window. Vincent abandoned his isolationist manner and threw himself into the melting pot; he organized an exhibition of his recently acquired collection of Japanese prints and enthusiastically participated in Impressionist exhibitions.

Toulouse-Lautrec, an independently wealthy painter, rendered a powerful profile of Vincent in pastels: Vincent is seated alone in a café, bristling with hair like a grizzly bear, drinking absinthe and intently gazing ahead, with such a menacing stare that he seems ready to bite someone's head off. Lautrec, a crippled dwarf, attracted the most beautiful women of the district as companions. Looking at life through pince-nez, he painted the exotic nightlife, immortalized the can-can in paint, and hobbled about Montmartre as though he owned it, in black top hat and black cape. He would become a celebrity, after Vincent's death, as the artist who designed posters for Le Chat Noire cabaret and other nightspots, showing patrons and performers having a good time. Vincent particularly admired the way

Lautrec painted some of the more unsavory inhabitants of Montmartre. Influenced by Japanese art, he gave his figures a flatness similar to that of Japanese prints, and his choice of colors presented a rawness that perfectly captured the seedier side of the district.

Vincent considered Paul Cézanne a kindred spirit. Cézanne attended gallery openings and exhibitions dressed in paint-stained overalls and a crumpled cloth cap. He slurped his coffee from a saucer, had bulbous bloodshot eyes, and, with his thick Provençal accent, sounded like a country bumpkin. He was painfully shy in the presence of women, and shrank from the touch of both women and men, yet he fathered a son by a young model, supported both of them, and kept the relationship a secret from his wealthy father for fear of losing his monthly stipend. "There is plenty of male potency in his work because he does not let it evaporate in merrymaking," Vincent decided.

Edgar Degas painted luminescent images of ballet dancers and prostitutes and had a reputation for being "impotently flabby." But Vincent described him as "a small lawyer who does not like women, for he knows that if he loved them he would become insipid as a painter. Degas' painting is virile and impersonal for the very reason that he has resigned himself to be nothing but a small lawyer with a horror of getting excited."

Vincent admired Monet's art. He could not understand his chaotic domestic life, however. Monet had lived with his wife, Camille, and their two children, and also with Alice Hoschede, the estranged wife of his main benefactor, Ernest, as well as her five children. All of them had occupied the same house, and it was presumed that Monet slept with both women. "Not so," insists Claire Joyes, Monet's biographer. "Monet was monogamous and Alice was far too religious."

Theo represented Monet, and Vincent met him at Theo's gallery. A Monet painting that particularly impressed Vincent was *Juan les Pins* (1888), in which unconventional colors were used to portray familiar objects. In it, Cap d'Antibes glows in the light of a setting sun across a sheet of glittering yellow Mediterranean Sea, and in the foreground seven writhing orange-hued pine trunks rise to create an immense canopy of dark foliage that frames a line of distant purple mountains and an apricot-colored sky.

Above them all in Vincent's estimation stood Paul Gauguin, who, like Cézanne, had studied with Camille Pissarro. Born in Paris to a Breton father and a Creole mother, Gauguin's father had to flee France to avoid political persecution, and so Gauguin was raised in Peru. His father, however, died aboard ship before the family reached Peru, where his mother had relatives. Paul traveled the world as a sailor aboard merchant ships, and is thought to have taken an interest in art as a result of an uncle's art collection and tutoring. After marriage to Mette Gad, the attractive daughter of a Danish banking family, he settled in Paris, where he used her family's connections to work as a stockbroker. At first he was successful and earned enough to acquire paintings by Cézanne, Pissarro, and Manet. After the financial crash of 1882, his savings gone, Gauguin decided to take up painting. From that time forward, he had little contact with his wife and five children because he could not support them as a painter. He became part of the Impressionist circle after one of his paintings, *Suzanne Sewing,* was accepted by the Paris Salon. Showing the Gauguin family's plain, slightly overweight young housekeeper sitting nude and sewing on the edge of an unmade bed, the painting impressed the art world with its aura of intimate domesticity and Vermeer-like quality; but Gauguin's intimidating looks, forceful

temperament, overly intellectual arguments, and ruthless ambition made his fellow Impressionists generally mistrustful of him.
"You know I have Inca blood in me," he wrote to Bernard, though
this was strictly untrue, "and it has influenced everything I do. It is
the basis of my personality. I try to confront rotten civilization
with something more natural, based on savagery." He declared that
he liked painting in Britanny because "here I find a savage primitive quality. When my clogs echo on the granite ground I hear the
dull, muted, powerful sound I am looking for in painting."

Vincent considered Gauguin a brilliant painter obsessed
with artistic expression, a quality that Vincent well understood.
Vincent also judged Gauguin to be addicted to sex, ambitious,
and self-centered, but he did not hold any of that against him.

Realizing a need to brighten his palette, through exposure
to the works of Monet, Renoir, and Adolphe Monticelli in particular, Vincent began painting floral bouquets that afforded him
complementary color contrasts—blue and orange, red and green,
yellow and violet—in his effort "to harmonize brutal extremes."

Vincent observed that individually, Cézanne's paintings did
not command special attention. When hung among other works,
however, a Cézanne washed all the color out of its neighbors.
Vincent also noticed that the color in all the Cézannes was com-
plemented and heightened by gold frames, because the color
schemes were exceptionally bright, "pitched high." He decided,
therefore, to avoid being hung next to Cézanne at exhibitions.
Only after he moved to Provence did Vincent believe that he had
at last captured and matched Cézanne's mastery of color, so that
he no longer needed to worry about competing with his friend's
art. "If you saw our paintings side-by-side mine would hold their
own," he declared.

When Vincent saw Edouard Manet's *Peonies* (1880)—now in

the Musée d'Orsay, in Paris—it was a revelation. He marveled at
Manet's use of a heavy impasto application of paint and at the
way he employed the edges of a palette knife to model the iridescent petals. The critics hated it, but Vincent was sufficiently impressed by Manet's peonies to later use a similar
technique for his own potent sunflower series. He explained in
a letter to Theo:

> Do you remember that one day we saw a very extraordinary Manet at
> the Hotel Drouot, some huge pink peonies with their green leaves
> against a light background? As free in the open air and as much a
> flower as anything could be, and yet painted in a perfectly solid
> impasto . . . that's what I call simplicity of technique. And I must tell
> you that nowadays I am trying to find a special brushwork without
> stippling or anything else, nothing but the varied brush stroke.
> [August 27, 1888.]

When he was living in Montmartre, Vincent became aware
of pointillism. Pioneered by Georges Seurat, pointillism used a
myriad of dots of color to create a vibrant image, and for a period
Vincent adopted this technique. He befriended Seurat, whom he
encountered at various gallery exhibitions, but Seurat proved to
be an aloof, reclusive person, and Vincent formed a deeper
friendship with the more outgoing Paul Signac, a twenty-four-
year-old artist whose work most closely matched that of Seurat.
Signac sometimes accompanied Vincent on painting excursions, during which they would set up their easels side by side
and challenge each other to create the best impression of what
they saw. Although Signac's style is almost indistinguishable
from that of Seurat, he never quite captured Seurat's grandeur
of composition. Both artists employed countless minuscule dots

from which emerge beautiful, evanescent images when the work is viewed from a distance. The effects achieved by placing colors in juxtaposition, where one color can impose its influence on another, fascinated Vincent, as in Seurat's most famous painting, *Sunday Afternoon on the Island of La Grande Jatte* (1886). Vincent's *Interior of a Restaurant* is one of his earliest paintings inspired by pointillism.

The Impressionists and the pointillists were so adept at imbuing their work with the effect of a sun-drenched, vibrant, and vibrating atmosphere that the sensation became known as the "Impressionist shimmer." Often this effect was achieved by placing tiny flecks of white next to bold colors to heighten their brilliance and make them shine. Similarly, in nature, the white centers of flowers like lupines and delphiniums make their vivid blues and reds even brighter.

The single most important influence on Vincent's work was Monticelli, an obscure French painter who died an alcoholic in Marseilles at sixty-two in 1886, the year Vincent arrived in Paris. His style of painting, which influenced both Cézanne and Manet, was pastois, or pasty, mostly abstract and extremely colorful, with brush strokes so saturated with paint that their raised edges cast shadows on the canvas. Theo had acquired one of Monticelli's floral still-life paintings, *Vase of Flowers* (1875), and introduced Vincent to more of Monticelli's work in a local gallery. Vincent would become teary-eyed on hearing stories about Monticelli's dedication to artistic expression, and he would sit transfixed by photographs of the elderly gentleman dressed flamboyantly in a variety of costumes, one even showing him costumed as an Arab sheik. Sponsored by Theo, Paul Gigon, author of a monograph featuring Monticelli's work, described him as "a handsome old figure whose face showed a majestic tiredness. His great bald head, a large beard reaching to his chest, a peaceful expression and slow gestures, gave him the appearance of an old monk." An obituary by artist Etienne Martin noted Monticelli's humility and total disregard for success or honors: "He kept himself aloof from artistic movements, not because he disliked them, but because he had no desire to make himself visible as an artist." Biographer Aaron Shion wrote: "He had detached himself from everything, no home, no family, or obligations." As long as he was not hungry and his palette had paint on it, Monticelli worried about nothing. This was a creed Vincent well understood, and he identified strongly with this painter who so completely submerged himself in his art. Vincent considered Monticelli his mentor.

Excited by his friendships with the likes of Lautrec, Signac, and Gauguin, stimulated by his exposure to the Impressionists, Vincent was working with new energy. Theo wrote home with news that Vincent was well: "Many people here like him . . . he has friends who send him every week a lot of beautiful flowers that he uses for still lifes. He paints chiefly flowers, especially to make the colors of his pictures brighter and clearer."

In spite of Vincent's opinion that an overly active love life diminished creative energy and reduced artistic expression, in a letter to Wil he admitted to being sexually adventurous in Paris. Still seeking revenge on the church by "worshipping the love which the theologians called sin, by respecting a whore," he found in Montmartre and other nearby districts of Paris plenty of sinful pleasures for him to worship. During this period, too, he developed a sympathy for homosexual behavior, although he acknowledged that he had not yet explored it himself. In a letter to Theo, soon after leaving Montmartre for the south of France, Vincent applauded the tendency for modern

novels to weave into their stories incidents of homosexuality.
Referring to homosexuality among both men and women,
he asked:

> Why should it be forbidden to handle these subjects? Unhealthy and
> overexcited sexual organs seek sensual delights such as da Vinci's. Not
> I, who have hardly seen anything but the kind of woman at 2 francs,
> originally intended for soldiers. But the people who have leisure for
> love-making, they want the da Vinci mysteries. I realize that these loves
> are not for everyone's understanding. But from the point of view of
> what is allowed, one could write books treating worse aberrations of
> perversion than Lesbianism. [August 13, 1888.]

One brief love affair that ended badly for Vincent was with
an older Italian woman, Agostina Segatori, the proprietress of
the Tambourin restaurant where Vincent staged an exhibition
of Japanese art and of his own work. Vincent's agreement was
that he could dine at the Tambourin in exchange for a few pictures per week; therefore, the establishment's walls were soon
covered with his work. Most of them were floral still lifes. This
lasted several months, until the restaurant went bankrupt.
When the restaurant was sold, all Vincent's paintings were
placed in a pile and auctioned for a ridiculous sum. Segatori had
posed for Courbet and Corot, and Vincent had also painted her
several times. When they broke up, she locked Vincent out of her
establishment and he had to force open the door in order to
recover his Japanese prints. A grotesque, full frontal nude portrait long thought to be Segatori is today housed at the Barnes
Foundation in Philadelphia, but it has recently been proven to
be an anonymous prostitute Vincent met on the street. (It shows
the woman diseased—her legs, face, and armpits swollen from

syphilis.) There is one interesting reference to Segatori in a letter to Theo, who at the time was away in Holland. Following his eviction from her restaurant, Vincent wrote:

> As for la Segatori . . . I still feel affection for her and I hope that she, too still feels some for me. But at the moment she is in a difficult situation . . . she is in pain and unwell. Although I wouldn't say so—I'm convinced she has had an abortion (unless, that is, she has had a miscarriage)—anyway in her case I don't hold that against her. [Summer 1887.]

Whether Vincent thought he was the cause of any pregnancy is not clear, and little is known about Vincent's other romantic entanglements because he was no longer corresponding regularly with Theo, now that the two brothers were living together.

Prior to Vincent's arrival in Paris, Theo had experienced a protracted relationship with a prostitute he referred to only as "S" in his correspondence. Like Sien, she was ill and needy, and when he found her abandoned in the street a year prior to Vincent's arrival, Theo had hastily invited her to share his apartment. The relationship had ended by the time Vincent arrived in Montmartre, but "S" still clung to Theo, and sought him out for help and comfort whenever she felt depressed. She went so far in her persistent neediness that she moved back into the apartment when Theo was out of town. In her, Vincent saw the opportunity to save another damsel in distress. He suggested to Theo:

> But, old fellow, the solution to the S problem . . . namely "either she gets out or I will," would be very succinct and efficacious—if it were practical. But you would run your head against the same difficulties Andre Bonger and I have had to face the last few days. . . . So no catastrophes

please! Well, I told Bonger what I told you, namely that you should try
to pass her along to somebody else . . . an amicable arrangement,
which would seem obvious, could be reached by your passing her on
to me. . . . I am ready to take S off your hands, preferably *without*
having to marry her, but if the worst [sic] comes to the worst *even*
agreeing to a marriage of convenience. [August 1886.]

Vincent rationalized that if he married S, she could then cook
for the two brothers and keep the apartment clean, besides helping Vincent out with his expenses by working—yet another glar-
ing example of his view of marriage as a way of enabling him to
pursue his art.

Vincent further advised Theo that in addition to S, their
mutual friend André Bonger, a Dutchman who would eventually
become Theo's brother-in-law, was also sleeping at the apartment. "These are queer days," Vincent commented. "At times we
are very much afraid of her, and at other times we are almighty
gay and lighthearted. But S is seriously deranged, and she is not
cured yet by a long shot." Bonger himself hastily wrote Theo,
advising him that Vincent's marriage suggestion was ridiculous:

The basis of Vincent's reasoning corresponds with my own conviction. The problem is that S's eyes must be opened. She is not the
least bit in love with you, but it is as if you have cast a spell on her.
Morally she is seriously ill. It goes without saying we cannot leave
her to her fate in this condition. On the contrary, we have been as
kind as possible to her. If we hadn't, she would have gone mad. . . .
The great difficulty is her obstinacy. . . . Nothing is to be gained by
harsh treatment. For the time being it is extremely difficult to
make a plan (Vincent's is impracticable, as far as I can see), but I
hope you are fully convinced that your handling of her has been

wrong; during the past year your relations have had no result other than getting her hopelessly muddled. If she could live a month with somebody else who would be able to satisfy her sensuality and take care of her . . . so she may recover her health, you would be forgotten. [August 1886.]

What is especially interesting about this liaison between Theo and S is the similarity to Vincent's relationship with Sien. Both Sien and S were undoubtedly loose women down on their luck, both were sickly, both were taken in out of sympathy for their distress.

Theo did leave S soon after this exchange of letters, because he had met André's older sister, Jo, who was to become his wife. The relationship ended abruptly when Jo found out about S, turned possessive, and insisted that she had to leave. However, this was not the first time Theo had saved a woman in distress. At the beginning of January 1883, Theo confided that he had taken in a young woman down on her luck. Her name was Marie, and she was a waif of a girl from Britanny whom he had found in the gutter. Deserted by a man who had stolen her money, she was suffering from a tumor on her leg. Theo took her in as his mistress and paid for an operation to remove the tumor. The incident was so similar to Vincent's recent experience with Sien that Vincent wrote to Theo and applauded him for such a noble deed: "Broadly speaking . . . a solemn, sorrowful figure of a woman has appeared on a cold, unmerciful pavement, and neither you nor I could have passed her by; instead we stopped and followed the dictates of our hearts."

This love affair worried Theo because the lower-class Marie was presumed to be a prostitute, and he hated the idea of his parents finding out. When he expressed this concern to Vincent and wondered how long he could continue to help her, Vincent replied: "From here to eternity." Vincent was even keen on Theo marrying the woman "because life becomes so very different with a woman." Theo did in fact contemplate marriage, but by 1884, the relationship must have ended, for her name mysteriously disappeared from his letters.

After his father's death, Vincent continued to harbor resentment toward his mother for her collusion in ending his relationship with Margot and for her unwavering conviction that he needed psychological treatment. On leaving the vicarage in Nuenen, Vincent kept in touch with news of home through his correspondence with Theo and his youngest sister, Wil. Although he corresponded with Wil intermittently during all his absences from home, the early letters are lost. The first of the surviving letters was written in the summer of 1887 after Vincent had moved to Paris. Wil had written to Vincent to lament her apparent lack of personal growth and development; for she yearned to be creative—as a writer, a painter, or a sculptor—but instead she found herself apathetic and forestalled. She felt like a wilted plant deprived of water, she said.

Vincent cared more deeply for Wil than he did for his other sisters, and in their evolving relationship the dynamic of the lady in distress with Vincent as her protector may have come into play. Wil had helped Vincent through many difficulties at home, and now she wanted his help. She was the only one of his sisters who had showed him any sympathy during his plight over Kee's rejection, and she was the only sister who had not blamed him for their father's death. Vincent proved to be a good listener and a supportive friend, and he responded to her letters in spiritual and enlightening terms. Over the next three years, this correspondence with Wil evidenced an almost Christ-like disposition in Vincent, as he counseled his sister with insights gained from his own inner turmoil—qualities not found in his letters to Theo.

Wil's admiration for Theo and Vincent—especially Vincent—can be realized in a letter she wrote in August 1886 to a Dutch girlfriend, Line Kruysse, following a visit by Theo:

My second brother, Theo, from Paris, left yesterday; he really is a dear boy. He told us so many good things about Vincent, the eldest, who is living with him. His paintings are getting so much better and he is beginning to exchange them for those of other painters, so everything's sure to come right in time. According to Theo, he is definitely making a name for himself. But we are under no illusions, and are only too grateful that he is having some slight success. You don't know what a hard life he has had, and who can say what is still in store for him. His disappointments have often made him feel bitter and have turned him into an unusual person. That was difficult for my parents, who could not always follow him and often misunderstood him. My father was strict, and attached to all sorts of conventions of which my brother never took any particular notice; needless to say, that often led to clashes and to words spoken in anger, which neither party was quick to forget. So during the past eight years Vincent has been a bone of contention with many, and all too often tended to forget all the God there was in him, the appearances to the contrary. During the past few years he has been working at home with us; after my father's death, Anna thought it would be more peaceful for Mother if he stopped living at home, and saw to it that he left us. He took that so badly that from then on he has not been in touch with us, and it is only through Theo that we have news of him.

Vincent's first surviving letter to Wil, a reply to hers of September 1887, was upbeat: it reflected his excitement to be among the Impressionists as, in an effort to comfort and counsel her, he assessed his own goals and progress as an artist. He began by reassuring Wil that Theo was well and that his sickly appearance had recently improved. Pale, bothered by a persistent cough, easily irritated, Theo constantly wore a look of worry on his face, but Vincent sprang ready to defend Theo's health whenever it was brought into question. "One must be strong to stand life in Paris as he has done," he asserted. "He goes on doing business, even though it is a difficult time for selling paintings nowadays."

Vincent then addressed Wil's concerns about her own inabilities. He suggested that a more active love life might help to stimulate her creativity; he even provided a tender definition of love as a "germinating force" in the process of "our natural development." The metaphor seems to stem from Vincent's own realization that love worked as a creative force in his creative life. He wrote:

Now, what shall I say about your little piece about plants and rain? You see yourself that in nature many flowers are trampled underfoot, frozen or scorched, and for that matter not every grain of corn returns to the soil after ripening to germinate and grow into a blade of corn—indeed, that by far the greatest number of grains of corn do not develop fully but end up at the mill—isn't this so? To compare human beings with grains of corn, now—in every human being who is healthy and natural there is a *germinating force,* just as there is in a grain of corn. And so natural life is *germination.*

What the germinating force is to the grain, love is to us.

Now we tend to stand about pulling a long face and at a loss for words, I think, when, thwarted in our natural development, we find

that germination has been foiled and we ourselves placed in circumstances as hopeless as they must be for a grain between the millstones.
[Summer or autumn 1887.]

Vincent noted that it was natural to seek for answers to
questions about oneself when life was not satisfying, but that
reading serious books was not enough to shed light on her dark-
ness. Because most people labored under melancholia and pes-
simism, Vincent believed that laughter was the best remedy.
Although he had found it difficult to laugh in his early years, he
told Wil that he often enjoyed a good laugh now, and humorous
books helped. In particular, he named Guy de Maupassant as an
example of a writer who made him smile. While he liked Voltaire
in *Candide*, for writers who bared the literal truth in life he recommended Emile Zola in *La Joi de Vivre* and Maupassant in his
masterpiece *Bel-Ami.*

They portray life as we feel it ourselves, thus satisfying our need for
being told the truth.

Is the Bible enough for us? These days I think Jesus himself
would say again to those who sit down in a state of melancholy, "It is
not here, it is risen. Why seek ye the living among the dead?"

If the spoken or written word is to remain the light of the world,
then we have the right and duty to acknowledge that we live in an age
when it should be spoken and written in such a way that, if it is to be
just as great and just as original and just as potent as ever to transform
the whole of society, then its effect must be comparable to that of the
revolution wrought by the old Christians. [Summer or autumn 1887.]

Vincent added that he was glad to have read the Bible more thoroughly than many people, because it eased his mind to know

that such lofty ideas once held dominion over human life. But as beautiful as he thought the old ideas, he saw the beauty in new ideas for better reasons, especially socially progressive ideas that might effect a revolution in society, and artistic ideas that could revolutionize artistic appreciation.

Not without a touch of self-mockery, Vincent then struck a more personal note as he considered the passing of his youthfulness—a loss redeemed by the pleasures he gained from his profession as a painter.

> My own adventures are confined chiefly to making swift progress toward growing into a little old man—you know, with wrinkles, a tough beard and a number of false teeth, and so on. But what does all that matter? I have a dirty and difficult trade—painting, and if I were not what I am, I should not paint; but being what I am, I often work with pleasure, and can visualize the vague possibility of one day doing paintings with some youth and freshness in them, even though my own youth is one of the things I have lost. [Summer or autumn 1887.]

Finally, speaking to Wil as an artist to an artist, he encouraged her to pursue her aspiration to write not by searching for strength and comfort through faith in an almighty power or by immersing herself in study; instead, she should open herself to life's joys and the sensations of romance, and so he urged her:

> No, my dear little sister, learn how to dance, or fall in love with one, or more than one, of the notary's clerks, officers, in short any who are within your reach—rather, much rather commit any number of follies than study in Holland. It serves absolutely no other purpose than to make people slow-witted, and I won't hear of it.

For my part, I still continue to have the most impossible and
highly unsuitable love affairs, from which as a rule I come away with
little more than shame and disgrace. [Summer or autumn 1887.]

People who embraced the possibilities of love, Vincent suggested,
were more serene and holy than those who sacrificed their
hearts to a theological idea, for love broadened and deepened
the human experience that artists brought to their work. "In
order to write a book, perform an action, paint a picture in
which there is life, one ought to be a live human being oneself,"
he insisted. Thus, he told Wil, to make any progress as a writer,
she must consider books to be of secondary importance. Rather,
she should first study how to enjoy herself by finding as many
diversions as possible, because what art required was vitality,
strength in color, intensity. "So intensify your own health and
strength and live a little," he advised.

Vincent's recent rebellious resolve—to worship passions that the
church found sinful—could be fully realized in Montmartre. Its
most infamous sinful pleasure was prostitution, a profession
that was legal in France and licensed. In addition to artists,
Montmartre had attracted writers, musicians, theatrical performers, and people of other creative professions who sought
heightened sensations of pleasure in their spare time.

"Those who led the country recognized that Montmartre
had its own vision, that it was an uncontrollable site and that
the only way it could be dealt with was by allowing its existence,"
wrote art historian Gabriel P. Weisberg. "Montmartre was a site
where pleasure and vice were equaled." And, as art historian
Karal Ann Marling has noted, "Of all the places for artists to

meet, *Le Lapin Agile,* with its saucy signboard rabbit jumping out of a saucepan, was the epicenter of sophistication, wit and intoxicating liberté."

Another famous nightspot was *Le Chat Noir*, where patrons were advised to leave their inhibitions at the door. Owner Aristide Bruant was famous for his biting wit and raucous insults when new patrons entered, calling out: "Attention, gentlemen, here come the women! Are they whores or are they ladies? In God's name it's all the same. This time it's not the toilet slops I see; we have choice trollops, the deluxe courtesan with her three lovers! And those gentlemen following behind, are they pimps or ambassadors?"

In addition to sophisticated enterprises, there were seedy brothels, striptease establishments, and private clubs that catered to every kind of sexual proclivity, including transvestism, mate-swapping, vampirism, and sado-masochism. Cultists performed erotic rituals, and disciples of the Marquis de Sade participated in bondage and discipline and even acts of bestiality. Although there is a description, by a fellow boarder at his rooming house in Dordrecht, of Vincent engaged in an act of self-flagellation, it was the brothels and the world of prostitution that captivated him. When Vincent had worked as a bookseller in Dordrecht, he had been in his deeply religious phase and it is thought that, like a penitent monk, he punished himself for thinking evil thoughts. In Paris, the very atmosphere of a brothel thrilled Vincent, as the following letter to his young artist friend Emile Bernard demonstrates. Expressing pleasure at some preliminary images Bernard had sent showing paintings of women in a Paris brothel, Vincent wrote:

I thank you furthermore for the batch of sketches entitled "At the Brothel." Bravo! It seems to me that the woman washing herself and the one saying: "There is none other like me when it comes to exhausting a man," are the best; the others are grimacing too much, and above all they are done too vaguely. . . . At the brothel! Yes, that's what one ought to do, and I assure you that for one I am almost jealous of the damned fine opportunity you will have of going there in your uniform, which those good little women dote on. [October 7, 1888.]

Others among the Montmartre painters were beguiled by prostitution, including Lautrec, Degas, and Cézanne. The impetus stemmed from depictions of prostitution in Japanese art. Until Japan had opened up its borders to world trade in 1853 after centuries of self-imposed isolation, and Europeans saw Japanese art and artifacts, painters wishing to impress the Salon jury had chosen grandiose themes, such as emotionally charged religious subjects, heroic battle scenes, and dramatic mountain landscapes, whereas Japanese art was rich in scenes from more common everyday life—especially prostitution and the theater. In Lautrec's painting *La Rue des Moulins*, he shows two prostitutes standing in line, their skirts hitched up over their naked thighs as they wait to be examined by a doctor in order to receive a permit to practice their trade. Lautrec had a talent for capturing the tragic look of degradation, abuse, and resignation in a prostitute's face, whereas Degas's images tended to glorify the profession by showing voluptuous women with pleasant features in elegant boudoir settings. Renoir also sentimentalized the profession; his painting *After the Concert* shows two angelic-looking young prostitutes soliciting two dignified top-hatted young gentlemen outside a theater. Though Renoir and

Vincent never met, Vincent valued his friendships with both Lautrec and Degas. For all his sympathy for prostitutes, however, Vincent never painted their louche world. In a letter to Bernard from Arles, he wrote: "I have already written you a thousand times that my night café is not a brothel. . . . But going in one evening I came upon a pimp and his whore making up after a fight. The woman pretended to be indifferent and haughty, the man wheedling." Vincent described painting the scene from memory and using an unusual color combination, but he did it only to please Bernard: "I have painted a study for you I should have preferred not to paint."

Gustave Courbet, precursor to the Impressionsts, had shocked the Paris art world with the realistic intimacy of peasant girls exposing their genital regions on cliff-tops. He even painted a surprisingly tasteful close-up view of a woman's vagina in his monumental canvas *The Origin of the World,* which at one time hung in the Louvre and today occupies a place of prominence in the Musée d'Orsay. However, it was the devoutly religious Cézanne, a self-described prude, who produced what was considered the most sacrilegious, most licentious image ever painted. Entitled *Lot's Daughters,* it shows the Biblical father conducting incest with one daughter in the presence of the other. Cézanne also catered to the public's prurient interest in bestiality in his painting *Leda with the Swan*—now in the Barnes Foundation—which even shows the swan's flaccid genital appendage retracting into its cloaca. Gauguin painted his own version of the Greek legend in *Leda and the Swan,* and then followed it with a reclining nude being fondled by a fox, entitled *The Loss of Virginity,* using the fox as a symbol of perversity.

Edouard Manet appealed to the public's interest in voyeurism and mate-swapping with his masterpiece *Dejeuner sur l'Herbe,* in which a naked woman sits intimately between two fully clothed young gentlemen in a woodland glade. He followed this controversial painting with the voyeuristic *Olympia,* which shows a nude woman displaying herself on a bed to an unseen admirer, while her black maidservant unwraps a gift of a bouquet of flowers. The controversy over the provocative image then prompted Cézanne to mock the painting in his *Modern Olympia,* which has him seated in a luxurious brothel and admiring the charms of a naked courtesan whose black maidservant is throwing back the sheets with an energetic flourish. This painting today is part of the Annanberg Collection, housed at the Metropolitan Museum of Art, New York.

To what extent Vincent explored the exotic pleasures of Montmartre with Gauguin can only be surmised. In one letter, Vincent described Gauguin as having "savage instincts"; he said that for Gauguin, blood and sex prevailed over ambition, and he noted that Gauguin interested him "very much as a man—very much." Vincent wished there were more men like him—"men with hands and stomachs of workmen. Men with more natural tastes—more loving and more charitable temperaments—than the decadent dandies of the Parisian boulevards have."

Although Gauguin was married, he was by then separated from his wife, who was living in Denmark with their children. Vincent, of course, was unmarried, and as, in later correspondence, he said he would eagerly anticipate exploring brothels with Gauguin in Arles, it's likely that the two of them visited brothels together in Paris. This could have established their special male bond. They exhibited their work side by side at the Grand Bouillon Restaurant du Chalet, and they exchanged paintings during Vincent's Montmartre period. These exchanges not only show the respect they held for each other's work; it might indicate, too, the special affection the two painters shared, as the swapping of paintings between artists often indicates intimate feelings toward each other. Moreover, Vincent's gift of two large paintings (both showing sunflower seed heads) for a small one of Gauguin's (a Martinique tropical landscape) might indicate Vincent's stronger affections for Gauguin. Conversely, it could be argued that the imbalance in the exchange merely exemplifies Gauguin's conceit and egotism, which would regard a straight one-for-one exchange as an insult. Nonetheless, there does seem to be a profoundly emotional element at play in this exchange of their art, especially when they were already discussing the possibility of moving south and living together in Arles.

Along the crest of Montmartre, above the street where Vincent lived, lay extensive vegetable plots tended by market -gardeners. The crops were planted in regimented blocks—bright green lettuce next to blue-green leeks, the dark green spinach next to yellow-green cabbages—with each block delineated by narrow dirt paths and drainage ditches so that the gardens assumed a quilt-like design. They also offered long lines of perspective that Vincent liked to exaggerate. This focus on the agrarian aspects of Montmartre is in complete contrast to Renoir's focus on the extraordinary gaiety of the district. Renoir's masterpiece, *Le Bal au Moulin de la Galette*, painted twelve years before Vincent's arrival, shows a Montmartre dance hall thronged with young people interacting socially around an outdoor dance floor, while Vincent's earthier paintings show a completely different side of Monmartre: deserted back alleyways, empty restaurants, sparsely populated streets, and cultivated plots dominated by windmills more reminiscent of the fenlands of Holland.

If the weather was inclement, Vincent painted indoors, and in his letters he explained that all his flower paintings were experiments in color contrasts and harmonies. When Vincent applied these experiments to his paintings of the countryside, he made even more significant advances, allowing two predominant colors to dominate a composition. He found blue and pink tones in a path through a woodland in *Path in the Woods.* He similarly used yellow and blue in *Wheat Field with Lark,* which conveys the sensation of the wind blowing through ripening stalks of wheat, and suggests the fluttering of the lark's wings in deft, energetic brush strokes.

Only his portraits left Vincent disappointed. Lacking funds to pay models to sit for him, time and again he painted self-portraits in an effort to apply his newly found knowledge about color to images of the human form. One exceptional painting for which Vincent used a model was *Woman Sitting at a Cradle,* a study that is predominantly a contrast of black and white. Vincent's most memorable self-portrait of this Paris period, *Self Portrait with Straw Hat,* partnered yellow and orange with blue, and in it the right side of his jaw shows a sunken cheek—the result of a recent tooth extraction.

Vincent's work rewarded him with more than satisfaction; it gave him a sense of serenity, if only briefly. It was a quality he also wished for Wil so that she would not remain melancholy or turn sour or bitter or ill-tempered:

> Now, having as much of that serenity as possible, even when one
> knows little or nothing for certain, is perhaps a better remedy for all

ills than what is sold in the pharmacy. Much of it comes by itself; one
grows and develops of one's own accord. . . . Enjoy yourself too much
rather than too little. [Summer or autumn 1887.]

Vincent wished, too, that Wil could study with him, as he
thought it would do her good to paint alongside him rather than
to write, because painting might better help her express her
feelings than did writing. But even as he asserts the benefits of
paintings—the peace and serenity he feels—he hints at still
being haunted by dark subconscious emotions.

"For me," he wrote, "it is a relief to do a painting, and without that I should be more miserable than I am."

Chapter Five

HIGH
EXPECTATIONS

ARLES, FRANCE, MARCH–SEPTEMBER 1888

A preliminary sketch of Vincent's *Yellow House*, in 1888, where he lived with the artist Gauguin for two months.

When Vincent first arrived in Paris, he declared: "The air in France is clarifying my ideas and is doing me good, a lot of good, all the good in the world." Two years later, he had produced 230 paintings, more than in any comparable time period, and all of them experiments in color. Now he wanted a different quality of light in which to work.

During his Paris period, Vincent had attempted to absorb every nuance of artistic expression the city had to offer. His work was often satisfying, but his love affairs were emotionally draining. So were his arguments with his brother. More and more, Vincent was complaining that Theo was not doing enough to sell his paintings, while Theo found his brother's messy habits around the apartment increasingly intolerable. Vincent's canvases and painting paraphernalia littered the rooms, soiled laundry lay strewn on the floor, his dirty dishes were piled high in the sink. The apartment often smelled so badly of linseed oil, mold, and rotting leftovers that Theo could not bring friends or clients home. He also resented having to collect Vincent from the police station, where he was frequently confined—if not for drunkenness, then for obstructing traffic by setting up his easel in a busy thoroughfare or for starting altercations with passersby who ridiculed his work.

Harassed, emotionally pummeled by this Parisian domi-
natrix of a city, Vincent sought out a new, more submissive
mistress—Japan.

By 1862, nine years after Japan had opened up its ports to
world trade, that long-isolated country's art and artifacts were
in big demand in Europe. Vincent had started collecting
Japanese woodblock prints when he was studying in Antwerp
and had expanded his collection in Paris.

Vincent admired the animation and simplicity of Japanese
art. Its lines drawn quickly with a reed pen, it had a visual spon-
taneity, and he admired its subject matter. Because Japanese art
could not be exhibited in Japan without a censor's stamp of
approval, artists avoided religious topics and depictions of war.
Instead, they chose more commonplace subjects, such as close-
ups of almond blossoms, and scenes of simple domesticity, like
a woman combing her hair, and images from the world of the
geisha. Japanese art also featured unusual viewpoints, often
from a high elevation to provide striking lines of perspective. In
paintings of gardens and landscapes, truncated forms in the
foreground were frequently used to frame the scene and
enhance the impression of distance.

Vincent, of course, did not have the financial means to travel
halfway around the world to live and work in Japan. Closer by,
though, in a quiet corner of France, was another place that, with
its serene landscapes, he was assured resembled the countryside
of Japan. It was Provence.

Vincent told Theo: "I believe that by looking at nature under
a brighter sky, one might gain a truer idea of the Japanese way
of feeling and drawing." And to find that sky, he left for Arles, in
Provence, where he hoped Gauguin would join him. Vincent had
noticed that of all the struggling painters in Paris, Gauguin was

the one most idolized among art students. He also drew a large following of aspiring artists to Pont-Aven, a coastal community in Britanny, where he painted during the summer. Vincent had a notion that with Gauguin as a drawing card, he might be able to establish a thriving artists' colony in the south. Theo was glad to see Vincent leave; he wrote to Wil that Vincent was unable to maintain normal social relationships and thus was his own worst enemy.

But why Arles? Why not Marseilles, just seventy miles farther from Paris to the east, where his mentor Monticelli had painted and drunk himself into madness? Or Aix-en-Provence, fifty miles to the east, where Cézanne lived in a bucolic landscape dominated by Mont St.-Victoire, its foothills cloaked with more vibrant foliage greens than anywhere else in France? Probably the following passage from one of Vincent's favorite books, Michelet's *L'Amour,* struck a chord in Vincent's heart: "In Paris a young man sees a beautiful young woman with regular features. He falls in love with her. He marries her, thereupon he wants to know his wife's country, the town of Arles, where she was born. Once in Arles, he finds her everywhere, this person that he thought unique. This miracle is in all the streets. He sees hundreds of girls, and a thousand, all equally lovely. It is the beauty of a whole people that he had loved, the Arlesian beauty."

Well-written books influenced Vincent immensely. He especially liked those with a philosophical, humane message, or romantic notions of women, love, and marriage, as well as depictions of the peasantry. And treatments of topics like revolution, life, death, reincarnation, metamorphosis, and resurrection. When Emile Zola wrote *Germinal,* a story about the harsh existence of French coal miners who ultimately rise up against the tyranny of the mine owners, Vincent was preaching to Belgian miners, and he immediately felt an affinity for Zola, whose works expressed so emotionally what Vincent himself felt in his heart and had started to represent in his sketches. As a consequence, Vincent read every book written by Zola, and eagerly awaited each new one.

On the train to Arles, Vincent wrote Gauguin that he felt a childish delight in looking out of the window at the countryside as it flashed by, to see if it looked like Japan yet.

What Vincent discovered in and around Arles delighted him. The sky was clearer and the sun warmer than in Paris; the vast fields of grain looked like rice paddies, bordered as they were with reed fences that resembled the bamboo palings in Japan; and the peasants wore wide, cone-shaped straw hats like those favored by Japanese coolies. The landscape even offered outcroppings of limestone boulders and stunted, weathered pines that recalled the trees of Japan's Inland Sea.

Vincent explained his admiration for Japanese art in a letter to Theo: "All my work is in a way founded on Japanese art ... isn't it almost an actual religion which these simple Japanese teach us, who live in nature as though they themselves are flowers ... I envy the Japanese the extreme clearness which everything has in their work. Their art is as simple as breathing, and they do a figure in a few strokes with ease." *Harvest at La Crau, with Montmajour in the Background,* in which the reed fences and fields of grain resemble rice paddies, is a beautiful example of the Japanese influence on Vincent's work.

Canvases that captured the intensity of light and the hot colors of the south were plentiful, but Vincent missed the intense discussions about painting technique with his friends Signac, Lautrec, and Bernard, in particular, and he continued to dream of starting an artists' community in Arles. Key to achieving that goal was to persuade Gauguin to join him from Britanny. He had written to Gauguin: "The noise of Paris was making such a bad impression on me that I thought it wise, for the sake of my mind, to get away from it and go out into the country." While he waited for Gauguin's response, he built up high expectations of what they might achieve together.

In Arles, Vincent resumed his correspondence with Theo and continued to write to Wil. For several years he had not written to their mother, as he could not forgive her threat to have him declared legally insane following Margot's attempted suicide.

Wil's first letter to Vincent in Arles brought news of the death of his friend Anton (Jet) Mauve, friend at The Hague School who had instructed him first in painting with watercolors and then in working with oils. Vincent sent her a brief reply in March 1888. He explained that he had gone south because his work and health demanded a milder climate. "Besides, what they want in pictures nowadays is a contrast of colors, and these colors highly intensified and variegated, rather than subdued gray tones," he explained. Reacting to Mauve's death, he wondered whether there was life in the hereafter: "I loved him as a human being. Now it is hard for me to imagine that those who penetrate to the core of life . . . can cease to exist."

Though Vincent continued to regard Wil as his protégé, in letters to Theo he confided the hope that through the two of them she would "manage to marry an artist," as he thought it would help further her career.

To bring that about she ought to be a little in the movement. Certainly it is not out of the question that she should come and live with us. It speaks well for her taste that she likes sculpture; I was

very glad to hear it. Painting as it is now promises to be more subtle—
more like music and less like sculpture—and above all it promises
color. If only it keeps this promise! [August 27, 1888.]

In his second letter to Wil, sent a month later, Vincent said:
"Work has got me in its grip now; and I think forever." He felt
good about his change of environment. Arles was surrounded by
orchards of almond, peach, apple, and pear trees, and Vincent
was painting them cloaked in shimmering blossoms. He was
eager to produce a lot of work for exhibition at the World's Fair
in Paris the following year. At the moment, he told Wil, he was
working simultaneously on six pictures of fruit trees in bloom,
one of which he had decided to set aside for Mauve's widow with
an inscription dedicating it to Mauve's memory. He described
the painting as "a dug up piece of earth in an orchard with a fence
of reeds and two peach trees in full bloom. Pink against a scin-
tillating blue sky with white clouds, and in the sunshine."
Predicting that the art world would soon clamor for works by
colorists, he continued:

> By intensifying *all* the colors one arrives once again at quietude and
> harmony. There occurs in nature something similar to what happens
> in Wagner's music, which, though played by a great orchestra, is
> nonetheless intimate. . . . You will get an idea of the revolution in
> painting when you think, for instance, of the brightly colored
> Japanese pictures that one sees everywhere, landscapes and figures.
> [March 30, 1888.]

Vincent wrote to Wil again in June 1888. First addressing
her recurring bouts of depression, he counseled that the best
cure for depression—and, indeed, all diseases—was to treat them

with profound contempt. What his own depression relates to, he does not say. Might it be connected with Agostina's abortion, the death of a child that may have been his? Might the accusations of a pregnant Margot still bother him? For he may have heard rumors that Margot had delivered a child out of wedlock and given it up for adoption through an orphanage. He advised Wil further that the remedy to her problem lay not in healing herbs but in a change of climate:

> The sun in these parts, *that* is something different . . . I assure you that in our native country people are as blind as bats and criminally stupid because they do not exert themselves more to the Indies or somewhere else where the sun shines . . . one gets stultified by introspection; one should not rest until one knows the opposite too . . . energy begets energy, and conversely paralysis paralyzes others. [June 22, 1888.]

Vincent then deplored the stagnation produced by the art establishment with its practice of not honoring a painter's work until after the painter was dead, and with its control over the public's appreciation of art, which was dictated by a few shortsighted critics and dealers. "Here we are now, living in a world of painting which is unutterably paralytic and miserable," wrote Vincent. "The exhibitions, the picture stores, everything, everything, are in the clutches of fellows who intercept all the money."

Vincent realized that the majority of people found his art difficult to appreciate. Yet he was certain that he had found his course and that, to succeed, he had to work directly from nature, but at the same time had to avoid "painfully exact imitation," and often had to depart far from the original. Nonetheless, he felt himself incapable of altering the paralytic situation in the art community; so, he told Wil, he had to remain dependent on Theo. In fact, Theo may have been the biggest obstacle to Vincent's making a sale, because prospective buyers regarded their relationship as blatant nepotism. If Vincent himself considered this a possibility, he dismissed the notion, no doubt out of a deeper conviction that by sticking with Theo, his goal of recognition would be realized eventually.

"All that one hopes for, independence through work, influence on others, all comes to nothing, nothing at all," he complained to Wil. For the future, though, he predicted that the work of the best of the underrated modern painters, like Gauguin, Signac, and Lautrec, would last a long time: "They will go on existing as long as there are eyes capable of enjoying something that is specifically beautiful. But I always regret that one cannot make oneself richer by working harder—on the contrary."

When Theo and his partner Tersteeg in Holland held an exhibition of Impressionist art, they did not make a single sale. "Well, this is to be expected," Vincent told Wil. "One has heard talk about the Impressionists, one expects a whole lot from them, and when one sees them for the first time one is bitterly, bitterly disappointed, and thinks them slovenly, ugly, badly painted, badly drawn, bad in color, everything that's miserable."

Vincent expected things to change. Alluding to the successes of Renoir's voluptuous nudes and Monet's atmospheric landscapes, he added: "And though some of the twenty painters who are called Impressionists have become comparatively rich men, and rather big fellows in the world, yet the majority of them are poor devils, whose homes are cafés, who lodge in cheap inns and live from hand to mouth, from day to day." To help more living

artists succeed was one of the reasons Vincent wanted to establish his artists' retreat in the south.

To illuminate for Wil the link between his art and that of the
Impressionists, Vincent explained the principles of color in terms
of planting a garden, for he knew how much she liked to garden:

> Cornflowers and white chrysanthemums and a certain number of
> marigolds—see here a motif in blue and orange.
>
> Heliotrope and yellow roses—a motif in lilac and yellow.
>
> Poppies and red geraniums in vigorous green leaves—motif in
> red and green.
>
> These are fundamentals, which one may subdivide further, and
> elaborate, but quite enough to show you without the help of a picture
> that there are colors which cause each other to shine brilliantly,
> which form a *couple,* which complete each other like man and
> woman.
>
> Explaining the whole theory to you would involve quite a lot of
> writing, yet it might be done.
>
> Colorings, wallpapers and whatnot could be made much prettier
> by paying attention to the laws of colors. . . . [June 22, 1888.]

"But I am writing far too much just about painting," he apologized. Yet he only wanted Wil to realize that in spite of poor
sales and an inauspicious beginning, the permanent exhibition
of the Impressionists that Theo had mounted now, just a year
before the World's Fair—where he hoped to show at least fifty of
Vincent's paintings—marked an important event in an art world
stultified by conventions.

"I hate writing about myself," Vincent told Wil. "And I have
no idea why I do it. Perhaps I do it in order to answer your questions." He did it, too, in order to assure her that he felt good about

his work, even though "*I still feel the want* of my models. If only I had them here—I feel sure my fifty pictures would turn out to be hits."

He concluded by encouraging Wil to accept an invitation from Theo to visit Paris:

I don't know how it would impress you. When I saw it for the first time, I felt above the dreary misery, which one cannot wave away, as little as one can wave away the tainted air in a hospital, however clean it may be kept. And this remained with me afterward—though later on I gained the impression that it is also a hotbed of ideas, and that people try to get everything out of life they can.... Other cities become small in comparison with it, and it seems as big as the sea. There one always leaves behind a considerable part of one's life. [June 22, 1888.]

Vincent had two consuming passions—painting and reading—and the two were intertwined, for it was his reading of richly descriptive passages in French and English novels that inspired him to paint unconventional subjects, like night scenes, in unconventional colors.

Vincent's search for unique subjects was ceaseless. Once he found a scene or a person that he wanted to paint, he quickly rendered a pen-and-ink sketch, but then deliberated a long time over perspective and composition before beginning the brush-work. Once he had decided on a particular viewpoint, however, he worked furiously, and sometimes completed a canvas in an hour. He explained his approach to Bernard:

My brush stroke has no system at all. I hit the canvas with irregular touches of the brush, which I leave as they are. Patches of thickly

laid-on color, spots of canvas left uncovered, here and there portions
that are left absolutely unfinished, repetitions, savageries; in short
I am inclined to think the result is disquieting and irritating . . . to
those people who have preconceived ideas about technique. [April 9,
1888]

This intense method of working–spending hours and days to
determine how he'd compose an image, and then attacking the
canvas savagely–resulted in paintings that seemed to throb
with energy. The entire process of creating a painting made
Vincent feel jubilant and alive, while the time in between paintings made him short-tempered and melancholy. "I work in the
middle of the day, in the full sunshine, without any shadow at
all, in the wheat fields," he wrote to his brother, "and I enjoy it
like a cicada."

Still, lack of sales among avant-garde painters in general
continued to dishearten Vincent. The Paris art establishment
was composed of painters, dealers, critics, and collectors. Most
of the dealers had galleries where they sold paintings privately
and at auction. Few artists sold directly to collectors, and a collector's choice was often influenced by critical acclaim, especially from the press, and, even more importantly, from the
judges of the Paris Salon.

Vincent complained bitterly to Wil and Theo that a few
wealthy collectors controlled the public's taste in art. At the top
of their ranks was the Tsar of Russia, Alexander III, whose
taste–like that of most art collectors among the European
aristocracy–was largely influenced by snob appeal. Along with
the great Italian masters like Leonardo da Vinci and Raphael,
the work of Courbet, Corot, and Millet had more recently become
recognized as collectable, following their recent deaths. At the

Vincent van Gogh at the age of thirteen. Physically, he was a strong, healthy boy, but his mother's continued mourning for her dead firstborn caused Vincent to feel unloved and unable to handle emotional rejection later in life.

(TOP LEFT) Vincent's father, the pastor Theodorus van Gogh. He ran an autocratic household and disapproved of his son's choice of artistic career and reading material. (TOP RIGHT) Vincent's mother, Anna Cornelia Carbentus. She lost her firstborn soon after childbirth and named Vincent after the dead child. (LEFT) Vincent's younger sister, Wilhelmina. They remained close throughout his life. Following Vincent's death, she spent more than thirty years in a lunatic asylum.

(RIGHT) Vincent's younger brother, Theodore van Gogh, supported Vincent's painting career financially, but threatened to put a halt to the allowance just weeks before Vincent's suicide. He died within six months of Vincent's death, in a lunatic asylum, after threatening to murder his wife and child.

(TOP) Vincent's sister-in-law, Joanna van Gogh-Bonger, named her son Vincent after her brother-in-law. Her tender-hearted letters to Vincent show she understood his art perhaps better than anyone of her day. Inheriting his vast cache of paintings after Theo's death, she dedicated herself to perpetuating Vincent's reputation in the art world.

(RIGHT) Vincent's cousin, Cornelia (Kee) Vos-Stricker, and her son Johannes Paulus. Kee firmly rejected Vincent's marriage proposal with the devastating words, "No, never never."

(TOP) Entitled *Sorrow* (1883), this pen-and-ink
sketch shows Vincent's common-law wife, Sien,
in a moment of depression.

(RIGHT) *Girl Kneeling by a Cradle* (1883)
shows Sien's two illegitimate children in a
tender moment of domestic bliss.

(RIGHT) Stein de Groot, Vincent's nineteen-year-old model. When it was discovered she was pregnant, it was assumed Vincent was the father. From his oil painting *Peasant Woman Standing Indoors* (1885).

The prostitute Rachel *(left)*, whom Vincent shared with Gauguin: from Vincent's painting *The Café,* also known as *The Brothel*. Rachel was sixteen when Vincent, in a fit of delirium, presented her with his severed ear.

Marguerite Clémentine Gachet was twenty-one years old when Dr. Paul Gachet, her father, asked Vincent to end their relationship. Note her resemblance to Stein de Groot. This photograph was taken in 1920.

Vincent's doctor in Auvers, Dr. Paul Gachet, photographed in military uniform. It is quite possible that Gachet loaned Vincent the gun that ended his life.

Entrance to the asylum of St. Paul at St. Remy, where Vincent admitted himself for continued mental care after treatment in Arles failed to cure him.

Vincent and Theo's gravesites, in a churchyard above Auvers. Visitors often decorate the gravestones with flowers.

bottom of the collectors' pyramid were the nouveau riche. What broke the stranglehold on public taste by the tightly knit European art-collecting community was the entry of wealthy American collectors into the game. At their vanguard was Mary Cassatt, the American-born Impressionist painter from Pittsburgh. Cassatt's association with an American couple, Henry and Louisine Havermeyer, who had amassed a fortune from a Philadelphia sugar refinery, profoundly affected the reputation and value of the French Impressionists. Cassatt advised the Havermeyers in the building of their exemplary art collection, later bequeathed to the Metropolitan Museum of Art in New York. Among the Havermeyers' prizes were paintings by Manet, Degas, and Pissarro.

In Vincent's second letter to Wil from Provence, he wrote enthusiastically:

> What strikes me here, and what makes painting so attractive, is the clearness of the air. You *cannot* know what this means, because this is exactly what we do not have in Holland—but one distinguishes the color of things at an hour's distance; for instance the gray-green of the olive trees, and the grass-green of the meadows, and the pink-lilac of a dug-up field. In Holland we see a vague gray line on the horizon; here even in the far, far distance the line is sharply defined, and its shape is clearly distinguishable. This gives one an idea of space and air. [June 22, 1888.]

Arresting as the scenery around Arles was, Vincent lacked models for studies of facial expressions. So Vincent began painting self-portraits that presented his face and features in a variety of different ways. "I want to emphasize the fact that the same person can furnish motifs for very different portraits," he told Wil, and then described a special self-portrait recently sent to Theo:

> A pinkish-gray face with green eyes, ash-colored hair, wrinkles on the forehead and around the mouth, stiff, wooden, a very red beard, considerably neglected and mournful, but the lips are full, a blue peasant's blouse of coarse linen, and a palette with citron yellow, vermilion, malachite green, cobalt blue, in short all the colors on the palette except the orange beard, but only whole colors. The figure against a grayish-white wall. [June 22, 1888.]

Although Vincent imagined that Wil might find the portrait more like the face of Death, because the skin was the color of a cadaver, he believed it was a good example of the advantage Impressionism had over other forms of art: "It is to be *different* from a photograph . . . it is not banal, and one sees a deeper resemblance than the photographer's."

Color film had not yet been invented, but not even the hand-tinting of a black and white photographic image could approximate the expressive power that lay in Vincent's painted portrait—in the skillful modeling of the forehead and cheeks, and the bristle-brush appearance of his closely cropped hair, in the emotional texture of the face. Now, he told Wil, he looked different from the self-portrait he had described, for he had shaved himself bald and beardless to look like a Buddhist monk, in an attempt to gain a closer affinity to Japanese artists.

> Furthermore, my complexion has changed from green-grayish-pink to grayish-orange, and I am wearing a white suit instead of a blue one, and I am always very dusty, always bristlingly loaded like a porcupine,

with sticks, painter's easel, canvases and further merchandise. Only
the green eyes have remained the same, but of course another color in
the portrait is the yellow straw hat, like a fieldworker's, and a very
black little pipe. [June 22, 1888.]

Vincent was actually referring to two portraits in this description: one that shows him with a shaved head and another somewhat more like a caricature of a gardener, in which he is wearing
a yellow straw hat.

Vincent had not only altered his mien, he had also now settled
into the upstairs apartment of a yellow house with a green door
and green shutters. The interior walls were whitewashed and
hung with brightly colored Japanese prints; red tile covered the
floors. Wil had meanwhile found accommodations in Holland
with a garden, rather than an apartment with a steep flight of
stairs. Vincent liked her choice, for "in Paris I could never accustom myself to climbing stairs, and I always had fits of dizziness in
a horrible nightmare which has left me since," he explained.

After closing the letter with "Your loving Vincent," he added
this postscript: "Theo is doing his best for all the Impressionists;
he has done something, or sold something, for every one of
them, and he will certainly go on doing so . . . he is quite different from the other dealers, who do not care the least bit about
the Impressionists." In fact, Theo's employers never acknowledged any benefit from his sales of Impressionist work. After
Vincent's death, when Theo fell ill, they instructed his replacement to move the remaining inventory of Impressionist work to
the basement, for they still felt the work of dead artists to be
more salesworthy.

* * *

When Vincent wrote to Wil again in July, he told her he was still working assiduously and continued to find Provence congenial. He thought the summer more beautiful than any he remembered in the north, but it was not typical for the south: frequently it rained in the morning or the afternoon, and an ill-natured, whining wind called *le Mistral* was proving to be troublesome as it invariably blew his easel over. The only way that Vincent could paint outdoors, therefore, was on his knees, with the canvas laid flat on the ground.

He described a painting he had recently finished under these very conditions:

> I have a study of a garden one meter wide, poppies and other red flowers surrounded by green in the foreground, and a square of bluebells. Then a bed of orange and yellow African marigolds, then white and yellow flowers, and at last, in the background, pink and lilac, and also dark violet scabiosa, and red geraniums and yellow sunflowers, and a fig tree and an oleander and a vine. And in the far distance black cypresses against low white houses with orange roofs—and a delicate green-blue streak of sky. [July 31, 1888.]

In the painting itself, not a single flower was drawn completely. The various flowers appeared instead as mere dabs of color—red, yellow, orange, green, blue, and violet—but nonetheless, in its juxtaposition of distinct colors, the painting conveyed the impression of nature's great variety. Because of Wil's particular love of flowers and her passion for gardening, Vincent supposed she would be disappointed by the painting's reliance on impression rather than realistic details. "But you will see that the subject is rather summery," he added.

Always watchful for interesting faces to paint, Vincent befriended his mailman, Joseph Roulin. He told Wil:

> I am now engaged on a portrait of a postman in his dark blue uniform with yellow. A head somewhat like Socrates, hardly any nose at all, a high forehead, bald crown, little gray eyes, bright red chubby cheeks, a big pepper-and-salt beard, large ears. This man is an ardent republican and socialist, reasons quite well, and knows a lot of things. His wife was delivered of a child today, and he is consequently feeling proud as a peacock, and is all aglow with satisfaction. [July 31, 1888.]

Vincent shared Roulin's joy in the birth of a healthy baby girl, and the fondness he expressed for the older man also appeared in letters to Theo:

> I do not know if I can paint old Roulin as I feel him; this man is a revolutionary. . . . But I watched him sing "The Marseillaise" and I thought I was transported back eighty-nine years in time. The scene was pure Delacroix, a Daumier, straight from the old Dutch. [August 11, 1888.]
>
> One portrait is the head, and one a half-length with hands. These portraits are more important to me than anything else. The good fellow, as he would not accept money for posing, cost more eating and drinking with me, and I gave him besides the *Lantern of Rochefort*. But that is a trifling evil considering that he posed very well. [August 6, 1888.]

Unfortunately, the painting Vincent gave Roulin has been lost. "I shall also paint the baby born today," he informed Wil, and then described another garden scene just completed, this one without flowers. Rather, it suggested in subtle shades of green and yellow the colors of foliage on trees and shrubs in a park.

In reply to an inquiry from Wil regarding a rumor that Vincent was planning to have someone live with him, he wrote:

> Well, this is rather probable, and with a very clever painter too [Gauguin] who, like the other Impressionists, is leading a life full of cares, and who is the proud owner of a liver complaint besides. Some time ago Theo bought a large picture from him portraying dusky women in pink, blue, orange and yellow cotton dresses under tamarind, coconut and banana trees with the sea in the distance. Like that description of Tahiti in *Le Mariage de Loti.* The fact is he has been to Martinique, and has painted among the tropical scenery there. [July 31, 1888.]

Another fact was that Theo had paid Gauguin a high price for the painting, and out of gratitude Gauguin had promised to visit Vincent. Theo believed that the companionship would brighten Vincent's outlook since he generally turned melancholy during long periods of solitude.

With excitement and admiration, Vincent reported to Wil that Gauguin worked "like one possessed, and he does all sorts of things; he is in Brittany at the moment." Indeed, the thought of being joined by the flamboyant Gauguin delighted Vincent, and he invested a lot of time and energy preparing for his friend's arrival. "We shall probably live together for the sake of economy, and for each other's company," he explained to Wil. To Theo he wrote: "I am hard at it, painting with the enthusiasm of a Marseillais eating *bouillabaisse*—which won't surprise you when you know that what I'm at is the painting of some great sunflowers." These sunflower paintings were intended specifically to decorate the rooms of his yellow house, in celebration of Gauguin's arrival.

In her most recent letter to Vincent, Wil had informed him of the death of their Uncle Cor, an art dealer, after whom their youngest brother was named. Vincent and his uncle had never been close—Cor was in fact one of his harshest critics—and Vincent was left nothing in his will. Theo, however, had been his favorite nephew, and he received a sizable inheritance. To make Vincent feel better about their uncle's slight, Theo sent him enough money to rent the yellow house; he also offered to pay Gauguin's travel expenses to Arles.

Despite his euphoria in anticipation of Gauguin's visit, Vincent confided to Wil: "Here I am afflicted now and then with an inability to eat, something of the sort you suffered from." Part of his eating problem could have been his uneasiness at the coldness of the local inhabitants. With few exceptions, such as the Roulin family, he was treated with suspicion. The Arlesians considered him to be a pervert, and children ridiculed him for his odd appearance and disconcerting habit of hanging around brothels in the evenings. But on the whole he managed to stay focused and clear-headed, a mental state that he attributed to the progress he believed he was making in his work as an artist.

Wil had told Vincent that she intended to visit Theo in Paris, and in his mid-August reply he again encouraged her to come south. He also suggested that when she left Paris, she "take along some study of mine to decorate your room."

Gauguin, though, remained uppermost in his mind. Vincent told Wil that with Gauguin he wanted to travel farther east, toward Nice, where the country was more rugged, since he had not yet in his life seen a mountain—an indication of the extent to which the lack of funds restricted Vincent's movements. "As soon as Gauguin is here, I suppose we shall do it," he announced. "But until then I am going to stay in Arles. And after he has come I should like to go on a walking tour with him all over Provence."

After repeating his plan to complete a series of sunflower paintings, Vincent abruptly closed the letter.

On September 8, 1888, Vincent wrote Wil that he was pleased that her visit to Paris had been a success, and then continued to fuel his excitement over Gauguin's prospective stay. He was busy furnishing the house, which at first had offered only sparse comforts. His bedroom, for instance, had just two straw-bottomed chairs, a table, and a bed of unpainted wood. Vincent wanted to decorate it with more portraits; he had already hung one that he had painted of the young Belgian Impressionist, Eugene Boch: "I have painted him a little like a poet, the fine nervous head standing out against a background of a deep ultramarine night sky with sparkling stars."

He wanted Gauguin's room to be more elegant, with a walnut bedstead and a blue coverlet. "And all the rest, the dressing table as well as the cupboard, in dull walnut. In this very little room I want to put, in the Japanese manner, at least six very large canvases, particularly the enormous bouquets of sunflowers." He reasoned that since the Japanese instinctively sought contrasts—sweetened spices, salted candy, fried ices, and iced fried foods—"it follows, according to the same system, that in a big room there should be very small pictures and in a very little room one should hang very large ones."

"For my part I don't need Japanese pictures here," he told

Wil, "for I am always telling myself that *here I am in Japan.* Which means that I have only to open my eyes and paint what is right in front of me, if I think it effective. . . ."

What had particularly captured his creative eye recently was the night, which he thought was more richly colored than the day, and he quickly noted that "putting little white dots on a black surface was insufficient to show a night sky." He proceeded by describing his work on a café exterior at night.

> On the terrace there are the tiny figures of people drinking. An enormous yellow lantern sheds its light on the terrace, the house front and the sidewalk, and even casts a certain brightness on the pavement of the street, which takes a pinkish-violet tone. The gable-topped fronts of the houses in a street stretching away under a blue sky spangled with stars are dark blue and violet and green, and in these surroundings the lighted square acquires a pale sulphur and a greenish-yellow citron color. It amuses me enormously to paint the night right on the spot. Others draw and paint such a picture in the daytime after a rough sketch. But I find satisfaction in painting these things immediately . . . it is the only way to get rid of the conventional night scenes with their poor sallow, whitish light, whereas a simple candle already gives us the rich yellows and orange tints. [September 9–16, 1888.]

The Night Café (1888) is an extraordinary work; the powerful complementary colors of golden yellow gaslight and rich violet tones for the street and the sky (opposites on the color wheel) are dramatic. Moreover, Vincent used neither black to paint the night sky, nor white to paint the stars. He explained his theories further to Wil:

My dear sister, it is my belief that it is actually one's duty to paint the
rich and magnificent aspects of nature. We are in need of gaiety and
happiness, of hope and love.

The more ugly, old, vicious, ill, poor I get, the more I want to
take my revenge by producing a brilliant color, well arranged,
resplendent. Jewelers too get old and ugly before they learn how to
arrange precious stones well. And arranging the colors in a picture
in order to make them vibrant and to enhance their value by their
contrasts is something like arranging jewels properly or designing
costumes. You will see that by making a habit of looking at Japanese
pictures you will love to make up bouquets and to do things with
flowers all the more. [September 9-16, 1888.]

Vincent himself continued to emulate the Japanese. He still
shaved his head like a Buddhist monk, and he told Wil that he
was pleased with a new self-portrait in which he had slanted his
eyes to make himself look more Japanese. Across the top he had
written a dedication to Gauguin.

He closed with a request for a photograph of his mother, to
whom he still had not written directly.

Vincent believed that an active sex life was healthy and even
sacred. He was sexually active, but all his relationships since
leaving Paris had been with prostitutes in the brothels of Arles.
Vincent's desire for a meaningful relationship with a woman,
and seeking women in distress, is no longer apparent, replaced
by quick, frequent, and convenient liaisons with prostitutes,
and a desire for Gauguin to come live with him. Vincent also
believed, however, that overindulgence was not good for an
artist seriously dedicated to painting.

In words that seem to announce the coming of Christ, he wrote Theo that someone even better than he would dominate the art world of the future: "You must feel as I do that such a one will come. . . . But the painter of the future will be a colorist such as never yet existed . . . this painter who is to come—I can't imagine him living in cafés, working away with a lot of false teeth, and going to soldiers' brothels as I do." Vincent seems here to be visualizing himself as John the Baptist foretelling the coming of the Savior, and he believed the ultimate colorist would be as pure as Christ. This Christ, though, is not incarnate in Gauguin, for Gauguin regularly and intemperately visited soldiers' brothels, as Vincent well knew; and in any case, Vincent predicted that this new art Messiah would appear in a future generation.

In Vincent's next letter to Wil, a month before Gauguin's arrival, he responded with delight to the news that she found herself more excited about sculpture than painting. He then declared his belief that watching artists at work was more important that seeing the results in a museum.

Wil had taken Vincent's advice that she read Maupassant's *Bel-Ami,* but she thought it wrong for the artist in the novel to end a relationship with a refined woman in favor of one with a servant girl from a farm. The man's rejection of an upper-class lady in favor of a common peasant reminded Vincent that life could be full of annoying fatalities, an allusion, no doubt, to his choice of Sien as a common-law wife over Kee, and his liking for Stien, the peasant girl in her faded blue dress, over a lady in a fine dress. "Well, painters die, or go mad with despair, or are paralyzed in their production, because nobody likes them personally," he mused.

A sad fatality lay behind Vincent's question to Wil about a painting of flowers in Theo's apartment. He wanted her opinion of it. It had been painted by Adolphe Monticelli, the recently deceased French artist whom Vincent identified as a father figure. According to Gauguin, Vincent could be reduced to tears by the mere mention of Monticelli's name. Addicted to alcohol, the old master had died in obscurity and poverty, his art virtually ignored during his lifetime. No doubt Vincent feared the same fate. To Wil, he reflected:

> I think of Monticelli terribly often here. He was a strong man—a little cracked or rather very much so—dreaming of the sun and of love and gaiety, but always harassed by poverty—of an extremely refined taste as a colorist, a thoroughbred man of a rare race, continuing the best traditions of the past. He died at Marseilles in rather sad circumstances, and probably after passing through a regular Gethsemane. Now listen, for myself I am sure that I am continuing his work here, as if I were his son or his brother. [August 27, 1888.]

With Gauguin, who he expected any day now, he would make a pilgrimage to Marseilles, where Monticelli had lived, he told Wil.

> It is my firm intention to go saunter in the Cannebiere there, dress exactly like him, Monticelli, as I have seen his portrait, with an enormous yellow hat, and black velvet jacket, white trousers, yellow gloves, a bamboo cane, and with a grand southern air.
>
> And there I shall find Marseillais who used to know him when he was alive . . . Monticelli is a painter who did the South all in yellow, all in orange, all in sulphur. The great majority of the painters, because they aren't colorists in the true sense of the word, do not use these colors there, and they call a painter mad if he sees with eyes

other than theirs. Of course all this is only to be expected. So I myself too have already finished a picture all in yellow—of sunflowers (fourteen flowers in a yellow vase and against a yellow background, which is certainly different from the previous one with twelve flowers on a blue-green background).

And I expect that I shall one day exhibit the former at Marseilles, and then there will be some Marseillais or others who will remember what Monticelli said and did in his time. [August 27, 1888.]

By the end of September, Vincent had built such high hopes of what he and Gauguin might accomplish together in Arles that he had worked himself into a state of nervous suspense. In a letter to Theo, he admitted frankly:

I am vain enough to want to make a certain impression on Gauguin with my work, so I cannot help wanting to do as much work as possible alone before he comes. His coming will alter my manner of painting and I shall gain by it, I believe, but all the same I am rather keen on my decorations, which are almost like French porcelain. And these days are magnificent. [October 3, 1888.]

In another letter to Theo, he wrote: "Do you realize that if we get Gauguin's support, we will be at the beginning of a very great event, which will open a new era for us," referring to Vincent's ambition to establish an artists' retreat in the south. He envisaged an educational institution where young, talented artists could interact and return to Paris like disciples to change the straitjacket thinking of the Salon.

In a letter to Gauguin, Vincent bubbled with enthusiasm: "I must tell you that while working I keep thinking incessantly of that plan to found a studio, which will have you and myself as permanent residents, but which the two of us would turn into a refuge and a place of shelter for comrades at moments when they are encountering a setback in their struggle."

He informed Gauguin that he thought of him with very strong emotions when he prepared his room, and concluded: "Let's be full of courage with regard to the success of our enterprise, and you must go on considering this your home, for I am very much inclined to believe it will last long."

Chapter Six

DESCENT
INTO MADNESS

ARLES, FRANCE, OCTOBER 1888-MAY 1889

Preliminary pen and ink sketch of Vincent's bedroom in Arles, 1888.

Vincent next wrote to Wil in November, several weeks after Gauguin's arrival in Arles, and although he said that he and Gauguin were getting along happily, the absence of details about their activities spoke volumes. While their time together passed smoothly enough for a few weeks, they soon began to have heated arguments about artistic technique and about the establishment of the proposed artists' colony in the south. Nor did Gauguin like Vincent's messy habits. Whereas Gauguin felt that Vincent should paint more from memory than from life, Vincent was critical of Gauguin's flat application of paint to the canvas and his anemic depiction of nature.

Gauguin was five years older than Vincent, and considered himself the superior artist. Strong-minded, self-centered, and egotistical, Gauguin could be cruelly acerbic and arrogant. ("A corpulent automaton with a stupid countenance" was his stinging description of the governor of the Marquesas Islands, Gustave Gallet, sparking a libel suit.)

An imposing man of sallow complexion, Gauguin was short in stature at only 5 feet, 4 inches in height, compared to Vincent's 5 feet, 9 inches. He had a prominent, aquiline nose and dark, malevolent eyes; he sported a bushy military-style moustache, a rakish forelock of dark brown hair, and a goatee. Always well-dressed, he wore a beret and painter's smock when painting *en plein air* and a dark business suit on social occasions. He was also an expert swordsman and a crack shot with a pistol.

Like Vincent, Gauguin was outspoken and confrontational about the plight of the poor, and he held liberal views on morality. No less than Vincent, he sought confirmation of his liberal ideals in contemporary romantic literature and the Bible; however, the two friends sometimes differed in their interpretations of passages from the Bible. Gauguin, for instance, quoted the Bible's exhortation to "increase and multiply" to justify sex outside marriage, whereas Vincent believed firmly in monogamy and envisioned the command only within a monogamous relationship.

The two shared a similar spirituality that did not recognize a God but believed in Godliness, and both painted numerous religious scenes. In artistic expression, they believed, lay the power to produce a more compassionate civilized society, one free of persecution from conventional religious edicts and mores. In the same way that British magazines like *The Graphic* and *Illustrated London News* raised public awareness of such social ills as slavery and child labor abuses, they felt that their art could move people to see the plight of poor and oppressed native cultures like the Polynesians and bring about needed changes.

Vincent, during his mission work with the Belgian miners, supported their cause to his own detriment. He had tried to demonstrate his sympathy for them both by personal deprivation and by speaking up against the mine management, and he was dismissed. When Gauguin traveled to Tahiti after Vincent's death, he deplored the French colonial policy of usurping native customs and rights. He also agitated against the attempts of Catholic missionaries to change the Tahitians' culture by teaching them absurd concepts of sin, destroying their naturalism and innocence, and encouraging them to wear Western clothes. As a result of Gauguin's persistent criticism, government officials made life difficult for him, and he had to leave Tahiti for the Marquesas Islands in a more remote part of French Polynesia; there he again locked horns with the Catholic missionaries, whom he called "absolutely unscrupulous." Vincent and Gauguin were champions of lost causes. Vincent thought it absurd when he read that two entire native tribes had been wiped out by colonial forces in the Marquesas Islands because of their cannibalism against each other. He railed against this injustice: "Those tattooed races, blacks, Indians, all of them, all, all are disappearing or degenerating. And the horrible white man with his bottle of alcohol, his money and his syphilis—when shall we see the end of him? The horrible white man with his hypocrisy, his greediness and his sterility."

Vincent and Gauguin discussed moving to the tropics to find new subjects to paint in a harsher light than Arles, in a Garden of Eden setting. Gauguin toyed with the idea of returning to Martinique or exploring Madagascar, and they both considered Australia a painter's haven; but in the end Vincent favored Tahiti, as he had seen an illustration of the island paradise in Pierre Loti's fictional work, *Madame Butterfly*. Eventually it would be Gauguin's Tahitian paintings of the natives and landscapes that would bring him fame. In 1893 the first exhibition of this work in France, the huge canvases dazzling in their luminescent colors and sensitive images of Tahitian men and women in exotic surroundings, established Gauguin's celebrity status, which only intensified after his death ten years later.

Neither Gauguin nor Vincent subscribed to edicts of aesthetic realism. Defending his penchant for exaggeration in his art when he was criticized for painting unrealistically, Vincent explained that he did not want his figures to be academically correct, that he did not wish to paint things as they were, but as he felt them: "My great longing is to learn to make those very incorrectnesses, those deviations, remodeling, changes in reality, so they become, yes, lies if you like—but truer than the literal truth." A prime example of this can be seen in Vincent's painting *The Sower,* which depicts a plowboy casting seed over a plowed field. Three quarters of the canvas is devoted to the plowed field which is cast in exaggerated colors under a blazing sun. The soil is a mosaic of yellow, orange, white, blue, and pink; and from a distance it looks violet. Vincent bestows on the soil a magnificence never before seen in art. The nurturing power of the earth, under an astonishingly sunny early-morning sky, is so forcefully presented that it is unlikely any other artist could suggest a greater reverence for such a humble, unglamorous element. It was Vincent's favorite painting after *The Potato Eaters.*

Gauguin expressed sentiments similar to Vincent's when he wrote: "Strict accuracy in depicting color creates an effect that is lifeless, frozen; impudently and stupidly it deceives. . . . In order to create the equivalent . . . it is necessary to put a greener green than that of nature. There you have the truth of the lie."

As different as chalk and cheese as they were in appearance and temperament, philosophically Vincent and Gauguin were remarkably similar. Both men were rebels; both shared an obsessive thirst for artistic expression. But when they differed, as they often did in their discussions about the work of contemporaries or dead artists, as well as in their views on new directions for artistic growth, the sparks flew. In a letter to Bernard, Gauguin wrote: "Vincent and I generally agree very little, especially about painting. He admires Daudet, Daubigny,

Ziem and the great Rousseau—all people I cannot endure. And on the contrary he detests Ingres, Raphael, Degas—all people whom I admire." To the locals they were an odd couple: the smooth, short, dapper Gauguin with his rapier repartee, and the clumsy, mumbling, seemingly distracted Vincent.

In spite of their disagreements over artistic merit, Vincent and Gauguin frequently painted the same subject, sometimes while sitting side by side. Soon after Gauguin's arrival, they both painted Roulin's wife Augustine after childbirth. In Vincent's portrait she is physically exhausted; her face is puffy and pale; her eyes are fighting sleep that has been lost to the baby's cries. In the background a window looks out onto a garden where, symbolic of childbirth, bulbs are sprouting out of pots. Gauguin's painting of the same title, *Madame Roulin,* is a similar composition, but it does not capture the look of physical exhaustion as successfully as Vincent's. Whereas Vincent's image of Madame Roulin is that of a pale French woman still bloated from her confinement, her hair hurriedly gathered loose at the back and her robe disheveled, open in front, Gauguin's portrait makes her look like a Creole, with a distinct resemblance to his own mother, pious and stiff, with her garment buttoned up to her chin as though she has dressed for church, not like a woman who has recently gone through the pain and labor of childbirth. And the garden in the background looks more like a wall decoration than a window.

There is a lot to question in Gauguin's portrait. Vincent thought his own rendering was faultless, and he was obviously pulling out all the stops to impress his friend. His painting is a triumphant exaltation of motherhood in a woman who was approaching menopause. Gauguin undoubtedly discovered that he was getting an education in artistic genius he had never expected. He had thought he would be the teacher, but Vincent proved to be relentless and eager to test his friend's mettle on any number of challenging subjects. Vincent undoubtedly considered his *Madame Roulin* the better. Shortly after this exercise in painting the same subject, Gauguin complained to Theo that Vincent was always finding fault with his work.

Vincent developed a special affection for Mme. Roulin. In a discussion with Gauguin about the world's most dangerous occupation, they concluded it was that of Icelandic fishermen, who ventured long distances from land in search of fish, often in bitterly cold weather and tempestuous seas, and spent long periods away from their women. So Vincent painted Mme. Roulin again, this time as the wife of an Icelandic fisherman. He gave her a sweet, plump face; he exaggerated her bosom and her girth to make her look warm and huggable. And he showed her holding the handle of a cradle. This image he painted five times, all titled *La Berceuse* (the cradle rocker). To Theo he explained the dynamics of the series:

> Of this picture I said to Gauguin when we once talked about the fishermen of Iceland and their melancholy loneliness, exposed to dangers on the desolate sea ... that ... the idea came to me to paint a picture that would make the seamen look like children and martyrs at the same time, seeing it in the cabin of an Icelandic fishing boat, get a feeling as if they were being rocked to sleep, as if they heard their own cradle song. [January 28, 1889.]

Vincent's *Red Vineyard,* painted near the end of Gauguin's stay in Arles, is a high-elevation view of a riverside vineyard; a gang of women is gathering grapes, and the vine leaves are imbued with rich autumn colors. It is a hot color harmony in red, yellow, and orange—the hottest assembly of colors Vincent ever painted—and he was delighted with the result. Gauguin, however, chose to paint a distressed woman who is sitting apart from the other workers, and whose face shows signs of misery and madness. Vincent congratulated Gauguin on producing a masterpiece, for it conveyed the kind of facial dynamic he found missing in Gauguin's *Madame Roulin* portrait. It also undoubtedly conjured up memories of Vincent's earlier sketch of Sien, entitled *Sorrow*.

Jo learned the true state of affairs between the two artists in Arles from Theo, to whom she was engaged at the time. In her translation of Vincent's letters, she noted: "The fact is that Vincent was completely exhausted and overstrained, and was no match for the iron-willed Gauguin with his strong nerves and cool arguing."

When Vincent first met Gauguin in Paris, Gauguin had recently returned from Panama and Martinique. He had worked briefly on the construction of the Panama Canal and then lived as a native on the Caribbean island of Martinique, where he painted native life. Jo believed that the friendship between Vincent and Gauguin in Paris was no more than a superficial acquaintance, but it must have been much deeper than she was led to believe, especially when one considers that it was in Paris that the two painters had discussed plans to journey south, live together, and start a colony for artists. In fact, Vincent idolized Gauguin. Though their individual painting techniques were distinctly different, Gauguin's being more careful and refined, Vincent admired Gauguin as a colorist, and appreciated the dignity in his portrayal of peasants and native people. He especially admired Gauguin's paintings of the Breton coast, particularly his portrayals of Breton shepherdesses in their traditional lacy headdresses, black ankle-length dresses, and wooden clogs. Perhaps he also saw in Gauguin faults that he recognized in himself—a confrontational, devil-may-care attitude and a tendency to be disliked for his abrasiveness. His esteem for Gauguin was such that Gauguin's name occurs 605 times in 177 letters.

In Arles the two friends enjoyed patronizing brothels together, Vincent excitedly telling Theo, after Gauguin's arrival, that it was one of the first items on their agenda. Vincent believed that drinking and womanizing fueled Gauguin's creative passion, although it often appeared to Vincent that with Gauguin, his thirst for blood and sex prevailed over artistic ambition, bullfights also being a major attraction for both men. In the blood and sex, the bullfights and brothels, they shared passionate, sometimes violent experiences. They also shared the same prostitutes; both relished the charms of a sixteen-year-old, swarthy, dark-haired ouvrière named Rachel. As a consequence, the two men formed a strong male bond—a profound one for Vincent.

Many psychoanalysts believe that Vincent intentionally revealed a homosexual attraction for Gauguin in his pair of paintings *Vincent's Chair* and *Gauguin's Chair*. In the former, Vincent's phallic pipe rests with a packet of tobacco on a wicker seat; in the latter, a lighted candle stands phallically erect between two books in the middle of an upholstered seat. Whereas Vincent's chair stands in a masculine setting, a tiled room, Gauguin's is in the more feminine setting of a richly carpeted boudoir.

Homosexuality in France did not carry the stigma attached to it in England, where it was illegal—a circumstance that would send novelist-playwright Oscar Wilde to prison in the 1890s. In France, homosexuality among women was considered exotic, while among men, especially among bisexuals, it was considered to be of little consequence.

Gauguin wrote frankly to Emile Bernard about the time he spent in Arles: "It was not until I had been there several weeks that I perceived the harsh flavor of Arles and its environs. All the same, we worked hard, especially Vincent. Between two human beings, the one like a volcano and the other boiling too, but inwardly, there was a battle in store, so to speak." Metaphorically, Gauguin was saying that their creative passions were so highly charged that there had to be an eventual fracture in their relationship. On a more mundane level, Gauguin had little tolerance for the messy state in which Vincent worked. "The paint box was barely big enough to contain all the tubes that had been squeezed, but never recapped, and yet in spite of the chaos and the mess," he confessed to Bernard, "his canvases glowed."

Gauguin believed that Vincent's anger toward him arose from a resentment of Gauguin's superior intelligence. Gauguin boasted that since his arrival in Arles, Vincent was still seeking ways for his art to grow, and benefited from the company and tutelage of a more enlightened, more mature individual. Gauguin wrote that both of them accomplished a lot of work in Arles, but at first Vincent had been so fixed on neo-Impressionism that his work was floundering. The soft tones did not correspond with Vincent's passionate nature. "With all his combinations of yellow on purple, all his random work in complementary colors, all he achieved were soft, incomplete, monotonous harmonies," Gauguin declared. This statement was quite an exaggeration. Vincent's portraits of postman Roulin, his *Flower Garden* series, *The Sower,* his *Langois Bridge at*

Arles, his *Street in Saintes-Maries,* and his night scenes were anything but monotonous, soft, and incomplete—and all were done before Gauguin's arrival.

"I undertook to enlighten him, which was easy enough, for I found rich and fertile soil," Gauguin bragged. "He seemed to glimpse all that he had in him, hence that whole series of sun after sun after sun, throbbing with sun." Again Gauguin exaggerated. Attempting to temper his claims with mock modesty, Gauguin continued by saying he did not wish to downplay Vincent's originality but thought the art world should know that he provided Vincent with helpful instruction. As an aside, he acknowledged a debt to Vincent for helping him consolidate his earlier ideas on painting.

In point of fact, judging from the body of work Gauguin went on to complete in Tahiti, where he moved within a year of Vincent's death, it was Vincent who had more influence over Gauguin's technique. Gauguin's color range, which had been characterized mostly by cool pastel shades, changed dramatically as it burst into a celebration of Vincent's hot colors, particularly orange and yellow. Also, Gauguin's Tahitian work is charged with the kind of symbolism Vincent liked to include in his paintings. *Nevermore* shows Gauguin's adolescent "wife" lying nude on a couch and casting an apprehensive glance at a sinister raven with no eyes. Gauguin explained that he used the sightless bird as a symbol of death, so its presence in the painting is unsettling. Another painting in Gauguin's Tahitian series is derived from Egyptian art. Entitled *We Shall Not Go to the Market Today,* it shows a group of Tahitian women sitting in a public square gossiping. It was Vincent who first realized that blending the art of two cultures could produce wonderful results. The cross-fertilization of European and Japanese art had inspired his own distinctive style, and he was exploring the potential for Egyptian art in his work. In fact, he had sketched an Egyptian pharaoh during his Arles period. Gauguin's amazing homage to Egyptian art shows the main figures of *We Shall Not Go to the Market Today* mostly in profile, the women with sleek, clean, flat human forms similar to those on the walls of Egyptian tombs and temples. Gauguin took this innovation a step further after he saw Maori art in the museums of Auckland, New Zealand. During a stopover there on his second trip to Tahiti, he was impressed with intricate Maori carvings, and started a series of wooden statues that combined elements of both European and Maori culture, an innovation Vincent would have applauded.

The hypersensitive Vincent had little defense against Gauguin's biting criticisms, which most people would have brushed off as thoughtless arrogance or professional jealousy. Always vulnerable in Gauguin's magisterial presence, Vincent often found his ego damaged and feelings hurt in his vocal confrontations with Gauguin about art. It is likely that Gauguin reveled in every bit of spirited argument with his impassioned opponent, saw Vincent as a rival, and even deliberately played devil's advocate to see how far he could goad him.

The meeting of Vincent and Gauguin in Arles is considered by art historians to be one of the most dramatic events in the development of modern art. During their two months together, Vincent completed thirty major oil paintings, and Gauguin sixteen. Their stormy friendship, their collaboration in finding new ways to express their talents, and their eagerness to be recognized as great painters produced work that inspired future generations of artists. If they had stayed together and worked co-operatively at founding an artists' colony and made a reality of

Vincent's cherished dream, it is unlikely that they would have ever made the impact they did by going their separate ways. Indeed, by meeting, exchanging ideas, clashing, then separating and pursuing their goals independently—at a safe distance from each other—they reached pinnacles of artistic acclaim that they could never have imagined.

During the tempestuous yet highly productive two months that Vincent and Gauguin spent together, Gauguin took total control. He decided how they should organize their day; he cooked most of their meals; he even negotiated for both of them how much they would pay women in the brothels. Vincent's emotional attachment to Gauguin became so strong that whenever Gauguin threatened to leave, Vincent became agitated, fearful of isolation, once even hurling a glass of absinthe at his friend.

At one point, to Gauguin's considerable discomfort, Vincent abruptly stopped speaking to him altogether. Several times at night during that uneasy period, Vincent left his room to stand over Gauguin's bed. He would then stare down at Gauguin until he sensed Vincent's presence and awoke. When Gauguin asked what was the matter, Vincent would silently return to his own room and fall fast asleep in his bed. One day, Gauguin did a portrait of Vincent painting sunflowers in a field. Vincent commented: "That's me all right; but me gone mad."

To Theo, Vincent wrote: "Gauguin and I talked a lot about Delacroix and Rembrandt. Our arguments were terribly electric. We come out of them sometimes as exhausted as an electric battery after it is discharged."

Their passions clashed, their intellects brawled, but no hint of the turbulence in their relationship appeared in Vincent's next letter to Wil. In it, Vincent remarked that, at Gauguin's insistence, he had painted a subject from memory, and he was pleased with the result: *Memory of the Garden at Etten,* which depicts one of the family's gardens in Holland, with Wil, their mother, and a maidservant walking through it. He further explained to Wil:

> I don't know whether you can understand that one may make a poem only by arranging colors, in the same way that one can say comforting things with music.
>
> In a similar manner the bizarre lines, purposely selected and multiplied, meandering all through the picture, avoid a vulgar resemblance, but may present to our minds the garden as seen in a dream, depicting its character, and at the same time stranger than it is in reality. [November 16, 1888.]

Vincent had also painted *A Woman Reading a Novel,* he told Wil. In the painting a young woman, her facial features sharp and her hair luxuriant, is wearing a green bodice, sleeves the color of wine, and a black skirt against a yellow background, and shelves filled with books. In her hands she is holding a yellow book. It is the beginning of a whole series of dynamic portraits using a host of local characters as models, including a man with one eye. The painting of the young woman was followed by *L'Arlesienne,* an older woman with sharp features. The entire Roulin family appears in the work of this period: their youngest, Camille, in *The Schoolboy;* Armand, their second son, as a young man in a trilby, in *Portrait of Armand Roulin;* Roulin's wife Augustine in numerous poses, mostly with her baby Marcelle, who is all big blue eyes and chubby cheeks.

Almost as an afterthought, Vincent added: "But I have not told you that my friend Paul Gauguin, an Impressionist painter, is now living with me, and that we are very happy together. He strongly encourages me to work more often from imagination."

Soon after he wrote this benign letter to Wil, two days before Christmas, Vincent suffered a devastating blow. His next letter to her would describe a harrowing period that he spent hospitalized, after a total mental collapse precipitated by a distressing downturn in his mercurial relationship with Gauguin.

Vincent and Gauguin had spent the day of December 23 at Montpellier, visiting an art museum, where they expressed divergent opinions about the work on display. After a tense evening meal, Gauguin simply walked out of the house. He later claimed that he wanted some moments alone, and he wanted to allow Vincent time to cool off. Vincent, however, mistook Gauguin's abrupt departure as a final farewell. He felt abandoned, all the more so since it was just two days before Christmas. Jo scoffed at Gauguin's claim that he intended to return, for he had already written Theo that he planned to leave Vincent and return to Paris: "Vincent and I simply cannot live together. He is a man of remarkable intelligence, I respect him highly, and regret leaving." Whether or not Gauguin intended to return, it was unkind of him to walk out on his fragile friend so close to the holiday.

Gauguin was walking across a cobbled square toward a hotel, where he planned to spend the night, when he heard a noise behind him. He turned and saw Vincent coming at him with a straightedge razor raised above his head. In response, Gauguin struck a combative posture. Vincent stopped, then turned away and vanished into the night.

Gauguin returned to the yellow house early in the morning to find the entrance thronged by neighbors and policemen.

Gaining entry, he followed a trail of blood that was splattered on the flagstones in the entryway, on the treads of the wooden staircase, and across the floorboards leading into Vincent's bedroom. Bloody handprints marked the whitewashed walls. On the bed, pale and near death, Vincent lay unconscious, his head swathed in blood-soaked towels.

Gauguin was arrested on suspicion of grievous bodily harm, but was released after he reconstructed the events of the night and his incredible story was corroborated by witnesses. After their encounter in the square, Vincent had sliced off his own ear and delivered it to the prostitute Rachel at their favorite brothel, with a request that she "keep this object carefully."

Roulin had found Vincent at the brothel. He was delirious, bleeding profusely, and the neighborhood was in an uproar. Roulin helped him back to his lodgings and asked for the police. The police summoned a doctor, and Vincent was transferred to Arles Hospital for treatment. A telegram from Gauguin called Theo to his brother's side, but not before Vincent suffered another violent breakdown the day after Christmas.

He had been bound in a straitjacket and locked in an isolation cell by the time Theo arrived by train from Paris. Theo feared that Vincent was close to death, and wrote home to Jo that he was wavering between consciousness and delirium:

> There were moments while I was with him that he was well; but very soon after he fell back into his worries about philosophy and theology. It was painfully sad to witness, for at times all his suffering overwhelmed him and he tried to weep but he could not; poor fighter and poor, poor sufferer; for the moment nobody can do anything to relieve his sorrow, and yet he feels deeply and strongly. If he might have found somebody to whom he could have disclosed his

heart it would have perhaps never have gone thus far. . . . There is little hope, but during his life he has done more than many others, and has suffered and struggled more than most people could have done. If it must be that he dies, so be it, but my heart breaks when I think of it. [December, 1888.]

Theo could stay only a short time, for he had just become engaged to Jo, who was waiting for him in Paris. They had made plans to visit her family in Holland and he did not want to disappoint her; but he made arrangements for a local minister, the Reverend Frederic Salles, to look in on Vincent. Postman Roulin also promised to keep Theo informed. Two days later, Theo left with Gauguin for Paris. The fact that Gauguin wanted no more involvement in the police inquiry left some of the locals wondering if Gauguin might have pulled a knife to defend himself from Vincent's razor attack, and in the melee sliced off Vincent's ear. Vincent's insistence, however, that he had mutilated himself is accepted by most biographers to be true. In any event, it is believed that the early departure of Theo and Gauguin caused Vincent to suffer another breakdown; again, he had to be isolated.

He would not speak; he refused all food. Roulin's wife paid Vincent a visit, and Roulin reported to Theo her distress at his condition:

My wife went to see him, and he hid his face when he saw her coming. When she spoke to him he replied well enough, and talked to her about our little girl and asked if she was still as pretty as ever. Today, Friday, I went there to see him, but the attendant told me that after my wife left he had a terrible attack; he passed a bad night and they had to put him in an isolation room. Since he has been locked up in

this room he has taken no food and completely refused to talk. That
is the state of your brother at present.

Yet, three days later, the Reverend Salles found Vincent
looking so perfectly well, chatting so amicably with the hospital
staff, that he was completely surprised by his confinement.
Vincent's physician, Dr. Felix Rey, wrote Theo that he thought
the crisis was over. Roulin persuaded the doctor to allow Vincent
to go home, and Vincent wrote both to Theo and to Gauguin, to
wish them well. Although Vincent was well aware that he had
endured mental seizures, he had no recollection of what he had
said or done during the episodes.

Vincent had placed far too much faith in Gauguin, whom he had
expected to enthusiastically help him establish an artists'
colony in the south. Vincent believed that Gauguin's admiration
among young artists and their own common goals for humanity
guaranteed success of the community center Vincent wished to
establish—a place where progressive artists could exhibit their
work and congregate for spirited, constructive debate and criticism, then return to Paris renewed and invigorated. Vincent
believed that in this way, the revolution in artistic expression of
which he so passionately dreamed would quickly become a reality.

Vincent's hopes had now been shattered. Gauguin had left,
and Vincent, alone once more, would be starved of intellectual and
cultural excitement. There would be no more joint excursions into
the countryside in search of stimulating motifs, no more cheering
with the crowd at bullfights, no more binge drinking and whoring
together, no more museum visits to study artists past and present
and determine what made them great or overrated.

Moreover, Vincent had become emotionally bound to Gauguin. When, in the middle of the night, Vincent stood over Gauguin while he slept, Vincent may have been responding to a desire to absorb some of the male potency he associated with Gauguin's singular artistic expression, a desire that psychologists call a "homoerotic impulse." Dr. Albert J. Lubin was the first to suggest that perhaps on one occasion, instead of discouraging Vincent, Gauguin opened up the sheets and they experienced closer intimacy, and Vincent enjoyed it: a love that the church considered sinful and possibly one that Vincent wished to experience—"a love that dare not speak its name," to quote Oscar Wilde.

Whether their relationship was latently homosexual or not, Gauguin's departure that night was too much for Vincent to bear. For sixty-three days, they had lived together in an atmosphere charged by their fiercely individualistic spirits. Vincent did not know how to process this monumental change and the profoundly painful feeling of rejection. It was harsher than Kee's "no, never never"; more disruptive than leaving Sien and her children; more confusing than Margot's attempted suicide; more unjust than the community that shunned him after the priests accused him of fathering Stien's child.

The remarkable aspect of Vincent's possible homosexual infatuation is that, at first glance, he seems to have painted Gauguin in the *woman's* role. Why so, when he regarded Gauguin as a man of iron, a swordsman who was also a crack shot with a pistol, a man's man, a man with a workingman's hands and a workingman's heart? If he imagined Gauguin as a man's man, why, in the pair of paintings symbolizing their friendship, did Vincent paint Gauguin's chair as an object of effeminate delicacy and place it in what is apparently a woman's bedroom? Was he projecting onto Gauguin the image of his mother, so that when Gauguin walked out on Vincent right before Christmas, it was not just Gauguin leaving him behind but also his mother turning her back on him again? And not only his mother, but Kee too—both of them haunted, the former by the ghost of her firstborn, the latter by the ghost of her husband. Since childhood, ghosts had starved Vincent of affection, and seven years earlier he had coldly imagined delivering Kee from the usurping ghost with a metaphorical surgeon's knife. The folding razor that Vincent grabbed from the bathroom was real. With it he ran out after Gauguin, into the street. Determined as he may have been, he did not advance, for Gauguin had struck a defensive pose. Vincent stopped in his tracks. Rebuffed, he ran off into the night and returned to the house they shared. There he sliced off his ear. Vincent's act of self-mutilation may have been his penitence for attacking Gauguin, a gesture to show his friend that he would rather harm himself. Whatever the case, he suffered a massive loss of blood, yet he had the strength and determination to carefully wrap the bloody ear in paper and take it to Rachel. But it was no mere severed ear he was presenting to her. "Keep this object carefully," he implored, as he extended to her the symbolic gift. Rachel fainted.

But why slice off an ear? Why not a finger, a toe, or even his penis if he wanted to show penitence? One explanation is that the victorious matadors at bullfights would slice off one of the bull's ears and present it reverently to a beautiful woman in the audience. He knew such a woman—Rachel! She had shown him compassion at the whorehouse; she was Gauguin's favorite, too.

Lawrence Decker has analyzed every scenario presented by the art establishment and other psychologists, including the possibility that Vincent projected onto Gauguin the image of his mother, as he had done previously in his relationship with Kee, who was obviously a mother substitute. Vincent had had other love interests that were also possible mother substitutes, including Sien and Margot . But in the case of Gauguin, Decker does not believe that Vincent projected onto him the image of his mother or that Vincent necessarily had a homosexual relationship with Gauguin. He finds another, more plausible, explanation:

> Vincent's desire to use a knife with Kee was to remove the influence of a dead husband, a threat to Vincent's attachment to Kee, similar to how the ghost of his dead brother had always threatened his relationship with his mother.
>
> In the case of Gauguin, however, I think a different dynamic plays out, but one remarkably similar. I believe that for Vincent, Gauguin represented the *ghost itself,* and Vincent's confrontation with Gauguin represented Vincent's best chance to finally change the unfolding reality he had been suddenly so cruelly presented with by his friend.
>
> Vincent idealized Gauguin, making him the longed for and now no-longer-dead brother, a kindred soul with fire and passion not unlike his own.
>
> Together with Gauguin, Vincent could correct all wrongs, provide his mother with the happy circumstance of two living brothers united in harmony and peace, able to create a safe haven for themselves and others to flourish, to be magnificent, not ordinary, to paint together and share profound ideas.
>
> That Gauguin tutored Vincent to paint from memory, to extol the virtues of the past, was balm to Vincent's ears, so damaged by the past that he had to correct it through his art.
>
> How disturbing it must have been for his idealized brother, his spiritual twin, the resurrected ghost, to abandon him.

But the painting places Gauguin's chair in a woman's bedroom! Vincent said so in a letter explaining its symbolism to Theo. On close inspection, the chair itself, though ostentatious, displays a candle standing stiffly erect. In contrast to this representation of Gauguin's maleness, Vincent's, represented by his pipe, is noticeably smaller and lies unassertively, curled on its side. Viewed together, the two paintings suggest sibling rivalry, and the erect phallus on Gauguin's chair stands potently agleam, like a gem in a feminine setting. In other words, the woman's boudoir is the womb, while the ostentatious chair and the lighted candle represent the idolized brother whom his mother has lost and who now lives again in the person of Gauguin. Vincent presents himself, on the other hand, as an inferior male in a sterile environment. His pipe is not lit. It is extinguished.

Despite the assumption of Vincent's and Gauguin's homosexuality, it seems unlikely that they ever had a homosexual relationship. Vincent never wrote about it and neither did Gauguin. In fact, in his autobiography of life in Tahiti, entitled *Noa Noa* (the Polynesian word for "fragrances", which serves as a metaphor for Gauguin's memories), written near the end of his life, Gauguin refers to only one homosexual temptation, which he says he declined, with a Polynesian youth, Totefa, whom he befriended in Tahiti. One day, Gauguin asked Totefa to lead him to a grove of rosewood trees in the mountains to collect wood for sculptures. The passage reads:

> We set out early in the morning.... Both of us went naked, the white and blue pareo around our loins, hatchet in hand.... The silence was absolute but for the plaintive murmur of water among the rocks. It was a monotonous sound, a murmuring so soft and low that it seemed an accompaniment of the silence.

And in this forest, this solitude, this silence where we two—he, a very young man, and I, almost an old man . . . whose body was tired . . . and . . . upon whom lay the long and fatal heritage of the vices of a morally and physically corrupt society.

With the suppleness of an animal and the graceful litheness of an androgynous person he walked a few paces in front of me. And it seemed to me that I saw incarnated in him, palpitating and living, all the magnificent plant life that surrounded us. From him, through him there . . . emanated a powerful perfume of beauty.

Was it really a human being walking ahead of me? Was it the naïve friend by whose combined simplicity and complexity I had been so attracted? Was it not rather the Forest itself, the living Forest, without sex—and yet alluring?

There is something virile in the women and something feminine in the men of Tahiti. . . . This similarity of the sexes makes their relationships the easier. Their continual state of nakedness has kept their minds free from the . . . excessive stress that among civilized people is laid upon the . . . clandestine and sadistic colors of love. It has given their manners a natural innocence, a perfect purity. Man and woman are comrades, friends rather than lovers, dwelling together almost without cease, in pain as in pleasure, and even the very idea of vice is unknown to them.

In spite of this lessening of sexual differences, why was it there suddenly arose in my soul, what my old civilization would consider a horrible thought? Why, in all this drunkenness of light and perfume with its enchantment of newness and unknown mystery?

The fever throbbed in my temples and my knees shook. But we were at the end of the trail. In order to cross the stream my companion turned, and in this movement showed himself full-face. The androgynous being disappeared. It was an actual young man walking ahead of me. His clear eyes had the limpid clearness of waters. . . .

Peace forthwith fell upon me again. I felt an infinite joy as I plunged
into the fresh water of the brook.

If Gauguin failed to respond to a homoerotic impulse on
such a rarefied and exotic occasion, it is unlikely that he experienced any temptation with Vincent. Although many writers have
interpreted Vincent's gazing upon Gauguin while he slept as a
sexual desire that could easily have turned into sexual contact,
Decker's analysis of their sibling rivalry suggests Vincent simply
could have been looking down in wonder at his resurrected
brother, with no sexual intent.

By December 31, in the care of Dr. Rey, Vincent was sufficiently
recovered to begin working again. In a letter to Theo, written January 2, 1889, he enquired about Gauguin: "Now let's talk about
our friend Gauguin. Have I scared him? In short, why doesn't he
give me any sign of life? He must have left with you. Besides, it
was necessary for him to go back to Paris. . . . Tell Gauguin to
write to me, and that I am always thinking about him."

After a month had elapsed, Vincent went to see Rachel to
apologize for his aberrant behavior. He reported to Theo:
"Yesterday I went to see the girl I had gone to when I was out of
my wits. They told me there that in this part of the country
things like that are not unusual. She had been upset by the incident and had fainted but had recovered her calm."

Vincent's first letter to Wil after his self-mutilation and hospi-
talization was dated January 7, 1889. It was also his first letter
to include his mother in the salutation. Having come to the

realization in light of recent events that he was mentally ill, he could finally forgive her for trying to have him institutionalized earlier.

> Dear Mother and Sister,
>
> For several weeks already I have firmly intended to write you a word or two to wish you a truly prosperous and Happy New Year. Well, I am pretty late in doing this.
>
> I think you may feel inclined to excuse me if I tell you that in December I was indisposed.
>
> But at the same time I can inform you that I have completely recovered, and am at work again, and everything is normal. [January 7, 1889.]

Vincent told them not to worry and optimistically noted that his illness had provided him the opportunity to meet a number of people who would be good subjects for his portraits. Framing his indisposition as a chance to refresh himself, he declared his determination to stay well for a long time to come. He asked them to write often, said that they were always in his thoughts, and closed with "Yours lovingly."

The brevity of this letter might have caused his mother and sister concern, except for a thoughtful letter written on the same day by postman Roulin to Wil:

> I acknowledge receipt of your kind letter, by which you do me too much honor, and I make haste to answer you that your amiable brother Vincent has quite recovered; he left the hospital today, January 7, 1889. What caused my reply to be delayed is the fact that we kept each other company all day long, and I beg you to write him a letter. I have not let him read your letter, for he would be too chagrined to know that he has caused you so much grief. When you

write him, please do not let him know that I informed you of the causes of his distemper; tell him you have learned through the mediation of your brother in Paris that he has been indisposed, and that you are very happy to hear he has recovered.

Three months later, on April 30, 1889, Vincent found the courage to write Wil in more detail about his breakdown. In response to her news that she was nursing a cancer patient, he explained how difficult it was for him to watch human suffering:

> Cancer is certainly a terrible disease—as for me, I always tremble when I see a case of it—and this is no rare occurrence in the South, though it is often not the real, incurable and mortal cancer, but cancerous tumors from which people occasionally recover. However this may be, I think it very brave of you, Sister, not to shrink from this Gethsemane. I feel I am less brave than you, when I think of such things, for I feel clumsy, unwieldy, awkward in their presence. [April 30, 1889.]

He likened cancer to the ivy that grows up the trunks of old willow and oak trees, and noted, "in the same way cancer, that mysterious plant, so often fastens on people whose lives were nothing but love and devotion." Vincent remarked, too, that not far from Arles an ancient tomb bore the inscription "Blessed be Thebe, daughter of Telhui, priestess of Osiris, who never complained of anyone," as he had been reminded of this epitaph by the fact that Wil's cancer patient never complained about her condition.

That same April, Theo had married Jo, and this caused Vincent to feel anxious about the future of his financial support.

* * *

Johanna Gesina Bonger (1862–1925) met Theo through his friend-ship with her brother, Andre, an insurance broker living in Paris. Born in Amsterdam, she had studied English at school, and then worked for a short time in the Library of the British Museum in London. At age twenty-two she began work as a teacher of English, first at a boarding school for girls in Elburg and then at the High School for Girls in Utrecht. She was twenty-six when she married Theo in April 1889. From the age of seventeen, she had kept a diary in which she described her experiences and feelings. The diary entries ended the day she married Theo. They resumed again in 1891 after his death with the words, "Everything is just a dream."

One diary entry, written while she was living with her parents in Amsterdam, reads like a passage from a Jane Austen novel. It relates the occasion when Theo first proposed marriage:

> Friday was a very emotional day. At two o'clock in the afternoon the doorbell rang: Van Gogh from Paris. I was pleased he was coming. I pictured myself talking about literature and art, I gave him a warm welcome—and then suddenly he started to declare his love for me . . . after only three encounters, he wants to spend his whole life with me . . . but I could not say yes to something like that, could I?
>
> He offered up visions of the ideal I have always dreamed of, a rich life full of variation, full of intellectual stimulation, a circle of friends around us who are working for a good cause, who want to do something for the world, my indefinable searching and longing would be changed into a clearly defined duty which is out there, just waiting for me: to make me happy! If only I could take the step, why does my heart feel numb when I think of him?

The question was rhetorical, for Jo was in love with another man, referred to only as "Mr. E" in her diary.

For Theo, it was love at first sight. In a letter to his sister Elisabeth (Leis), he confided shortly before his marriage proposal: "I am planning at one time or another to ask Jo Bonger's hand. I surely don't know her enough to be able to tell you much about her. As you know, I have only seen her a few times, but the things I know about her appeal to me. She gave me the impression that I could trust her in a completely indefinable way, more than anyone else. I think I could talk with her about anything."

Theo proposed twice more before Johanna accepted him. Only after her love for Mr. E was firmly rejected did she accept Theo's proposal of marriage.

Vincent imagined his mother would be pleased with Theo's marriage, as Theo himself seemed to be so happy. However, with some cynicism, Vincent commented to Wil on Theo's married status:

> He has very few illusions about it all, for he possesses to a rare degree that strength of mind which enables him to take things as they are without expressing himself about the good or the bad of them. And he is quite right in this, for what do we know about what we are doing?
>
> As for myself, I am going to an asylum in St.-Remy, not far from here, for three months. I have had in all four great crises, during which I didn't in the least know what I said, what I wanted and what I did. Not taking into account that I previously had three fainting fits without any plausible reason, and without retaining the slightest remembrance of what I felt. [April 30, 1889.]

Vincent's "four great crises" referred to his seizures, and his determination to admit himself to an asylum for the insane shows how fearful he was of more such crises endangering his life and his work. Apparently, he and his doctor in Arles were unaware of any link between his psychological problem and his perceptions of emotional rejection, a pattern that has already been established.

Despite these attacks, Vincent reported that he was feeling much calmer. He felt perfectly well physically, and he had finished two new paintings of the hospital where he had convalesced after severing his ear. He described one as:

> A very long ward, with rows of beds with white curtains, in which some figures of patients are moving. The walls, the ceiling with big beams, are all white, lilac-white or green-white. Here and there is a window with a pink or bright green curtain. The floor paved with red bricks. At the end a door with a crucifix over it. It is all very, very simple. [April 30, 1889.]

While Vincent's painting of the ward was claustrophobic and austere, with its figures looking like phantoms, the second painting, of a courtyard flower garden at the hospital, was extremely colorful. Vincent invested *The Courtyard of the Hospital at Arles* with his personal symbolism. In his mind the flowers represented gaiety, an escape from melancholia, yet sinister elements representing Vincent's hidden demons also lurked threateningly in his garden.

> And then, as a pendant, the inner court. It is an arcaded gallery like those one finds in Arab buildings, all whitewashed. In front of those galleries an ancient garden with a pond in the middle, and eight flower beds, with forget-me-nots, hellebores, anemones, ranunculus, wallflowers, daisies and so on. And under the gallery orange trees, and oleander. So it is a picture quite full of flowers and vernal green. However, three gloomy black tree trunks pass

through it like serpents, and in the foreground four big dismal clusters of somber box shrub. It is probable people here won't see much in it, but nevertheless it has always been my great desire to paint for those who do not know the artistic aspect of a picture. [April 30, 1889.]

Signaling some return to normalcy, Vincent's April letter to Wil resumed their discussion of books. Wil had previously expressed disappointment in some of Vincent's recommendations—Voltaire's *Candide,* for one—as she could not follow their arguments. "These are books written by men for men," Vincent reasoned, "and I don't know whether women can understand them. But the memory of them often sustains me in the hours and days and nights that are hardly easy or enviable," for Vincent himself was suffering badly from insomnia, poor appetite, and recurring nightmares of people trying to poison him.

Vincent said that he had recently read *Uncle Tom's Cabin* by Harriet Beecher Stowe "with *extreme attention,* for the very reason that it is a book written by a woman, written—as she tells us—while she was making soup for the children." He had followed Stowe with Charles Dickens's *Christmas Tales.* "I read a little in order to meditate," he continued. "It is very probable that I shall have to suffer a great deal yet. And to tell the honest truth, this does not suit me at all, for under no circumstances do I long for a martyr's career. For I have always sought something different from heroism, which I do not have." His reference to the probability of more suffering indicates his fear of recurring seizures, while the martyr's career manifests his fear of dying while doggedly pursuing his passion for art at the expense of his health.

Vincent then recommended books by Joseph Ernst Renan to

Wil because Renan spoke to his readers in a French unlike the French spoken by anyone else:

> A French that contains, *in the sound of the words,* the blue sky, the soft rustling of the olive trees, and finally a thousand *true and explanatory* things which give his History the character of a Resurrection. One of the saddest things I know is that prejudice of people who in their self-conceit oppose so many good and beautiful things which were created in our own time. Ah, the eternal "ignorance," the eternal misunderstandings—and how much good it does one to come across a word which is really serene.... [April 30, 1889.]

Speaking to Wil's desire to become a writer, Vincent here explains Renan's technique as an analogue of his own, for Renan did with words what Vincent was attempting to do with paint, in spite of his work being largely unappreciated. Renan's serenity could only help a little, however. Vincent remarked that his own mind was uneasy and needed to be more calm: "All those bitter disappointments, adversities, and changes," he said, "keep me from developing fully and naturally in my artistic career." Perhaps rueful of Gauguin's departure and hindered by his attacks, he complained that whereas last year he had painted a dozen or so orchards in bloom, this year he had managed only four. He felt his work was not progressing fast enough.

Then, reflecting on the people in his life, he mentioned that there were some very interesting nuns at the hospital, but he had discovered the majority of the priests to be in a wretched state, probably because they looked depressed and undernourished like him.

I have been so afraid of religion for so many years. For instance, do
you happen to know that love may not exist in the way people
imagine?—the resident physician here, the worthiest man you could
possibly imagine ... the most devoted, the most courageous, a warm
and manly heart, amuses himself now and then by mystifying the
good women here by telling them that love is a microbe. And when on
hearing this, the good women and even some men raise a loud out-
cry, he does not care a rap, and remains imperturbable on this point.
[April 30, 1889.]

Two years earlier, in his first surviving letter to Wil, Vincent had
eloquently described love as "the germinating force in a grain of
corn." Now he offered her a skeptical physician's definition of
love as a microbe, a germ, the cause of a heart's malaise—or perhaps, in Vincent's case, the cause of his mind's disorder, his
fears of rejection and abandonment, and even the seizures that
left a void in his memory. Given Vincent's history of crushing
rejection—as his mother's son, as Kee's would-be suitor, as
Gauguin's friend—his musing that love might be a sickness was
not so far-fetched.

While physicians might prove to be powerless in treating
the mystifying disease of love, they were not ineffectual, in
Vincent's estimation, in dealing with diagnoses like cancer. He
told Wil that simply by pressing your hand more cordially and
gently than did other people, doctors in such apparently hopeless cases could by their very presence be sympathetic and reassuring. Could the lack of his mother's gentle hand pressing his
when he was young have brought Vincent to such a sensitive
realization?

At this point in the letter, Vincent apologized for his ram-
bling, as his diverse ideas seemed to come to him in such an

incoherent fashion. Yet, even if he could not write two sensible lines, he still wanted Wil to know his thoughts:

> I am unable to describe exactly what is the matter with me; now and then there are horrible fits of anxiety, apparently without cause, or otherwise a feeling of emptiness and fatigue in the head.
>
> I look upon the whole thing as a simple accident. There can be no doubt that much of this is my fault, and at times I have attacks of melancholy and of atrocious remorse; but you know, the fact is, that when all this discourages me and gives me spleen, I am not ashamed to tell myself that the remorse and all the other things that are wrong might possibly be caused by microbes too, like love. [April 30, 1889.]

Vincent's self-analysis here, and his remarkable view of love as a disease, does not lie far from the truth, according to those modern psychologists who view his breakup with Gauguin as an emotional upheaval so traumatic that his feelings were vulnerable and as sensitive as exposed, raw nerves. What Vincent seems to be saying is that remorse and melancholia may be caused by a microbe that the resident physician named love. Either way, Vincent seems to be attributing his instability and mental disorder to a physiological, rather than a psychological, cause, as do those theorists and practitioners in modern psychiatry who treat and attempt to control many aspects of mental disease by medication. From this point on in Vincent's life, any perceived rejection, whether by man or woman, would trigger the same sort of erratic psychological behavior and physiological responses like blackouts and delirium.

For his anxiety, remorse, and melancholia, Vincent had devised his own special treatment. "Every day I take the remedy the incomparable Dickens prescribes against suicide," he declared. "It consists of a glass of wine, a piece of bread with cheese and a pipe of tobacco." He thought Wil might find it hard to believe that his melancholia could induce a contemplation of suicide, but at some moments he had come close to it.

Nor did Vincent any longer seek, or even see, a release from his melancholia and redemption in love. It was a microbe, after all. He had already confided to Theo that he had given up any hope of finding a woman to love and marry. While he did not find this situation always pleasant, he tried to treat his malady with contempt, and he avoided the idea of being a hero or a martyr. "In short, I do my best not to take lugubrious things lugubriously," he concluded to Wil.

Still grappling with melancholia while planning his move to the asylum at St.-Remy, Vincent received a letter in unfamiliar handwriting. Letters were Vincent's lifeline to the world, and though he wrote prolifically—usually after dark—his correspondents were relatively few: Theo, of course, his sister Wil, Rappard, the young artist Emile Bernard, and even, occasionally, Gauguin. Since Vincent recognized handwriting immediately, any script he didn't know aroused his curiosity. The careful penmanship hinted at a woman's hand. The crisp, clean envelope may have smelled slightly of perfume. He opened it to read words that shined like jewels. Although he had no way of knowing it then, the young woman who had sent that letter would ensure his immortality and raise his stature as an artist well above that of the duplicitous Gauguin.

It was three weeks since Theo's wedding, and Vincent had not yet met his brother's wife Johanna (Jo), although she had

Vincent's favorite self-portrait, in a yellow straw hat and blue smock.

Self-portrait by Paul Gauguin, during the time he lived with Vincent.

(TOP LEFT) Two paintings that some psychologists consider symbolic of Vincent's homosexual interest in Gauguin: *Vincent's Chair* (1888) shows a rustic chair with a pipe and bag of tobacco. (TOP RIGHT) *Gauguin's Chair (1988)* shows an ostentatious chair with a plush seat, in a boudoir setting with a luxurious carpet. The lighted candle and pair of books represent Gauguin's manhood. However, a new analysis of the two artists' relationship suggests that the two men were not homosexual.

(LEFT) Vincent's *Pink Peach Tree* (1988), which Jo placed on a wall facing the bed she shared with Theo. She wrote to Vincent that the reflected sunlight from the peach blossoms bathed her body in warmth and gave her comfort.

Vincent's *The Baby Marcelle Roulin* (1888), with his blue eyes and chubby cheeks, gave Jo comfort during her pregnancy, alleviating fears that her child might be born sickly. The baby Marcelle was born to the postman Roulin and his wife in Arles.

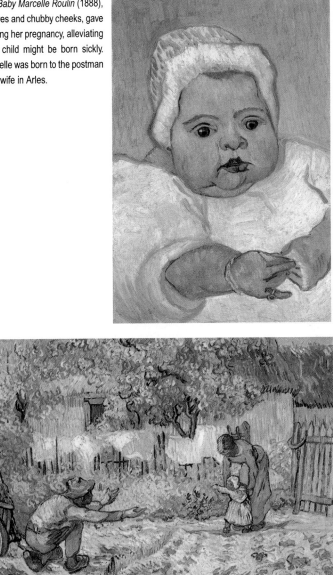

First Steps (1889) was painted soon after Vincent's sister-in-law Jo announced she was pregnant and declared that she wished to name the child after him. It depicts a gardener who, with open arms, is ready to catch his child as it takes its first steps. Symbolically, in trademark yellow hat and presenting himself as a provider, Vincent appears to be projecting himself as the father of the child.

Vincent's portrait *Marguerite Gachet at the Piano* (1890) shows the twenty-one-year old dressed in a romantic pink gown, though the pink has faded to white over the years. Vincent's use of Marguerite as a model, including the possibility that they might be lovers, undoubtedly caused Dr. Gachet much anxiety.

(BELOW) Vincent's *Undergrowth with Two Figures* (1890). Could this painting represent Vincent and Marguerite, in wedding attire, walking down the aisle of a church or cathedral? A top hat was traditional wedding attire for a groom.

Although Dr. Gachet gave Vincent permission to paint his daughter a second time, the resulting motif deepened his concern over their relationship. With its white and pale yellow overtones, *Marguerite Gachet in the Garden* (1890) could be interpreted as a wedding garden scene, with Marguerite dressed as the bride.

Within a year of Vincent's death, Gauguin traveled to the French Polynesian colony of Tahiti. Vincent had urged Gauguin to go there, and his influence on Gauguin's Tahitian paintings is obvious. This painting, *Tahitian Mountains* (1891), appears to evoke memories of his friendship with Vincent. Note the man in Vincent's trademark straw hat and the wheel tracks and golden wheat field effect in the foreground, similar to Vincent's final masterpiece, *Wheat Field with Crows*.

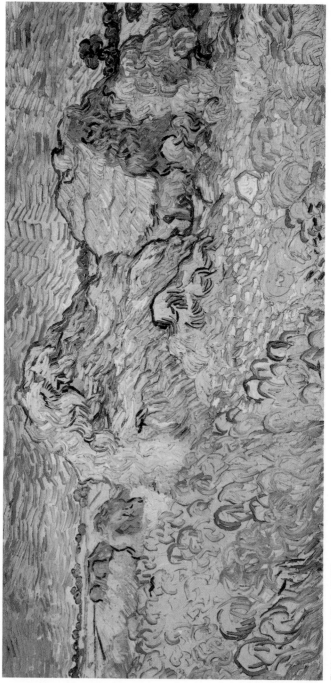

Field with Wheat Stacks (1890).

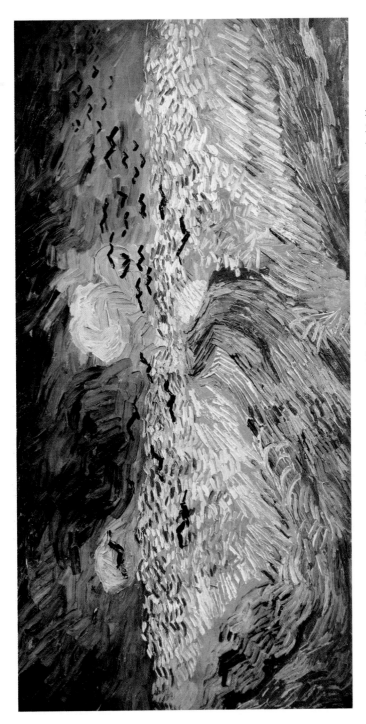

Vincent's *Wheat Field with Crows* (1890) is considered one of his greatest masterpieces. Vincent shot himself in a wheat field similar to the one depicted here.

Gauguin's *Van Gogh Painting Sunflowers* (1888).

been introduced to Vincent some time before through Theo's correspondence. Theo had tried to describe for her something of Vincent's undeniable if unappreciated genius.

That head of his has been occupied with contemporary society's insoluble problems for so long, and he is still battling on with his goodheartedness and boundless energy. His efforts have not been in vain, but he will probably not live to see them come to fruition, for by the time people understand what he is saying in his paintings it will be too late. He is one of the most advanced painters and it is difficult to understand him, even for me who knows him so intimately. His ideas cover so much ground, examining what is humane and how one should look at the world . . . one must free oneself from anything remotely linked to convention to understand what he was trying to say, but I am sure he will be understood later on. It is just hard to say when. [April, 1888.]

Theo's enthusiasm for Vincent's work and her own admiration of it, as well as her amiable curiosity about the person behind it, prompted Jo to write to her new brother-in-law independently of her husband. The letter, cheerful and frank, filled with tender feelings, was dated May 8. It follows in its entirety:

Dear Brother,

It is high time at last that your little sister had a chat with you herself, instead of leaving it to Theo to send her regards. When we were not yet married I was always thinking, Oh, at present you haven't yet got the courage to write about everything to Vincent, but now we are really truly brother and sister, I should be so very happy if you knew me a little too, and, if possible, loved me a little.

As for me, this has been the case for quite a long time . . . Wil as well as Theo have told me so many things about you, and here in the house there are so many things that remind one of you; the moment I come across a charming little jug or vase or some such thing, I am sure to hear *This* was bought by Vincent, *that* Vincent thought so pretty. Hardly ever a day passes without our speaking of you. You see, I still speak of "our house," and do not seem to be able to accustom myself to saying "the apartment"; I should so much like you to see how pretty and cozily Theo had everything arranged before I came. The bedroom especially is so sweet, very light and a great deal of pink in it—in the morning, when I am lying in bed, I have to look at that fine little peach tree in bloom of yours, which looks at me so kindly in its turn. Over the piano (we have one; Aunt Cornelia gave it to us) in our drawing room there also hangs a picture by you—a large one I like very much. It is a landscape in the neighborhood of Arles. The dining room is also full of them, but Theo is still dissatisfied with the arrangement, and every Sunday morning is spent hanging pictures in other places and rearranging everything.

It is so delightful on Sundays when Theo is at home all day; I well remember how as a child I always loved Sundays, because at home they were so pleasant and cozy (something which most people could not understand), and now they are much more so. So Monday meant a double festivity for me, for all the art shops were closed on account of the opening of the exhibition—of course we did not go to the exhibition, but enjoyed ourselves in our own way. Paris certainly looked beautiful that day—I so hope I shall come to love it as much as Theo does—but at times I am very much afraid it won't be possible. It is so noisy that we are living in our quiet cité—it may not be an aristocratic quarter but it is certainly a highly typical one—a big painter's studio across the way, a little arbor and a few lilac trees, which are in deliciously full flower at the moment. What a lot of beautiful flowers there are in Paris—if I should have to enumerate some good qualities of Paris, this would surely be one of the very first things!

A great number of Theo's acquaintances have already come to see us in the evening–last night, for instance, there was quite a reunion. Pissarro and his son, Isaacson and young Nibbrig and my brother–who for some time now has been dining with us every day because his wife has gone to Holland.

I certainly wish I could speak French a little better–I can manage on my own when I do my shopping or when I speak to the housekeeper, but I think carrying on a conversation, especially when Theo is present, is something horrible. So I do not attempt a letter in French–although I know in point of fact you would have preferred it, but Wil told me she also confines herself to writing in Dutch. As soon as I feel I am getting to be a bit of a Parisienne, I'll start writing in French–is that a bargain?

Leis and Wil have laid a little plot to come here this summer, the two of them; how pleasant it would be particularly to have Wil here. How she would laugh at me–for she herself is such a clever little housekeeper. She can do everything–whereas I–to make a clean breast of it–I don't know how to do anything–twice already I've let the rice burn and once the prunes–poor Theo, he has to swallow it all.

For the rest we are getting along very well together–we have been married three weeks today–it seems to me it happened long ago and also only a short while ago–it doesn't seem the tiniest little bit strange to us–it's as if we had always been together. What is worse is that I don't look at all like a married lady yet–yesterday I went to pay our baker, and the good man could not possibly understand that I myself was Madame van Gogh, and he persisted in calling me mademoiselle, which is really something too frightful!

Now I have to prepare lunch, for Theo will be coming home in a minute or two–so I will say goodbye for today–I hope I have not bored you too much, but the fact is I have grown so accustomed lately

to writing about all these little things, which they like to hear about
so much in Breda and Amsterdam that I am no longer able to write a
serious letter—this will improve later on, I hope.

With most cordial regards, and wishing you all the best,

Your affectionate little sister, Jo.

Jo's warm, cordial letter with its declaration of sisterly love and
appreciation of Vincent's art arrived during a bleak period of his
life: he lived in fear of recurring attacks; he felt friendless and
had lost faith in love. With buoyant spirit, she would not cease
trying to alleviate some of her new brother's strife. He was
touched by her tender sentiments. And with Jo's description of the
effect one of his peach-tree paintings had on her as she lay in
bed, bathed in its reflected light, a spark of understanding was
suddenly ignited in his dark, tormented life. In time, Jo would
turn the spark into a conflagration.

In his next letter to Wil, written the third week of June, Vincent's
spirits were low, and for good reason. Although often in his
letters he criticized the local population for not working as
hard as the Dutch, he did not reveal to Wil their increasing
hostility toward him. Regarded as a madman and a danger to
the community, he was often taunted while painting, the
street urchins throwing stones at him whenever he set up his
easel within the town. One of these street urchins, remi-
niscing as an adult, explained the reason: "Along with other
young people I used to poke fun at this strange painter. Well,
we were only children then. His appearance made a highly
comical impression on us. His long smock, his gigantic hat,

the man himself continually stopping and peering at things, excited our ridicule."

Vincent indicated that he was taking time out to write to Wil while his canvases dried in the sun. He was carrying on the work that he had left unfinished in Holland, that of rendering portraits of peasants and the elderly, he said, and felt his health gradually returning, but still he was depressed. His low spirits were reflected perhaps in two landscapes he had just finished: one, an orchard of twisted, gnarled olive trees with gray leaves; the other "one in which a wheat field on the slope of the hills is all devastated and smashed to earth by the pouring rain and the rushing water of a cloudburst."

Then, responding to a question from Wil as to whether he thought all people in love might be infected with a virus, Vincent jokingly suggested that if a person indeed believed he was in love in a healthy way, he ought to seek out Dr. Pasteur and get an inoculation against its potentially harmful effects. While Vincent's reply showed some humor, the humor was dark, the viewpoint grim, the message low-spirited. Love had been shorn of hope, of optimism, of its germinating force.

Once again Vincent had come close to identifying perhaps the primary factor causing his mental illness—extremely painful rejection in his relationships—and he could think of no way to produce a cure.

Vincent soon overstayed his welcome in Arles. He was locked out of his yellow house by the landlord and barred from entering, even to recover personal property, by the police, who were reacting to public pressure to have Vincent imprisoned.

It is little wonder that the neighborhood turned against

Vincent. The Arlesians found his behavior bizarre, and they could not understand, for example, that he shaved his head like a Buddhist monk in order to feel a closer affinity to Japanese artisans. Instead, they considered him a troublemaker, someone to be feared, what we would today call a "skinhead." Not only had eighty people signed a petition to have him incarcerated; he had angered the chief of police by showing him a still-life painting of two fish—kippered herring, called bloaters. The police chief was not amused, because "bloater" was a term of derision for a gendarme. It sounds farcical, but "The commissioner of police then gave the order to have me locked up," wrote Vincent to Theo. "Anyhow, here I am shut up in a cell all the lifelong day, without my guilt being proven. So you understand what a staggering blow between the eyes it was to find so many people here cowardly enough to join together against one man, and that man ill."

The petition grieved Vincent very much, according to the Reverend Salles. He quoted Vincent as saying "If the police had protected my liberty by preventing the children and even the grownups from crowding around my house and climbing the windows as they have done (as if I were a curious animal), I should have more easily retained my self-possession."

The feeling of rejection by so many people caused Vincent to suffer another attack in his jail cell, and so Vincent was readmitted to the Arles Hospital. Here he received a visit from his friend Paul Signac, the young pointillist painter from Paris, who had accompanied Vincent on some of his painting expeditions there.

Vincent continued to be completely mystified about his seizures and failed to see any link to Gauguin's rejection. Instead, he blamed himself for retreating into his solitary work as a painter, for missing meals, for drinking too much alcohol. He also blamed a dependency on coffee for killing his appetite.

"I have a craft that I do not know well enough to express myself as I should," he told Signac. As it came time for Signac to leave, Vincent showed signs of another attack, and Signac had to escort him back to his hospital bed. "When Vincent drank a bottle of turpentine, I knew it was time to take him back to the hospital," Signac commented wryly.

After painting in other parts of Provence, Signac returned to Paris and categorically blamed Gauguin for Vincent's breakdown. This diagnosis was taken so seriously by the Paris art community that in later years, after Vincent's death, Gauguin felt the need to "correct an error that circulated in certain circles" by writing his own account of what had happened between them, and categorically denying that Vincent's collapse was any of his doing.

With hospital treatment, Vincent soon recovered, and Dr. Rey refused to declare him a lunatic. Without the doctor's written diagnosis of lunacy, the police could no longer keep him in jail. Vincent was so thankful of the young doctor's support that he painted his portrait and gave him a particularly compassionate countenance. Vincent realized, though, that if he did not do something, his painting career and his life would be jeopardized. Four months after his first attack, reluctant though he was to leave Arles, Vincent admitted himself as a mental patient to the Asylum of Saint-Paul-de-Mausole, near St.-Remy-de-Provence. Convinced that the move to St.-Remy was a road to oblivion, he was filled with despair. "As a painter I shall never amount to anything important now, I am absolutely sure of it," he wrote to Theo.

Chapter Seven

DEAR
SISTER

St.-Remy, France, May 1889–June 1890

A preliminary sketch of *Starry Night* (1889), while Vincent was living in the Asylum of St. Paul at St. Remy.

We hope to have a baby,
a pretty little boy—whom we are going to call Vincent.

—Letter to Vincent from Jo, July 5, 1889,
announcing she is pregnant

On May 8, 1889, Vincent entered the austere Asylum of St. Paul at St.-Remy, where he placed himself in the care of its director, Dr. Theophile Peyron.

The facility is only fifteen miles from Arles, yet to Vincent it seemed to belong to another world. Built beside a Roman limestone quarry located between the edge of town and the mountains, the stone buildings of the asylum—originally a monastery complete with cloisters—were enclosed by a high stone wall, the top of which was embedded with iron spikes. Inside the walls, the asylum sat amidst tall umbrella pines and a sheltered, park-like garden.

Vincent's discharge from Arles Hospital was dated May 7, 1889, signed by a Dr. Urpar. It read: "I, the undersigned medical superintendent of the hospital in Arles, declare that six months ago Vincent van Gogh, 36 years old, was affected by complete mania and general mental derangement. At that time he cut off his ear. At this moment his state of mind is much improved, but he nevertheless thought it useful to have himself treated in a mental institution."

On May 25, Dr. Peyron made the following written report of Vincent's condition: "I, the undersigned physician, Director of the Lunatic Asylum of Saint-Remy, declare that Vincent van Gogh, native of Holland, entered here May 8 1889, suffering from a severe nervous attack accompanied by hallucinations of the sight and hearing, has experienced a noticeable improvement, but there is reason to keep him in the establishment to continue his treatment."

Vincent was given two small adjoining rooms with bare whitewashed walls, one to serve as his studio and the other as his bedroom. Both had steel bars at the windows and stout oak doors that were locked at night. Shut off from the outside world and working in what had been a monastic cell, Vincent felt like a monk, and he attributed his inclination to paint religious motifs to the ecclesiastical architecture of the buildings. He resumed his work immediately, as he firmly believed that painting was the best therapy for staving off the frightening and delibitating effect of seizures. In a letter to Theo again, he likened his illness to an ivy-girdled tree, the ivy being a burden the tree might not relish but could survive.

Though the food was poor and the corridors smelled like a musty, cockroach-infested restaurant, the regimented life of the asylum enabled him to accomplish a monumental amount of work. As the institution practiced hydrotherapy, Vincent was made to take frequent baths, administered by nuns, so that he might benefit from the soothing influence of water on his mind. During attacks of delirium, however, Vincent's body was submerged in water and restrained with a hinged wooden lid that left only his head exposed. Icily cold water was then showered upon his head to shock his system into recovery, and as he calmed down warm water was added. Regular bathing was also used as a preventative treatment. The director was congenial toward Vincent, whom he considered an unusual case because of his overall intelligence. The other inmates were friendly, if curious; they often looked over his shoulder while he painted, but respected his need for silence while he worked.

Vincent spent long periods without incident, and the garden delighted him as a subject to paint. Its gravel paths were edged with fragrant pink shrub roses, deep blue irises, and golden yellow feverfew. The scent of the umbrella pines and the spicy aroma of lavender from a nearby farm pervaded the atmosphere. Vincent imagined the garden to be a secret place where lovers could meet, an indication of his return to his old faith in the potential of love to cure all that ails the world.

During his periods of stability, Vincent was allowed to wander beyond the walls, but only in the company of a male attendant. Then the nearby quarry, Roman ruins, wild woodland, and olive groves were his favorite places to set up his easel.

When he was recovering from seizures and confined to his rooms, Vincent painted what subjects he could see from his windows, or else rendered his own interpretations of famous paintings by Delacroix and Millet. His rooms offered a view of cultivated fields enclosed by rough fieldstone walls, and in the background the foothills and high peaks of the Alpilles mountain range. These paintings reflected the extremes of his mood swings, from menacing black beetles and the sinister, hooded arum lilies that grew wild in moist meadows, to poppy fields and olive orchards under a blazing sun when he felt euphoric.

In his first letter to Wil from the asylum, dated May 9, the day after his arrival, he sounded in good spirits. He told her he found it rather strange that as a result of his attacks he felt less desire to marry, then continued:

Though here there are some patients very seriously ill, the fear and horror of madness that I used to have has already lessened a great deal. And though here you continually hear terrible cries and howls like beasts in a menagerie, in spite of that people get to know each other when their attacks come on. When I am working in the garden, they all come to look, and I assure you they have the discretion and manners to leave me alone—more than the good people of the town of Arles, for instance. . . . I have never been so peaceful as here and in the hospital in Arles. [May 9, 1889.]

Vincent was part of a male ward with only ten other patients, and he consoled himself on being the least mad among his companions. "There is someone here who has been shouting and talking like me *all the time,* for a fortnight," he told Theo. "He thinks he hears voices and words in the echoes of the corridors, probably because the nerves of the ear are diseased and too sensitive, and in my case it was my sight as well as my hearing." Another patient, who shouted all day and into the night, tore his shirts to shreds and smashed everything in sight, including mirrors and furniture.

Tireless in his work, Vincent hoped eventually to earn enough money from his art to pay for his care, "for it worries me a lot when I think that I have done so many pictures and drawings, without ever selling one," he added.

Theo still had not made a single sale from his gallery, despite Monet's endorsement that he admired Vincent's work at a gallery exhibition. Monet was a collector of Impressionist art, especially the work of Renoir and Cézanne, and for him to have purchased a van Gogh would clearly have thrilled Vincent. Since Theo was his dealer, perhaps Monet was hoping some day to receive one of Vincent's paintings as a gift. Not all the Impressionists liked each other's work. Manet thought Cézanne's paintings "foul," and Cézanne described Vincent's paintings as "the work of a madman," while he thought Gauguin's paintings "plagiarism"—an attempt to copy Cézanne's own style. Vincent kept reminding himself that his work was difficult for many people to understand because the public's taste was still firmly fixed on realistic-looking images, but he never lost faith in his belief that in time, his paintings would earn respect and live on after he was gone.

Having introduced herself in a letter to Vincent early in May, at the end of his stay in Arles, Jo divulged startling news in her second letter to Vincent on July 5: she was pregnant. Predicting that the child would be a boy, she told Vincent she wished to name the baby after him and to name Vincent the godfather as well.

In both these two letters, Jo expressed lucidly and with comprehension the dynamics of Vincent's painting, so that he began to view her as a true friend rather than a threat to his financial well-being. Jo's admiration of Vincent's art brought more than a ray of light into the darkly troubled life of a sensitive, misunderstood painter with a mutilated ear. It brought him real hope for his work and restored some of his faith in love. For even though Jo was his brother's wife, Vincent was moved to love her: for the youthfulness and energy he perceived from her engagement photograph, for the conviction and maturity that characterized her written thoughts, for her optimism in wanting him to be a godfather, for her perceptions and insight into his art.

Jo's sentiments were powerful, and many of them were centered on him. Jo and Vincent had yet to meet. Still, her second letter brims with tender thought and sisterly affection:

My dear brother,

This time I shall try to write you in French; in the first place I know you like it better, and then . . . if two people express themselves in the same language, they will understand each other in the end, I think. Only, as for me, I am not in the habit of writing in French, and I am afraid I will make mistakes which will seem very ridiculous to you—but I shall do the best I can. After some time I hope to be able to express myself—but at the moment, if the strangers I meet do not speak English, the conversation is far from animated, I assure you.

I am now going to tell you a great piece of news, on which we have been concentrating a good deal of our attention lately—it is that next winter, toward February probably, we hope to have a baby, a pretty little boy—whom we are going to call Vincent, if you will kindly consent to be his godfather. Of course I know we must not count on it too much, and that it may well be a little girl, but Theo and I cannot help imagining that the baby will be a boy. When I told them at Amsterdam and Breda, they all replied, "Aren't you pleased, what happiness, etc., etc."—and yet, to tell the honest truth, I was not pleased at all when I found out about it; on the contrary, I was very unhappy, and Theo had a lot of trouble consoling me. It's not that I don't like babies—take my little brother, who is now twelve years old; I held him in my arms when he was hardly two hours old, and I think there is nothing prettier in the world than a baby—but this is something of a selfish pleasure. When I think how neither Theo nor I are in very good health, I am greatly afraid that we are going to have a weak child, and to my way of thinking the greatest treasure that parents can give to their child is a strong constitution. But in this respect the doctor has reassured me a good deal, and then taking good food and taking good care of oneself may do a lot; the baby will have nothing to complain of in this respect.

Do you remember the portrait of the Roulin baby you sent to Theo? Everybody admires it greatly and people have already asked me many times, "Why have you put this portrait into such an out-of-the-way corner?" The reason is that from my place at the table I can just see the big blue eyes and the pretty little hands and the round cheeks of the baby, and I like to imagine that ours will be equally strong, and equally healthy, and equally beautiful—and that his uncle will one day paint his portrait!

In one of your last letters you asked Theo whether he was still dining at restaurants? Oh, dear no—never—what would be the good of being married if one could not dine at home? He always comes home at twelve o'clock to lunch and half-past seven for dinner. Often in the evening, somebody drops in, Isaacson or Hart Nibbrig. Tersteeg dined with us twice, and De Haan has come to see us too—and when he was there Mr. Pissarro and his son came too. In general we are very tired at night, and we go to bed early, but notwithstanding this I think Theo is looking far from well, but that Sacretan sale caused him a lot of fatigue, and besides, the heat is so overwhelming! Don't talk to me of Paris in such weather as this, and Theo says that in August it is even worse!

I read with great pleasure what you wrote to Theo about reading Shakespeare. Isn't it beautiful?—and so few people know him. "It is too difficult" (they say)—but that is not true—I for my part understand him much better than Zola. But when I think that such beautiful things were written nearly three hundred years ago, I think the world has not made much progress since then. I once saw *The Merchant of Venice* at the theater when I was in London, and the impression it made on me was a good deal stronger still than when I only read it. I have also seen *Hamlet* and *Macbeth*, but that was in Dutch—and then it loses much of its beauty.

Now I am going to say goodbye—please write us your opinion about our little boy, for a boy it must be.

Your sister, Jo

As Jo's pregnancy advanced, Vincent began a painting dealing with the subject of fatherhood. In *First Steps* he portrays a gardener, a provider, on bended knee with open arms, in a bountiful vegetable garden, while the mother of his child nudges a toddler toward him. Although the gardener could be Theo, the gardener wears Vincent's trademark yellow hat. Considering Vincent's keen interest in gardening, an interpretation of the painting is that *First Steps* fulfills a fantasy in which the child becomes Vincent's and Jo becomes his wife.

Vincent replied to Jo's letter in July 1889 and expressed his interest in the expected child's welfare. After congratulating her and Theo, he counseled them not to worry about the baby's health because what mattered to the well-being of a child was not the parents' health but the depth of their love for their child. He advised them, therefore, to be patient and to let nature take its course. As to Theo's health, he shared Jo's anxiety but felt that though Theo's health seemed often to be changeable, it was not feeble like Vincent's own. "I very much like to think that illness sometimes heals us, that is to say, when the discomfort comes to a crisis, it is necessary for the recovery of the body's normal condition," Vincent counseled.

After thanking Jo and Theo for sending paints and canvas so he could continue his work, he expressed concern about the responsibilities that fell upon a godfather. He wondered how he could provide for the child's religious education in the event of their deaths, if he was still in a mental institution. His treatment was expected to take at least a year. Also he suggested that they name their firstborn, if it was a boy, after Vincent's late father, Theodorus. Perhaps with this request was a reluctance to see a third child in the family named Vincent, when he was the second and the first had caused him so much grief.

In the meantime, Vincent had been churning out a phenomenal amount of work, and, in a letter to Wil in early July 1889, he revealed that he'd had another severe mental setback. He had recently gone to Arles to recover some of his canvases from Joseph Ginoux, owner of the Café de la Gare, and to collect money owed him by the Reverend Salles. Neither was at home, however. Their absence he interpreted as an intentional avoidance of him, and it caused him to feel another crushing instance of rejection that brought on the attack.

Not since the summer of 1884, when his parents had opposed his engagement to Margot Begemann, had Vincent communicated to his mother. Soon after his breakdown in Arles, he began including her in his letters to Wil, and in August 1889 he started writing to her directly.

In his first letter to his mother, Vincent comforted her over the news that her youngest son Cor had accepted a job in South Africa. Vincent believed that his younger brother would be happy in another country, especially if he was living away from large cities. Cor had experienced emotional problems since childhood and, like Vincent, was subject to periods of depression, yet Vincent had never felt close to him.

Vincent then turned his thoughts to Theo. He told his mother not to worry about Theo's persistent coughing and expressed the wish that Theo could live with Jo in a cottage outside Paris and commute to the office because "Theo needs action, business and friends in Paris itself. Let his wife take care that he gets back to his old Dutch food as much as possible, for he has been deprived of this for about ten years, and has been fed with restaurant food without any family life."

In closing, he urged his mother to trust Jo to take care of Theo, for Vincent had every confidence in her. He signed the letter, "Your loving Vincent."

In the next letter to his mother, dated early September, Vincent admitted that he had suffered another attack, but he continued to believe that his isolation at the asylum was good for his art because there was little to do except paint. He reported that during lucid periods, he felt fine. Even if the food was poor, he was eating regular meals and had plenty of mental and physical strength. For two weeks he had been well, and he was working from morning till evening day after day: "I lock myself up in the studio to have no distraction. Thus it is a great consolation for me that the work is progressing instead of declining, and that I do it with absolute calmness and that in this respect my thoughts are quite clear and conscious. And so, compared with others here who cannot do anything, I certainly have no reason to complain."

In closing, he wished his mother a happy birthday.

The extent of Vincent's output during this period is astonishing. It included *Starry Night,* which shows the village of St.-Remy nestled beneath a cloudless moonlit night sky, and two canvases entitled *Wheat Field with Cypresses,* the night scene playing with yellow and blue as a color harmony, the others using orange and blue.

In *Starry Night,* Vincent incorporated several of his original techniques into a single painting. The artist's eye is looking down on an idyllic village from a high elevation, but Vincent in fact painted the scene from memory, a new approach for Vincent that recalls Gauguin's instruction. Like his *Sower* masterpiece, where three quarters of the canvas presents soil in myriad colors to signify its hidden power for growth, in *Starry Night* three quarters is devoted to sky, and what a sky! Swirling stars radiate energy and yellow light as though they are trailing sparks; a crescent moon the color of Gouda cheese radiates golden yellow light that shimmers like ripples from a stone thrown into a pond. The village sleeps. A few lamp-lit windows show human presence, and a rakish church steeple connects the village to the universe, but the villagers remain oblivious to the incredible light show taking place above their heads. Some art historians who have attempted to decipher the symbolism in this immensely popular work see in its vibrance a menacing element. But just as *The Sower* glorifies the earth in its transformation of what most people see as nothing more than dirt, so *Starry Night* seems to be a celebration of celestial inspiration, as well as a comment on the ignorance of humanity and its inability to see beauty and cause for veneration in a night sky. What most people see, instead, are a black void and cause for fear. *Starry Night* thus becomes a metaphor for Vincent's art—something that is worthy of appreciation, but to which most people are blind.

Vincent's self-portraits of this period show him looking dejected, apprehensive, and sad, while the undergrowth in his paintings of woodland shows tortuous ivy-covered trunks that suggest the demons still haunting his mind.

Vincent was seriously thinking about returning to Paris, but he was continually nagged by the fear of another attack, which his physician could predict no more than he. Agonizing over his predicament, he told Wil: "In the beginning I was so dejected that I had no desire even to see my friends again and to work, and now the desire for these things is stirring, and then there is the fact that one's appetite and health are perfect during the intervals. And so I am longing for Theo and his wife, whom I haven't even seen yet."

Gradually, Vincent regained his confidence. In a letter to Theo, he expressed his desire forcefully: "My surroundings here begin to weigh on me more than I can say—my word, I have been patient for more than a year—I need air; I feel overwhelmed with boredom and grief. I am at the end of my patience. I must make a change."

Vincent's letter to Wil in late September 1889 followed one of his darkest periods at the asylum. He confessed to feeling terribly lonely and to not having left his two tiny rooms in two months. In the interim, he had suffered several attacks and had even attempted suicide by swallowing his paints and the mentholated spirits used in the asylum's lamps, although he may have actually drunk the mentholated spirits to satisfy his cravings for alcohol. During this severe depression, he hallucinated that people were trying to harm him, so he would not venture from his rooms even in the care of an attendant. Attempted suicide, hallucinations, paranoia, severe depression: this is an extremely low point in Vincent's life. Yet little is known about the details, because the asylum's records are either nonexistent or lost. When he showed signs of recovery and his paints were returned, he still felt fearful around people and therefore concentrated on religious motifs and a new series of self-portraits.

He was painting religious motifs because he found such subjects less disturbing when he felt agitated. He sought solace in copying Delacroix's *Pieta,* in which a grieving Mary is seen trying to revive a dead Christ; Delacroix's *The Good Samaritan,* showing a deathly pale, beaten traveler being helped onto a horse; and Rembrandt's *The Raising of Lazarus,* which depicts an emaciated Lazarus being brought back to life from the grave.

None of Vincent's previous paintings revealed his mental crisis more dramatically than these, as the facial features of the dead Christ, the wasted Lazarus, and the battered traveler in the Good Samaritan become Vincent's own.

He explained the significance of his rendition of *The Pieta* to Wil. The figure of the dead Christ obviously represents himself as a dead brother:

> The Delacroix is a "Pieta," that is to say the dead Christ with the Mater Dolorosa. The exhausted corpse lies on the ground in the entrance to a cave . . . it is the evening after a thunderstorm, and that forlorn figure in blue clothes . . . is sharply outlined against a sky in which violet clouds with golden edges are floating. She too stretches out her empty hands before her in a large gesture of despair, and one sees the good sturdy hands of a working woman. The shape of this figure with its streaming clothes is nearly as broad as it is high. And the face of the dead man is in the shadow—but the pale head of the woman stands out clearly against a cloud—a contrast which causes these two heads to seem like one somber-hued flower and one pale flower, arranged in such a way as mutually to intensify their effect.
> [September 19, 1889.]

After explaining the dynamics of his *Pieta* to Wil, he defended portrait painting in the face of photography, which he considered abominable: "Those photographic portraits wither much sooner than we ourselves do, whereas the painted portrait is a thing which is felt, done with love or respect for the human being that is portrayed." During his adult life, Vincent never posed for a photograph, but his surviving self-portraits total thirty-eight. When he received a photograph of his mother, he was so disappointed with her cheerless expression that he used it to paint her portrait in oils and to put strength and dignity into her features. The result delighted him: "Ah, what portraits could be made from nature with photography and painting," he wrote to Theo.

Regarding the two months he had spent isolated in his rooms, he told Wil:

> What I need is courage, and this often fails me. And it is also a fact that since my disease, when I am in the fields I am overwhelmed by a feeling of loneliness to such a horrible extent that I shy away from going out. But this will change as time goes on. Only when I stand painting before my easel do I feel somewhat alive. Never mind, this is going to change too, for now my health is so good that I suppose the physical part of me will gain the victory. [September 19, 1889.]

In his next letter to Wil, sent in October 1889, Vincent announced with great delight that the attending physician did not consider him insane. He now had long stable periods in which he was calm and clear-headed, conversed intelligently, and doggedly worked at his art, unlike other inmates, many of whom walked around in a trance-like state or threw fits of temper at the slightest provocation. He was also pleased to hear that Wil and their mother's new lodgings in Leyden had room for his paintings, for he had just completed an exciting collection he wanted Wil to see, in particular "an orchard of olive trees—a field of wheat with a reaper—a field of wheat with cypresses—an interior—a plowed field, early morning effect—orchard in bloom—and a self portrait."

He speculated that Wil might find his wheat fields too yellow, too blue, or too green, and that she might not care for the painting of his empty bedroom in Arles, which he had painted twice, on a large scale. Vincent believed that the extreme simplicity with which he tried to render life in his paintings might be unappreciated by modern society, so his bedroom painting would never be understood. The Japanese would understand it better, he said, for they lived in very simple interiors, whereas wealthy painters in Europe tended to live in overly ornate, cluttered rooms. For too long he had lived in chaos, and his messy habits had blinded him to the benefits of simplicity that he now sought in his work.

Vincent had learned that an art critic wanted to write an article about his recent work for a Dutch newspaper, but, he told Wil, he was apprehensive about giving his consent. He thought that reading an article about his art would make him feel sad, since he believed his best work was yet to come.

He then described another unconventional painting that he thought many people would find ugly because of its claustrophobic feeling: "It is a ward in the hospital at Arles, with a big black stove surrounded by a number of gray and black figures of patients; behind this the very long room with a red tile floor, with two rows of white beds, the walls white, but a white which is lilac or green, and the windows with pink and green curtains, and in the background the figures of two sisters in black and white. The ceiling is violet with big beams."

This painting reminded him that, as one writer had observed, people under stress often saw others at a great distance, as if they were at the far end of a great arena, and that even their voices seemed to come from afar. Vincent explained to Wil that during his attacks, he had suffered the ordeal of exactly this experience: all the people he saw, even if he recognized them, seemed to come toward him from a great distance, and they looked like distorted and sometimes even grotesque versions of their own reality. Sometimes they might assume a pleasant aspect, but at other times they bore unpleasant, disturbing resemblances to people he had known in his past.

With that macabre thought, he bade Wil "au revoir."

In a letter to his mother, undated but probably sent in November 1889, Vincent echoed many of the sentiments he had expressed in his letter to Wil: that she, too, might find some of the paintings he was sending unattractive; but that disapproval of his art did not concern him, as he was trying to form "several original ideas into a whole" that would be understood by the art establishment in the course of time. His belief that photography was an unsatisfactory way to memorialize a person, yet could be a tool by which to achieve great art through exaggeration, was undoubtedly one of these ideas. Another involved his copying—or, more accurately, interpreting—the work of other artists. He did at least twenty-four versions of Millets, and explained why in a letter to Theo:

> Let me try to explain what I am looking for and why it seems to me worthwhile to be copying these things. People always say we artists should compose our own works, and be composers only. Very well; but in music it is not like that—if someone plays Beethoven, he adds his own personal interpretation—in music, particularly in singing, the way a composer is interpreted is an art in itself, and it is by no means necessary that only a composer play his own compositions. Very well; but at present, being ill, I want something that will afford me a little pleasure and consolation. I take the black and white copy of a Delacroix or a Millet, as my motif. And then I improvise in color. But do not misunderstand me—this is not altogether my own, I am trying to preserve memories of their pictures—but the remembering,

and the approximate harmony of emotionally registered colors (even if they are not quite the right ones), are my own interpretation. [September 19, 1889.]

In the November letter to his mother, Vincent also shared his concern that everything go well with Jo's confinement. Probably referring to the pain and labor women had to endure in order to deliver a child, he noted that it was a humbling experience, the way in which a human being entered this world. He closed with a lament to his mother that his paintings had yet to create a public demand. "And yet never have such high prices been paid for pictures as these days. . . . And those high prices one hears about, paid for work of painters who are dead and who were never paid so much while they were alive."

Vincent explained more about his painting technique in a November letter to Wil, and admitted that some of his paintings might show the effects of a sick mind. He mentioned olive trees, twisted and gnarled, some against a pink sky, others against a lemon sky, and sinister fir trees towering high above the asylum garden against a red sky. Still, he intended to send to a Brussels exhibition a number of paintings featuring: "sunflowers, a quiet red vine in autumn, an orchard in bloom, tree trunks covered with ivy, and finally a field of young wheat at sunrise."

Vincent had heard that Theo was still coughing, but he thought his brother's health was likely to improve once he became a father, since Vincent expected him, Jo, and the baby to move to the country where the fresh air would benefit both Theo and the child. In addition to the coughing, Theo often had bouts of paralysis and his face would become swollen. Vincent wished that Theo would get out more instead of spending day after day in his office with his head filled with financial problems and with his good nature aggravated by an inconsiderate employer, Boussod & Valadon, a partnership that Theo found to be proud and tyrannical.

Vincent might have been trying to set Wil up for romance by praising the work and character of his young painter friend Emile Bernard and suggesting that she allow him to paint her portrait during her forthcoming visit to Paris. "Well, he is a nice boy, very Parisian, very elegant," he wrote. Although Emile Bernard was four years younger than Wil, who was twenty-four at this time, this small discrepancy in their ages never bothered Vincent. Bernard developed close friendships with Vincent, Gauguin, and Cézanne, and his enthusiastic writings about all three not only helped others to more clearly understand these men and their art, but also helped to establish their reputations. Wil certainly could have learned a great deal from this inquisitive, well-connected young painter.

Returning to the subject of his paintings, Vincent remarked that he'd taken a break from writing his letter to add a few brush strokes on a canvas showing the weatherbeaten old fir trees of the asylum garden against a red, orange, and yellow sky:

I don't know what thoughts came into my head while I was writing, but when I looked at my canvas I told myself it wasn't right. Then I took a color that was there on the palette, a dull dirty white, which you get by mixing white, green and a little carmine. I daubed this greenish tone all over the sky, and behold, at a distance it softens the tones, whereas one would think that one would spoil and besmirch the painting. Don't misfortune and disease do the same thing to us, and to our health? And if fate ordains that we

be unfortunate and sick, are we not worth more than if we were
serene and healthy? [December 10, 1889.]

He seems to have concluded here that his illness is aiding his
creative expression by providing him with an alternate view of
reality. If people judged his paintings to be the work of a madman, that was their right, but he hadn't gone mad. What he did
on purpose was paint.

Vincent wrote to his mother just prior to Christmas and offered
an insightful analysis of his strained relationship with his late
father, and it forgave his mother for having considered him
mentally ill long before his attack in Arles. He blamed his condition on himself—on his immoderate use of alcohol and irregular eating habits, which brought on continual mood swings and
violent attacks—and admitted to throwing tantrums and having
been a difficult son. The letter, obviously a painful one for him
to write, was a lucid document. He alluded to having looked on
Theo as a father figure after his own father's death:

> I discovered that in Paris, how much more Theo did his best to help
> Father practically than I, so that his own interests were often neglected.
> Therefore, I am so thankful now that Theo has got a wife and is expect-
> ing a baby. Well, Theo had more self-sacrifice than I, and that is deeply
> rooted in his character. And after Father was no more and I came to
> Theo in Paris, then he became so attached to me that I understood how
> much he had loved Father, and now I am saying this to you and not to
> him—it is a good thing I did not stay in Paris, for we, he and I, would
> have become too attached to each other. [December 20, 1889.]

He reminded his mother that a year had now passed since he had fallen so desperately ill and said he found it difficult to determine to what degree he had recovered, as he had, for such a large part of his past, been an unhappy character: "In the beginning when I fell ill, I could not resign myself to the idea of having to go into a hospital. And at present I admit that I should have been treated even earlier, but to err is human."

After quoting a French writer who claimed that all great painters were more or less crazy, Vincent found the assertion invalid, although he admitted that an artist could get too wrapped up in painting: "Whatever the truth of it may be, I imagine that here, where I don't have to worry about anything, the quality of my work is progressing. And thus, I go on with relative calmness, and do my best in my work, and don't consider myself among the unhappy ones." While the last statement may read like a contradiction, since Vincent has explicitly discussed his unhappiness with his mother, a contradiction it is not. The unhappiness Vincent earlier confessed to his mother referred to his life in general and to his perception of himself as an unsociable, disagreeable member of society. Here, however, he is speaking of himself as a pioneering artist, dedicated to his work. In that work, in art, in the act of painting, he is happy.

Another letter to his mother, probably written on Christmas Eve, soon followed. In it, Vincent sounded apprehensive, as though he sensed an attack coming on, and indeed a seizure occurred the next day. Judging from events referred to in this letter, the attack was prompted by memories of the traumatic events during the preceding Christmas period, when Gauguin had left him in Arles. "It is a year since I fell ill," he remarked. "But reasoning and thinking about these things is sometimes so difficult, and sometimes my feelings overwhelm me more than before. And then I think so much of you and of the past."

The fact that he was thinking of Gauguin and his mother in the same context shows that Vincent was once again wrestling with his own identity. If he made any connection between Gauguin and the ghost of his brother and his mournful mother, however, he does not reveal it. Perhaps when a flicker of reality entered his tangled emotions, the horror of his thoughts triggered the attacks. Given their history of melancholy moods and violent outbursts, one wonders if Vincent's two brothers, Cor and Theo, were also haunted by ghosts. Did Cor try to escape his ghost by leaving the country? If so, it followed him all the way to South Africa, where he committed suicide ten years after Vincent's death. And did Theo try to escape his ghost through workaholic habits as an art dealer, just as Vincent submerged himself in his art? In the end, Theo would suffer a fate similar to Vincent's.

In closing, Vincent told his mother that he thought of her often, "here where I spend my days more withdrawn into myself than to me seems desirable." But in spite of this, he said he was feeling stronger and healthier than a year ago, when he had wished only to die.

Vincent wrote three letters to Wil in January 1890, after he had recovered from his Christmas Day attack.

In the first of these letters, he expressed his pleasure to hear that Wil was staying with Theo and Jo in Paris, where she was helping them with preparations for the birth of their first child. He then discussed his latest relapse: "Fortunately, another rather violent attack of exaltation and delirium is at an end, and if I may say so, I don't feel any after-effects at all; I feel the same as I do on ordinary days. And tomorrow I shall start working again if the weather permits."

He referred to the anniversary of his relapse again in his second letter: "I'm adding a word to you in great haste; it is exactly a year ago that I had that very bad attack; I have no reason to complain too much, as things are going better for me at the moment, but it is to be feared that it will come back from time to time."

In his third January letter, Vincent addressed his concern about the effect Paris might have on him if he visited Theo and Jo in the spring. He wrote: "I have been forcing myself to forget Paris on account of the trouble and excitement a prolonged stay there causes me. As far as the painters are concerned it is right to say, 'One works better in the country; there everything speaks a distinct language, everything is firm, everything explains itself. And in a big city, when one is tired, one feels lost.'" Certainly his germinal canvases, *The Sower* with its vast expanse of plowed soil, and his *Starry Night,* could never have been painted in the city, with its pavement and smog.

Vincent then rued the fact that he was aging, "for it seems to me that life is passing by more rapidly, and that the responsibilities are more serious, and that the question of how to make up for lost time is more critical, and that it is harder to do the day's work, and that the future is more mysterious and a little more gloomy." With this remark, Vincent seems to have a presentiment of difficult days to come.

Before closing, he asked Wil if she had met his friend Bernard yet. She hadn't and never would. Bernard married a Lebanese girl, Hanenah Saati, in 1894. At least Vincent's romantic streak and belief in love was returning.

Dated January 30, 1890, Jo's next letter to Vincent was written close to midnight and mailed just hours before her delivery. An extraordinarily intimate letter, it was penned while Theo, Wil, and Jo's mother were dropping off to sleep; a doctor dozed close by while she was waiting to go into labor.

Dear Vincent,

Ever since Christmas it has been my intention, every day, to write to you—there is even a half-finished letter to you in my writing case—and even now, if I should not make haste to write you this letter, you would get the news soon that your little namesake had arrived. Before this moment, however, I want to say goodnight to you. It is precisely midnight—The doctor has gone to sleep for a while, for tonight he prefers to stay in the house—Theo, Mother and Wil are sitting around the table with me—awaiting future events—it is such a strange feeling—over and over again that question, "Will the baby be here tomorrow morning?" I cannot write much, but I so dearly wanted to have a chat with you—Theo brought along the article about you from the *Mercury* this morning, and after we had read it, Wil and I talked about you for a long time—I am eager for your next letter, which Theo is anxiously awaiting too—shall I read it? So far all has gone well—I must try to be of good heart. Tonight—and all through these days for that matter—I have been wondering so much whether I have really been able to do something to make Theo happy in his marriage—he certainly has made me happy. He has been so good to me, so good—if things should not turn out well—if I should have to leave him—then *you* must tell him—for there is nobody on earth he loves so much—that he must never regret that he married me, for he has made me, oh, so happy. It is true that such a message sounds sentimental—but I cannot tell him now—for half of my company has fallen asleep, he too, he is so very tired. Oh, if I could give him a healthy, sweet little boy, wouldn't that make him happy! I must stop now, for I have attacks of pain every now and then which prevent my thinking or writing in an orderly way. When you receive this, all will be over, believe me.

Yours affectionately, Jo.

Jo's thought of leaving Theo may have emerged from her fear of dying in childbirth, or from her guilt at not being able to make him happy. She certainly had good reason to leave him. Theo, she had discovered after their marriage, had syphilis. That she herself had not contracted syphilis from him was probably due to the fact that after the first two years, the disease is no longer contagious through sexual contact. He suffered a chronic cough, which was presumed to be tuberculosis but in fact had never been diagnosed. He experienced severe mood swings that resulted in the verbal and physical abuse of his wife, though Vincent was unaware of this until he returned to Paris and firsthand witnessed the abuse.

Deeply touched that Jo would write to him just hours away from her delivery, Vincent dashed off this reply on January 31:

Dear Jo,

It moves me so much that you write to me, and are so calm and master of yourself on one of your difficult nights. I am longing to receive the news that you have come safely through, and that your child is healthy. How happy Theo will be, and a new sun will rise inside him when he sees you recovering.

Forgive me if I warn you that in my opinion recovery takes a longer time and is no easier than being ill. Our parents knew this too, and following them in this might almost seem our duty.

Well, I myself am also thinking of you people these days. I am feeling better, but have again had a few days like the others, when I did not know exactly what was going on, and was upset.

But you see that the quietness is coming back. I read Theo's letter with the enclosed 50 francs along with your letter; he writes me things that give me much pleasure. And I hope to send him some of my work shortly.

But how I am longing to hear the good result of your struggle.

Tell him that I got a good letter from Gauguin. And if Wil is still with you, tell her that I received her letter and hope to answer it soon.

She too will be happy if you and your child are well, and it is so very good to be present at times like these. And Mother at Leyden will rejoice in it more than anybody else, for I believe she has been longing for life to be happier for Theo. Well I shall be glad when I may congratulate him and you, and I hope that time has already arrived.

In thought always with you and him,

Your brother, Vincent

PS—I cannot write more as I am not yet calm. Good-bye for now. [January 31, 1890.]

The day after shortly after sending this letter, Vincent received news that Jo had delivered a boy and both mother and baby were in good health. The same day, he wrote to Theo:

Today I received your good news that you are at last a father, that the most critical time is over for Jo, and finally that the boy is well. That has done me more good and given me more pleasure than I can put into words. Anyhow, here it is, the thing I have so much desired for a long time. No need to tell you that I have often thought of you these days, and it touched me very much that Jo had the kindness to write to me the very night before her delivery. She was so brave and calm in her danger it moved me deeply. Well,

it contributes a great deal to helping me forget the last days when
I was ill; at such times I don't know where I am and my mind wan-
ders. [February 1, 1890.]

In mid-February, Vincent's next letter to Will expressed his joy
at the birth of baby Vincent and thanked her for being on hand
at Jo's delivery: "I am touched by what you write about Jo's confinement—how very brave and very good you have been, staying
with her all the time. In those circumstances in which we feel
the strain of anxiety, I should probably be like a frightened wet
chicken."

To celebrate the birth, Vincent told Wil that he had decided
to paint a picture of pale pink almond blossoms against a blue
sky. And he was planning another trip to Arles to tie up some
loose ends and to test his ability to travel. Though he felt it was
normal for an artist to behave eccentrically at times, he wondered if he could ever lead an ordinary life. There were still
paintings stored in Arles that he wanted to collect, and since he
had let his hair grow back he wanted to test the reaction of people in his old neighborhood.

By this time, Vincent had of course learned of Wil and Jo's
excitement over the article about his work that had appeared in
the Paris publication, the *Mercury.* The writer, Albert Aurier,
began the piece: "Beneath skies that sometimes dazzle like
faceted sapphires or turquoises, that sometimes are molded of
infernal, hot, noxious and blinding sulphurs . . . there is the disquieting and disturbing display of a strange nature. . . . Such,
without exaggeration, is the impression left upon the retina
when it first views the strange, intense and feverish work of
Vincent van Gogh."

Vincent told Wil that it was overly flattering:

I thought the article by Aurier—leaving out of consideration whether I deserve what he says of me—very artistic and very curious in itself. But it describes what I *ought to be,* instead of the sad reality of how I do feel. I wrote to tell him, that it seems to me both Monticelli and Gauguin are more the innovators—and it seems to me that my work is of secondary, very secondary order. . . .

When I read that article I felt almost mournful, for I thought: I ought to be like that, but I feel so inferior. And pride, like drink, is intoxicating, when one is praised, and has drunk in the praise. It makes one sad, for reasons I feel and cannot express—but it seems to me that the best work one can do is what is done in the privacy of one's studio without praise. And then you do not always find a sufficiently friendly disposition among artists. Either they exaggerate a person's qualities, or else they neglect him too much. However, I believe justice will prevail in the end. . . .

I feel the desire to renew myself, and to try to apologize for the fact that my pictures are after all a cry of anguish, although in the rustic sunflower they may symbolize gratitude. You see that I do not reason well yet—it would be better to know how to calculate the price of a pound of bread or a quarter of a pound of coffee, as the peasants do. And here we are again in the same spot. Millet set the example by living in a hovel, and talking only with people who did not know the bounds of pride and eccentricity. [February 20, 1890.]

The lack of self-esteem in this letter is painful to read. Instead of raising his spirits and making him feel good, Aurier's complimentary article worries Vincent instead, because it makes no mention of the influence of Gauguin and Monticelli. Vincent also worries that the praise might go to his head and affect his future progress in a negative way, since he feels his best work is done in solitude, free of outside influences.

Though no one would think it from reading the previous letter, suddenly things were looking up for Vincent—first a favorable review by a leading art critic and then a sale. *The Red Vineyard* (1888) was purchased for the respectable sum of four hundred francs by Anna Boch, the sister of a Belgian Impressionist painter, at an exhibition of Vincent's work in Brussels. He had painted it in Gauguin's company, the leaves a riot of purple and fire red, the sky a lemon yellow and the soil violet, "like the Virginia creeper of Holland." It was the only painting he sold in his lifetime.

Success, however, did not enter Vincent's mind in a mid-February letter to his mother. Instead, he expressed his increasing frustration at being cooped up in the asylum: "I must try to get out of here, but where to go? I do not think I could be more shut up and more a prisoner." He said he thirsted for a taste of Paris again; he wanted to do more portraits.

In a subsequent letter to his mother and Wil, in early March 1890, Vincent repeated his desire to leave the asylum: "What one has to endure here is hardly bearable," he insisted. Work alone enabled him to tolerate his existence, and he described his painting of a lawn with yellow dandelions in the blazing sun—proof of his ability to paint even when his illness was at its height.

In a postscript he suggested that one reason for his latest seizure may have been the favorable article about his work: "As soon as I heard that my work was having some success, and read the article in question, I feared at once that I should be punished for it; this is how things nearly always go in a painter's life; success is about the worst thing that can happen." Again, Vincent demonstrated a warped sense of reasoning. He can only imagine that, as a result of some favorable press, he is fated to suffer a calamity. It is a premonition that will soon prove to be insightful.

Two months after the birth of his nephew and namesake, Vincent received more news from Jo. Dated Paris, March 29, 1890, her letter was short, but the words warmed his heart:

Dear Vincent,

Among all the letters from brothers and sisters which you will receive tomorrow, I wish you the best of luck, which I do at the same time on behalf of your little namesake, who cannot do so very well himself as yet. What he does is look at uncle Vincent's pictures with a good deal of interest—the tree in blossom especially, which is hanging over his bed, seems to enthrall him—and further the Rembrandt, although I cannot assert confidently that it is not the gilt frame which attracts him in the latter case. I am happy to say he is growing well, and we long to show him to you. But being a father and a mother is quite an art—perhaps because I have had to learn and get used to so many things in the course of that one year. . . . What amazes me most is that such a little child has so much of a personality, against which you are utterly powerless. Now and then he looks at me as if he wanted to say, What are you doing to me—I know much more about things than you do. His are the eyes of an adult and then with a lot of expression. Is it possible that he has the makings of a philosopher?

He does not allow his mother much leisure, but I managed to escape for a little while at the opening of the Independents' Exhibition to see your pictures—there was a seat directly in front of them, and while Theo was talking to all sorts of people I sat there for a whole fifteen minutes enjoying the delicious coolness and freshness of your painting entitled "Undergrowth"—it's as though I knew this spot, and had been there several times—I'm so fond of it.

Here it is the height of summer—indescribably hot—and I dread the hot days yet to come. I know it sounds a bit like sacrilege now that there is that fine delicate haze of green over all the trees, but I prefer winter after all. I shall have to close this letter in a hurry, for Theo is waiting to take it to the post office.

With best wishes,

Affectionately yours, Jo.

Vincent's desire to escape the asylum and return to the north to see Jo and his godson persuaded him to discharge himself from the institution. Jo sympathized with his desire to make a bid for freedom: "Vincent had spent a full year at the asylum, and described his art during that period as 'No longer the buoyant, sunny triumphant work of Arles.' There sounded a sadder, deeper tone than the piercing clarion call of his symphonies in yellow during the previous year: his palette had become more sober...."

Reluctantly Theo gave his approval for Vincent to be discharged. However, he voiced his concerns in a letter to his mother and Wil on April 15:

The last time the doctor wrote he said that it is very rarely that he is completely himself. He mostly sits there with his head in his hands and when someone speaks to him he looks as if it hurts him and he makes signs that he wants to be left alone. What a sad business and Dr. Peyron says that, although he has hopes that the crisis will soon be ended, it will leave an impression on his constitution.

Theo wrote again to his mother on May 3, saying he had not heard from Vincent in a while and had been getting worried;

then a letter arrived. Theo conveyed his impressions to their mother:

> It appears he is not yet strong and calm, but it is an improvement that he is able to write again. At this time he still did not have the courage to read your letters and mine, as a particular characteristic of his illness are those fits of despondency and everything that reminds him of the past makes him sad and melancholic. Above all he longs to leave the asylum . . . if only that might happen without harm to him. Dr. Peyron would rather that he stayed somewhat longer but Vincent has already written before that he thought he would be cured sooner in a home where there would be no nuns.

Remembering how Vincent had angered the police during his previous stay in Paris, and fearful that the neighborhood might turn on him for his antisocial behavior like the citizens of Arles had, Theo agreed to accommodate Vincent in his apartment for a temporary period, but he insisted that Vincent should then move on to stay with their mutual friend Camille Pissarro in the country near Auvers. As it turned out, Pissarro himself was suffering some health problems, and he recommended to Theo that Vincent instead take lodgings close to a local homeopathic doctor, Dr. Paul Gachet. Fearing that Vincent might suffer a mental seizure during his journey north, Theo had offered to pay for an attendant to accompany Vincent from the asylum to Paris, but Vincent thought it would be a good test of his improved mental health if he traveled alone, and promised to ask the train conductors to keep an eye on him. However, he left St.-Remy against the advice of Dr. Peyron. Of his disagreements with the doctor, Vincent wrote Theo: "Peyron speaks vaguely so as to escape responsibility, but we shall never see the end of it this way, never, the thing will drag on and we shall end up by getting angry with one another . . . I can't stand any more— I must make a change, even a desperate one."

In spite of his misgivings about Vincent's determination to leave the asylum, Dr. Peyron wrote in his record book only one word concerning Vincent's discharge: "Cured."

Chapter Eight

FINAL
REJECTION

AUVERS, FRANCE, MAY–JULY 1890

A preliminary portrait of Dr. Paul Gachet, Auvers-sur-Oise, May 1890, a month before Vincent's falling out with the doctor.

I was afraid—not entirely—but nevertheless a little—that my being a burden to you was something you found intolerable.

—Letter to Theo and Jo, July 10, 1890,
after Theo informed Vincent that their child was ill

On his release from the Asylum of St. Paul on May 17, 1890, Vincent traveled first to Paris, to visit his brother and Jo in their apartment in the Cité Pigalle. It was a year since he had been admitted to the asylum. On May 20, he then moved to the village of Auvers, where he placed himself in the care of Dr. Paul Gachet.

Jo described the suspenseful moments as she waited for Theo to return from picking Vincent up at the Gare de Lyon: "It seemed an eternity before they came back. I was beginning to be afraid that something had happened when at last I saw an open coach enter the Cité; two merry faces nodded to me, two hands waved—a moment later Vincent stood before me." She had expected a sick man, "but here was a sturdy, broad shouldered man, with a healthy color, a smile on his face, and a very resolute appearance. . . ." She observed that he looked stronger than Theo.

Vincent's nephew was sleeping in his cradle, and quietly she ushered the two brothers into the baby's room. Silently the two brothers looked down on the infant, and, Jo noted, "both had tears in their eyes." During the next three days, Vincent was cheerful and lively all the time. He was pleased to see his paintings decorating every room of the apartment: in the bedroom, *The Orchards in Bloom;* over the mantelpiece in the dining room, *The Potato Eaters;* in the sitting room, *Landscape near Arles* and *Starry Night over the Rhone,* which was the first of his night scenes. *Blossoming Almond Tree,* just recently painted to commemorate his nephew's birth, hung on a wall over the child's cradle. More paintings were stored under the bed, under the sofa, inside cupboards. Vincent pulled huge piles of unframed canvases out from their hiding places and spread them on the floor so he could study them with critical attention.

Receiving visitors at the apartment, Vincent caught up on the latest developments in the Paris art world, while Jo made him feel welcome with some wholesome Dutch cooking. Lucien Pissarro, Toulouse-Lautrec, and Bernard stopped by. From Lautrec, Vincent learned about significant changes to the district of Montmartre—a new cabaret theater called Le Moulin Rouge, which had opened the previous October, was catering lavishly to thrill-seeking middle- and upper-class patrons. It was also providing Lautrec with a rich source of subjects to paint. Work was progressing, too, on the Cathedral of Sacre Coeur on the highest part of the Butte. Gauguin did not stop by; he was in Britanny, at Pont-Aven, attempting to scrape enough money together to buy a one-way ticket to Tahiti, where Vincent had urged him to go as a potentially triumphant phase in his artistic career.

Vincent also ventured outdoors. With Theo, he visited Père Tanguy's artists' supply store to check on the condition of paintings that he still had in storage there, and the two brothers viewed several gallery exhibits.

But Vincent sensed there were too many distractions in Paris, and just three days after his arrival from Arles he took a train from Paris to Auvers, where he rented a room above a café on the main street. In the widowed Paul Gachet, Vincent found not only a doctor who felt he could help Vincent if his mental problems returned, but also a friend and a painting enthusiast. Gachet had treated several Impressionists—among them Pissarro, Cézanne, and Renoir—and had acquired a fine collection of their work, which he displayed in his home. The doctor no longer practiced at his Auvers house, but had an office in Paris where he held consultations several days a week. His consultation office in Auvers had been converted into a printmaking workshop, and this Jo described as looking like an alchemist's shop from the Middle Ages, with its massive wooden printing press and bulbous glass jars filled with strange liquids of different colors. The doctor also had a medieval-style physic garden of healing herbs.

Sandwiched between the house and the bottom of a perpendicular cliff was a shaded flagstone courtyard with a large slate table for outdoor picnics. Shade trees were girdled with English ivy, which also cloaked the cliff face. Marguerite Gachet, the doctor's twenty-year-old daughter, cultivated a colorful flower garden along a terrace in front of the house, overlooking the main street. The front door was accessible by a steep, narrow flight of stone steps that led up directly from the street. More stone steps ascended the rock face to a belvedere where Cézanne had stood to paint a spectacular panoramic view of Auvers's orange-tiled rooftops.

Directly opposite the back door of the house, across the courtyard, a cave penetrated the cliff. This connected to miles of passageways—catacombs that had been used as a refuge in times of warfare, dating back to the Viking raids. Just inside the cave entrance was a spacious cavern where the doctor had created a theater for the performance of plays and concerts. The back yard had pens for ducks, chickens, and turkeys, and a pair of peacocks walked about in the company of five cats.

The house was solidly built, architecturally austere with straight gables, rakish brick chimneys, and a black slate roof. It had three levels plus a loft. The interior was poorly lit by narrow, shuttered windows, and the rooms were filled with paintings and antiques. "It was the home of an original," wrote Jo, "but an original of great taste."

Dr. Gachet lived on this sinister property with his fifteen-year-old son Paul, Jr. and Marguerite. Jo found it curious that Dr. Gachet himself, though much older than Vincent, resembled Vincent physically, while his son Paul looked like Theo.

Viviane Forrester, writing about Vincent's last days in Auvers in a history of the village, described Gachet "as a strange person, disturbed and impassioned, who practiced medicine after having published a thesis on melancholia. Yet politics, hypnosis—everything interested him . . . he painted and above all he did engravings. Gachet had bought the works of his friends: Renoir, Monet, Cézanne, Pissarro, yet under conditions that had caused constant upsets. He had proved hard and aggressive. Friendships had dwindled."

Feeling rejuvenated now that he had escaped the claustrophobic atmosphere of the asylum and the noise of the city, Vincent set to work and began painting the rural streets and quaint thatched cottages in the village. He was pleased with the results. To friends in Arles, the Ginoux family, he wrote: "And, incidentally, now that I am no longer drinking . . . a definite progress when all is said and done . . . I am doing work that is certainly better than before." All traces of despondency or depression had disappeared, his productivity had increased, and his chronic nightmares had ceased.

In just a few weeks, Vincent had accomplished his two goals on leaving the asylum: he had escaped its stultifying atmosphere, and he had met his godson. He had reason to be feeling better than he had in a long time, and this is reflected in the optimism and confidence expressed in his letters.

This new-born optimism is apparent in a letter Vincent wrote to Theo and Jo dated May 21, of his new friend Gachet: "I have seen Doctor Gachet, who gives the impression of being rather eccentric, but his experience as a doctor must keep him balanced enough to combat the trouble from which he certainly seems to be suffering at least as seriously as I." He described the doctor's house as being "full of black antiques, black, black, black," except for the Impressionist pictures, mostly Cézannes and Pissarros. Vincent added, "The impression I got of him was not unfavorable. When he spoke of Belgium and the days of the old painters, his grief-hardened face grew smiling again, and I really think that I shall continue to be friends with him and that I shall do his portrait."

In a second letter to Jo and Theo, also dated May 21, Vincent continued to be optimistic: "And I already feel that it did me good to go South, the better to see the North." For the area around Auvers offered him a great deal of color. In addition to thatched cottages, there were many pretty middle-class timbered houses with colorful flower gardens to paint. Moreover, there were people willing to pose for him. In Auvers, his work could only progress. Vincent believed that everything else—like his relationships with others—was now secondary to his art, "because I haven't the gift for that and can't help it." He added that if he sometimes felt a little low, he could be confident that a sense of serenity would return as soon as he completed more work. One consistency in Vincent's psychological history was that his work as an artist proved always to be the best antidote for depression, and though he was well aware that he lacked social graces around people, ultimately it didn't matter to him.

Vincent continued to keep Theo and Jo apprised of his progress. He grew increasingly confident about his work and life in Auvers, particularly as he had Dr. Gachet close at hand to give him medication if he felt an attack approaching. But he had sensed that not all was right with Theo and Jo when he had seen them in Paris. Neither of them was eating well, and they had looked worn down by stress. When he wrote to them again, at the end of May, he expressed concerns about their health, and suggested they drink lots of beer to fatten themselves up.

After thanking Theo and Jo for sending his allowance, he said that he had again seen Dr. Gachet and that he was planning to paint at his house. The two often dined together, and afterward the doctor would view Vincent's most recent work. "He seems very sensible, but he is as discouraged about his job as a doctor as I am about painting," Vincent wrote, referring to the lack of recognition for his art and his inability to earn a living from it. He then suggested that Theo and Jo might visit Auvers for some country air and rest: "Often, very often, I think of your little one, and then I wish he were big enough to come to the country. For it is the best system to bring up children there. How I wish that you, Jo and the little one would take a rest in the country."

Repeatedly Vincent refers to Theo's and Jo's frail constitutions. He felt that Jo especially needed nourishment, as she was still nursing her baby. He fussed: "Really, she ought to eat twice as much."

It is likely that Theo and Jo were stressed from the financial strain of Vincent's allowance and additional expenses brought on by having a baby, particularly as Theo had recently been forced to take a salary cut. They may indeed have had to cut back on their allowance for food in order to save money.

* * *

On May 25, Vincent reported to his mother that he was feeling well but that he was concerned about Theo's health, particularly his persistent coughing. In the week since his trip to Paris, Vincent remained focused on his work. He assured his mother he was in good spirits because of:

> The pleasure of seeing Theo again and making the acquaintance of Jo, who seems to me sensible and cordial and simple, and my new little namesake, and further, to be back among painters and interested in all the struggle and discussions and especially in the work of the little self-contained world of painters—all this distraction has, it seems to me, a favorable effect and the symptoms of the disease . . . have quite disappeared these days—though, as I have learned, one must not count too much on this. [May 25, 1890.]

Vincent told his mother, as he had told Wil, that work was helping him to maintain his mental balance, and he noted with satisfaction that Dr. Gachet was willing to take his paintings as payment for medical services.

In a letter to Wil on June 5, Vincent retained his confidence in his ability to keep his spirits high. He said he continued to be bolstered by Dr. Gachet, whom he regarded as an older brother, "so much do we resemble each other physically and also mentally." He then elaborated on Gachet's character:

> He is a very nervous man himself and very strange in his behavior; he has extended much friendship to the artists of the new school, and he has helped them as much as was in his power. I painted his portrait the other day, and I am also going to paint a portrait of his daughter. . . . He lost his wife some years ago, which greatly contributed

to his becoming a broken man. I believe I may say we have been friends from the very first, and every week I shall go stay at his house one or two days in order to work in his garden. . . .

What impassions me most—much, much more than all the rest of my métier—is the portrait, the modern portrait. I seek it in color, and surely I am not the only one to seek it in this direction . . . I should like to paint portraits which would appear after a century to the people living then as apparitions. By which I mean that I do not endeavor to achieve this by a photographic resemblance, but by means of our impassioned expressions—that is to say, using our knowledge of and our modern taste for color as a means of creating the expression and the intensification of the character. So the portrait of Dr. Gachet shows you a face the color of an overheated brick, and scorched by the sun, with reddish hair and a white cap, surrounded by rustic scenery with a background of blue hills; his clothes are ultramarine—this brings out the face and makes it paler, in spite of the fact it is brick-colored. His hands, the hands of an obstetrician, are paler than the face. Before him, lying on a red garden table, are yellow novels and a foxglove flower of a somber purple hue. [June 5, 1890.]

Vincent had obviously developed a strong attachment to Dr. Gachet. In his care-worn face Vincent had found an appealing subject to paint, and in his person he had found a sympathetic friend, a man who had also experienced tragedy in his life. Not only did they physically resemble each other; they were intellectually compatible, too. They enjoyed each other's conversation, and the doctor seemed genuinely impressed with Vincent's groundbreaking artistic ability.

On June 8, Theo and Jo traveled up to Auvers from Paris with their baby to spend a Sunday with Vincent. They enjoyed a pleasant, sunny day and lunched outdoors in Dr. Gachet's garden. Vincent's next letter to them left no doubt that the visit had been one of the happiest days of his life. He wrote that their Sunday together had left him with a very pleasant memory and that he would like them to have a *pied-a-terre* in the country near to him. In a brief letter to his mother several days after the visit, Vincent reaffirmed his pleasure at their visit, and concluded: "It is reassuring for me to live so much closer to them."

In a recollection of that sunny June day, Jo described the idyllic visit with Vincent in Auvers:

> Vincent came to meet us at the train, and he brought a bird's nest as a plaything for his little nephew and namesake. He insisted on carrying the baby himself and had no rest until he had shown him all the animals in the doctor's yard. A too loudly crowing cockerel made the baby cry, and Vincent consoled him.
>
> We lunched in the open air on the terrace, and afterward took a long walk; the day was so peacefully quiet, so happy, that nobody would have suspected how tragically our happiness was to be destroyed a few weeks later. [June 10, 1890.]

In his letter to Theo and Jo after the visit, Vincent said he felt a little upset that furniture sent from Arles had failed to arrive, but at least in Auvers the nightmares had ceased; he only wished that Dr. Peyron had supported his decision to return to the North. In the delicate days of his mental condition at the asylum, an incident like the failure of furniture to arrive on time would have produced a feeling of dejection, and might have triggered a seizure, so again Vincent's general contentedness, his patience and persistence, seemed to be keeping the disease in check.

Vincent's letters during June 1890 generally reflected a

renewed sense of well-being. They were lucid and lively, with no mention of melancholy moods. He delighted in the closeness he shared with Theo and his family, and he reveled in his work, which did not want for subjects to paint. He was particularly satisfied with his portraits of Dr. Gachet.

In a letter to Wil dated June 12, he reported that he had finished three landscapes and explained that he had painted a portrait of Dr. Gachet with an expression of melancholia to contrast with the calmness seen in "old portraits." He described the portrait as "sad and yet gentle, but clear and intelligent–this is how one ought to paint many portraits." By "old portraits," Vincent probably meant portraits as they had traditionally been painted in the past, with the subject stiffly posed and masked in a forced or benign smile. Vincent preferred to paint the anguish, stress, pain, horror, madness, fear, loneliness, tragedy written in the faces of his subjects. One of his goals was to make the Paris art establishment and the general public more aware of his criteria for a good portrait painting, which relied for its effect on color intensity rather than the mere exaggeration of an expression.

Affirming his desire for artists to paint more portraits of people with passion in their features, so as to arrive at the truth of their nature, Vincent wrote: "Knowing what I know now, if I were ten years younger, with what ambition I should work at this! Under the present circumstances I cannot do very much, for I do not talk with, nor should I know how to talk with, the people I want to influence." The people he wished to influence, of course, were the Paris Salon judges who still dictated artistic merit. Exposure at a Salon exhibition was still essential for an artist to gain public recognition.

In closing, he told Wil that he wanted to paint her portrait some day.

* * *

Vincent's world indeed seemed bright that June. His happiness was reflected in his letters and evident in his work. The dark, tortured images that haunted his canvases in the year he spent at the asylum had been vanquished by cottage gardens, sunny landscapes, and smiling children. Gone were the indices of his depression. Instead it was color, color, color—red roofs, indigo skies, vibrant foliage greens, wildflower meadows. He returned to painting floral arrangements as well, and the flowers he used bloomed with iridescent petals—scarlet poppies, orange and yellow anemones, and mallows in all shades of pink.

Then a letter arrived from Theo. It was dated June 30, 1890. It said that little Vincent was ill, and that Theo, short of money due to his drastic cut in pay, could no longer afford to support his family in their Paris apartment. Vincent was shattered as he read:

My dearest brother,

We have gone through a period of greatest anxiety; our dear little boy has been very ill, but fortunately the doctor, who was uneasy himself, told Jo, "You are not going to lose the child because of this." Here in Paris the best milk you can buy is downright poison. We are now giving him ass's milk, and this is doing him good, but you never heard anything so grievously distressing as his almost continuously plaintive crying all through many days and many nights, when you don't know what to do, and all you do seems to aggravate his sufferings. It's not that the milk isn't fresh, but what's wrong is the fodder and the treatment of the cows. It's abominable . . . Jo was admirable, which you can imagine too. A true mother, but for all that she wore herself out a good deal too much; may she recover her strength and not be subjected to new trials. Fortunately she is asleep at the moment, but she is moaning in her sleep, and there is nothing I can do for her. If only the baby, who is sleeping too, will let her sleep for some hours, both of them will wake up with a smile, at least I hope so. In general she is having a hard time of it at the moment.

At present we do not know what we ought to do; there are problems. Ought we to take another apartment—you know, on the first floor of the same house? Ought we to go to Auvers, to Holland, or not? Ought we to live without a thought for the morrow, and when I work all day long not earn enough to protect that good Jo from worries over money matters, as those rats Boussod and Valadon are . . . keeping me on a short allowance?

. . . What do you have to say to this, old fellow?

Beside himself with worry, Theo attempted to relieve Vincent of the burden of concern and to raise his spirits with acknowledgments of his progress as an artist and his recovery from illness. Soon, though, Theo lapsed again into self-pity:

Don't bother your head about me or about us, old fellow, but remember what gives me the greatest pleasure is the knowledge that you are in good health and that you are busy with your work, which is admirable. You have too much ardor as it is, and we shall be ready for the battle for a long time to come yet, for we shall have to battle all through life without eating the oats of charity they give to old horses in the mansions of the great. We shall draw the plow until our strength forsakes us, and we shall still look with admiration at the sun or the moon, according to the hour.

In the next two paragraphs Theo seems to be drunk as he sinks into maudlin melodrama. Despite that, the images he conjures and the ideas he bandies—like "love's germinating force"—allude to views and a vision that the brothers shared.

Look here, old boy, watch your health as much as you can, and I shall do the same, for we have too much in our noodles to forget the daisies and the lumps of earth freshly cast up by the plow, neither do we forget the branches of the shrubs which put forth buds in spring, nor the bare branches of the trees shivering in winter, nor the sun rising over our aunt's garden, nor the red sun going down to the sea at Scheveningen, nor the moon and stars of a fine night in summer or winter—no, come what may, this is our profession.

Is it enough? No—I have, and hope from the bottom of my heart that you too will someday have a wife to whom you will be able to say these things; and as for me—whose mouth is so often closed, and whose head is so often empty—it is from her I receive the germinating force, which in all probability comes from afar, but which was found by our beloved father and mother—perhaps they will grow so that at least I may become a man, and who knows whether my son, if he can stay alive and if I can help him—who knows whether he will not grow up to be Somebody. As for you, you have found your way, old fellow, your carriage is steady on its wheels and strong, and I am seeing my way, thanks to my dear wife. Take it easy, you, and hold your horses a little, so that there may be no accident, and as for me, an occasional lash of the whip would do me no harm.

Having spilled his guts, so to speak, Theo seems to regain some composure. "Now listen," he urges, "as soon as Jo is a little stronger and the little one entirely recovered, you must come and stay with us for a day or two, at least on a Sunday and some days after."

Theo closes with a final tug at Vincent's heart: "Goodbye, dear old brother. The paints are going off. I shake your hand most cordially, and I am glad that the little one and his mummy are sleeping so soundly."

There was a lot here for Vincent to worry about. Though Theo wasn't explicit about the consequences of all this turmoil, the message was clear—he wanted to reduce or end Vincent's allowance, for the sake of Jo and his baby son's health. Theo even appealed to Vincent on the basis of their special friendship and the goals for artistic expression that they shared. The last thing Vincent would want to hear was that the baby was sick. Jo had drawn Vincent into a huge emotional investment by sharing with him her most intimate thoughts during labor pains and concerns for a healthy child—even by naming the child after him. Vincent's stability was being tested to the limit.

Theo's letter turned Vincent's life suddenly sour. The press had praised him as a bold new artist with a rosy future. Theo had sold his *Red Vineyard.* Vincent was at last approaching the point of recognition for his art. And he was working well. He had made a successful transition from the asylum to society. He was living in a picturesque village. He had built an intellectual friendship with Dr. Gachet. His drinking was under control and his nightmares had vanished. Only now Theo was pulling the financial plug.

Vincent's reply expressed concern for his brother's family, and especially for the health of his godson. Yet, however much he shared their anxiety, he felt powerless to help since he was earning nothing from his art, and what Theo needed most was money. Nor did he feel that visiting them in Paris would solve matters. He suggested that instead, they move to the country, that perhaps they could stay with Dr. Gachet. "I think that country air has an enormous effect," he reasoned.

> As for the little one, really, I am beginning to fear that it will be nec-
> essary to give him fresh air and, even more, the little bustle of other

children that a village has. I think Jo, too, who shares our anxieties and risks, ought to have a change of air in the country from time to time. . . .

I honestly believe that Jo would have twice as much milk here. . . .

I myself am also trying to do as well as I can, but I will not conceal from you that I hardly dare count on always being in good health. And if my disease returns, you would forgive me. I still love art and life very much, but as for ever having a wife of my own, I have no great faith in that. I rather fear that toward say forty I declare I know nothing, absolutely nothing as to what turn this may take. But I am writing to you at once because I think that you must not be unreasonably worried about the little one; if it's just that he's cutting teeth, well, to make the job easier for him, it would perhaps be possible to distract him more here where there are children, and animals, and flowers, and fresh air.

I shake your hand and Jo's in thought and a kiss for the little one.

[July 2, 1890.]

Despite his initial reluctance to visit them, Vincent went to Paris. The baby was undeniably seriously ill. Worry had settled in the faces of his brother and sister-in-law. The household was in fear. The meeting became so argumentative about financial concerns that Vincent left, returning to Auvers in a state of anger, confusion, and shock.

It seems unlikely, however, that Theo and Jo aligned themselves as one powerful entity against Vincent. If they had, Vincent would probably have suffered an attack right there in the apartment, or as soon as he stepped out into the street. Rather, it seems, Theo had been browbeaten by Jo to force the issue of suspending Vincent's support payments. There are clues that she instigated the confrontation, as she felt torn between her admiration for Vincent's art and her instinct as a mother to protect the baby's health. When Vincent arrived at the apartment, he apparently received a friendly reception, for Theo had arranged for several friends in the art community to stop by to meet Vincent. Toulouse-Lautrec arrived before noon and stayed for lunch; with him, he brought a painting that Vincent admired. It showed a woman playing the piano in a pose identical to one Vincent had recently painted of Marguerite Gachet in profile. But Lautrec's painting showed a more mature woman in a black gown instead of pink. Even the woman's facial features resembled Marguerite. It was as if Lautrec had transformed Marguerite into Vincent's ideal woman—his dark lady, or woman in black. Vincent wrote that it affected him emotionally. Then came the journalist Aurier, who had written the glowing account of Vincent's art. After they had left, Jo apparently got down to business and presented Vincent with an ultimatum: for the baby's sake, and for the money they needed to pay for medication, they wished to terminate Vincent's allowance. Jo declared that Theo simply could not support everyone any longer—himself, his child, his wife, his mother, and Vincent. Theo probably argued for a compromise, perhaps a deep cut in Vincent's allowance, and Vincent left the two of them arguing between themselves. If Vincent had stayed and faced the fear and anger of both parents, he could well have felt the way he did when his mother and father took sides against him in the past, and the consequences would have been predictable—a seizure.

That Jo alone forced the issue is suspected because of her actions after the confrontation. In a memoir written as an introduction to her published translations of Vincent's letters, she states only that after Aurier left, an artist friend, Jean-Baptiste Guillaumin, was expected, but before he arrived "the

visit became too much for Vincent, so he did not wait for this visit
but hurried back to Auvers." She does not explain why Vincent
had to leave. Jo undoubtedly believed that the purpose of the
meeting had been to discuss her baby's health and to obtain
more money for medication and food, but to her distress she saw
Theo and Vincent turning the occasion into a social gathering
to benefit Vincent. There was probably much joviality, bawdy
humor, noisy conversation, intense discussion about art
appreciation, social drinking, toasting to Vincent's future success, and demands on Jo as a hostess. Frustrated at seeing
Vincent being worshiped and coddled while her baby lay near
death in its crib, she could have simply exploded, and before
the next guest, Guillaumin, arrived, demanded a resolution to
the problem. Torn between her sisterly concern for Vincent
and her maternal love and duty to her child, naturally Jo would
choose to save her child and ask Vincent to make a sacrifice.
If Theo tried to take Vincent's side against the welfare of her
baby, a domestic argument would have ensued. Any normal
mother in similar circumstances would have lost patience and
done the same.

Tossed between being lionized and being upbraided about
money, immediately following this roller-coaster of a meeting
on July 7, Vincent wrote a brief letter:

> Dear brother and sister,
>
> My impression is that since we are all rather distressed and a little
> overwrought besides, it matters comparatively little to insist on hav-
> ing any very clear definition of the position in which we are. You
> rather surprise me by seeming to wish to force the situation. Can I
> do anything about it, at least can I do anything that you would like
> me to do?

However that may be, once again a good handshake in thought, and in spite of everything, it gave me great pleasure to see you all again.

Be very sure of that.

Ever yours, Vincent [July 7, 1890.]

Though Vincent drafted this letter, he never mailed it. Four days later, on July 10, Vincent wrote a longer letter. He needed to know if his support payments would continue—150 francs a month—as before. "Theo fixed nothing and so to begin with I left in confusion," he explained. Of course, he did not want to see the health of his godson jeopardized, he told his brother and Jo, but neither did he wish to see his career terminated. Remarkably, in spite of the fact that this encounter with Theo and Jo resulted in one of the severest instances of emotional rejection he had ever had to endure, surely comparable to Gauguin's walking out on him, Vincent remained relatively calm; he did not suffer an attack. Evidently, he still had enough fortitude to keep the anguish of rejection and anxiety over his future under control.

Addressing Theo and Jo together, Vincent said he regretted not hearing from them in the past few days, but he could imagine why:

Considering how things have happened—honestly—I think that Theo, Jo and the little one are a little on edge and are worn out—and besides, I myself am also far from having reached any kind of tranquility.

Often, very often I think of my little nephew—is he well? Jo, believe me—if ever you happen, as I hope, to have more children—don't get them in the city, have your confinement in the country and stay there until the child is three or four months old. At present it seems to me that while the child is still only six months old, your

milk is already drying up—like Theo—you are too tired. I do not at all
mean to say exhausted, but anyway worries are looming too large,
and are too numerous, and you are sowing among thorns....

I take an interest in my little nephew and am anxious for his
well-being: since you were good enough to call him after me, I should
like him to have a soul less unquiet than mine, which is foundering....

Now about Dr. Gachet. I went to see him the day before yesterday, I did not find him in . . . I think we must not count on Dr. Gachet
at all. First of all, he is sicker than I am, I think, or shall we say just
as much, so that's that. Now when one blind man leads another blind
man, don't they both fall into the ditch? [July 10, 1890.]

Vincent volunteered to find cheaper lodgings, but he begged his
brother and Jo not to stop his support payments, as then he
would have to stop painting and would lose the skills he had
acquired. He pleaded for a prompt reply.

Immediately, Vincent received a sympathetic letter from Jo.
The letter has apparently been lost, but it is more likely that Jo
may have destroyed it later in order to hide the nature of her
involvement in the altercation. Judging by Vincent's reply on
July 10, however, it eased his anxiety, especially as Jo evidently
confirmed that his support payments would continue.

Dear brother and sister,

The letter from Jo has really been like a gospel to me, a deliver-
ance from the distress caused by the hours I had shared with you,
which were a bit difficult and trying for us all. It is no slight
matter when we are all made aware of the precariousness of our
existence.

Back here, I, too, still felt very sad and the storm which threat-
ens you continued to weigh heavily on me as well. What is to be

done? Look here, I try to be fairly good humored in general, but my life too is threatened at the very root, and my step is unsteady too.

I was afraid—not entirely—but nevertheless a little—that my being a burden to you was something you found intolerable—but Jo's letter proves to me clearly that you do realize that I am working and making an effort just as much as you are.

So—having arrived back here, I set to work again—although the brush almost slipped from my fingers—and because I knew exactly what I wanted to do, I have painted three more big canvases since.

They are vast fields of corn under troubled skies, and I did not have to go out of my way very much in order to try to express sadness and extreme loneliness. I hope you will see them soon since I'd like to bring them to you in Paris as soon as possible. I'm fairly sure that these canvases will tell you what I cannot say in words, that is, how healthy and invigorating I find the countryside.

The third canvas is Daubigny's garden, a picture I have had in mind ever since I came here. [July 12, 1890.]

At this point in his career, Vincent felt too old to retrace his steps or to follow any pursuit other than being a painter, even to the exclusion of marriage and children. "That desire has left me, though the mental suffering of it remains," he professed in the same letter.

It is significant that Vincent should receive an apology from Jo and not from Theo, for it suggests that the attempt to cut off Vincent's allowance was against Theo's wishes. Other clues support this notion. First, there is Theo's initial letter broaching the subject, in a manner that suggests he was drunk and had been browbeaten into doing something against his will. Indeed, he could not even verbalize the intent of the letter—to stop Vincent's financial support. Then there is Vincent's account of their meeting, which he left early because Theo and Jo were arguing with each other over his support. As a result, nothing was resolved. Most revealing is Jo's account of the events. She provides only the barest specifics. She merely states that when Vincent arrived for their meeting, "they were exhausted by a serious illness of the baby," and that the meeting "became too much for Vincent," so he "hurried back to Auvers overtired and excited." Biographer Jan Hulsker concludes, "The talks with Theo and Jo had a stormy and—at least in Vincent's case—desperate character." He believes this is the only possible conclusion from the letter Vincent addressed to them upon his return to Auvers. The most revealing passage in that letter states: "You rather surprise me by seeming to wish to force the situation *while there are disagreements between you.* Can I do anything about it—*perhaps not—but have I done anything wrong,* or finally can I do anything that you would like me to do?" The italicized portions, which show clearly that Theo and Jo were not in agreement, were omitted from Jo's translation of the letter. Vincent, then, was not dealing with a mother and father united. If he had been—if Theo and Jo had ganged up to cut off his support—this could have been an unbearable form of rejection, and cause for a seizure. But it didn't happen. With great fortitude and presence of mind, he left the apartment to let them argue it out between themselves, and when he returned to Auvers wrote earnestly to ask what had been decided.

His anxiety apparently alleviated by Jo's apology, the very next day Vincent wrote to his mother and Wil in a state he described as calm. But it was to be his last communication with them. Across the top of the surviving document, his mother wrote "Very last letter from Auvers."

He wrote, "For the present I am feeling much calmer than last year, and really the restlessness in my head has greatly quieted down. In fact, I have always believed that seeing the surroundings of the old days would have this effect."

For the sake of their health, he urged Wil and his mother to "work in the garden and to see the flowers growing."

He concluded: "I am in a mood of almost too much calm."

This sense of foreboding is revealing. Vincent had walked into an emotional minefield and was standing up to significant pressure. First he had suffered an emotional rejection from Jo, whose desire to end his allowance threatened the very root of his artistic campaign; then he had experienced a betrayal of some kind from Doctor Gachet, something so serious he declared him a blind man, a person he could no longer rely on *at all.* Either of these emotional traumas would have been devastating a year earlier when he was in the asylum, and would have caused a seizure. Yet he seems to be perfectly centered and calm, and the satisfaction he gains from his art makes him buoyant. His brush strokes are firm and confident, the results gratifying in their strength of color. This calmness in the face of catastrophe is a new, and strange, experience for him.

In a matter of days, Vincent's anxiety over Theo's problems returned. He felt that the stress created by his brother's financial support of him only added to the turmoil in Theo's household. For his part, Theo realized that Vincent was feeling continually more depressed and guilty about the entire difficult situation. He wrote to Vincent and tried to assure him that things were not as bad as they seemed, that the boy was making a recovery; but Vincent was not convinced. In his mind he had become the reason for Theo and Jo's distress: the money they were sending him was money they could be spending on better medical attention for their child and on nourishing food to restore their health.

The following blood-stained letter, dated July 23, was never mailed. It was found in Vincent's pocket after he shot himself in the wheat fields above Auvers, in an area located between Dr. Gachet's house and his own lodgings:

My dear brother,

Thanks for your kind letter and for the 50 franc note it contained.

There are many things I should like to write to you about, but I feel it is useless. . . . Your reasurring me as to the peacefulness of your household was hardly worth the trouble, I think, having seen the weal and woe of it for myself. And I quite agree with you that rearing a boy on a fourth floor is a hell of a job for you as well as Jo.

Since the thing that matters most is going well, why should I say more about things of less importance? My word, before we have a chance of talking business more collectedly, there is likely to be a long way to go.

The other painters, whatever they think of it, instinctively keep themselves at a distance from discussions about actual trade.

Well, the truth is, we can only make our pictures speak. But still, my dear brother, there is this that I have always told you, and I repeat it once more with all the earnestness that can be imparted by an effort of a mind diligently fixed on trying to do as well as one can—I tell you again that I shall always consider that you are something other than a simple dealer in Corots, that through my mediation, you have your part in the actual production of some canvases, which even in the cataclysm will retain their quietude.

For this is what we have got to, and this is all or at least the
chief thing that I can tell you at a moment of comparative crisis. At
a moment when things are very strained between dealers in pictures
of dead artists, and living artists.

Well, I have risked my life for my own work, and it has cost me
half my reason—all right—you can still choose your side, as far as I can
tell you are not one of those dealers in men, I am sure you act with true
humanity, but what do you expect? [July 23, 1890.]

Most studies based on Vincent's correspondence with Theo portray Vincent shooting himself while in the grip of a seizure, and
though there is a lot of gloom expressed in this letter, it does not
appear to be a suicide note. On the contrary, Vincent talks of the
future when he says: "there is likely to be a long way to go" and
"I shall always consider that you are something more than a simple dealer in Corots." Also, his declaration that he is risking his
life for his art does not suggest that Vincent has given up hope.
This letter was actually the draft of a longer letter Vincent
mailed to Theo the next day, July 24, which he toned down considerably, and in it requests more paints. Biographer Claude
Millon noted that Vincent mentioned the possibility of death
frequently in his letters, but Millon does not believe Vincent's
death was a premeditated suicide, stating: "In his July 24 letter
to Theo, Vincent asks for several tubes of paint, and then three
days later pulls the trigger on himself. There is no sign of crisis
here. He is perfectly lucid."

In his final letter, Vincent made reference to Theo's
stormy marriage; and Theo's reply showed he lived in deep
denial of spousal abuse. "Where did you see these violent
domestic quarrels?" Theo demanded. "That we were tired by
these interminable preoccupations on the subject of the

future of all of us, yes . . . but truly I don't see these intense domestic quarrels."

Vincent's motivation for shooting himself has been the subject of much speculation. One explanation biographers have given for his suicide is his conviction that he had become "a thing to be dreaded," a burden on his brother and his family; that his needs were taking the bread from their table and threatening their well-being, especially that of their cherished child, his godson. Another baby boy named Vincent had gone to an early grave—a brother whose name he bore as a memorial to his mother's grief. He surely did not want a second baby Vincent to depart the world—not if he could prevent it.

Vincent's small, oppressive room at Ravoux's Café on the main street was in the attic and had only a tiny window for ventilation. It was a mere fifteen-minute walk from Dr. Gachet's house. The ridge at the back of the doctor's house runs parallel to the River Oise above the village. Between the two is a chateau with a high boundary wall, and beyond the wall, above the ridge, are vast fields of wheat. It is believed Vincent shot himself between the wall and the wheat fields, close to the doctor's property, before sunset.

Dr. Gachet was called in to attend his wounded patient shortly after nine P.M. on July 27, after Ravoux had found Vincent curled up on his bed like a wounded dog. His knees were up to his chin, and he was moaning heavily. "Are you ill?" Ravoux asked, whereupon Vincent lifted up his shirt and showed him the bloody wound above his stomach. "I wanted to kill myself," Vincent replied.

Vincent refused to give anyone Theo's home address, so Dr. Gachet had to send a messenger to contact him through his employer, at the showroom of Boussard & Valdon. Because Jo was away visiting family in Holland with her baby, Theo traveled alone. He arrived the next morning to find Vincent reclining in bed and smoking a pipe. He seemed to be contented. A second doctor's opinion was sought, and it was concluded that the bullet should not be removed, and that Vincent should not even be moved to a hospital for better care. Anton Hirschig, an artist who occupied the room adjacent to Vincent, recalled: "The heat in the room under the roof was suffocating." He heard Vincent complain: "Is there no one to cut open my belly?"

Theo stayed by Vincent's bedside and watched as his will to live weakened. Vincent lingered until dawn of July 29, when he died at the age of thirty-seven. His last words to Theo were, "I wish it were all over now."

Vincent's funeral was attended by artist friends and locals who knew him. The journalist Albert Aurier wrote of the occasion: "On the walls of the café where the body lay all his last canvases were nailed, forming a sort of halo around him, and rendering his death all the more painful to the artists who were present by the splendor of the genius which radiated from them. On the coffin was a simple white linen, masses of flowers, the sunflowers that he loved so much, yellow dahlias, yellow flowers everywhere. It was his favorite color . . . a symbol of the light he dreamed in hearts as well as in his paintings. His easel, his folding stool and his brushes were placed on the ground before the coffin . . . at three o'clock the coffin was raised up and friends carried it to the hearse. In the assembly some people cried. Theodore van Gogh, who adored his brother, who had always supported him in his struggle for art and independence, did not stop sobbing painfully. . . . Outside there was a terribly hot sun; we climbed the hills of Auvers, talking of him, of the bold push he has given to art, of the great projects he always had, of the good he has done to all of us. We arrived at the cemetery, a little new cemetery dotted with new tombstones. It is on the hill overlooking the harvest fields, under the great blue sky which he would still have loved. Then he was lowered into the grave. Who could not have cried at that moment; this day was so much made for him that one could not help thinking that it could still have made him happy. . . ."

"Vincent's fear of an impending attack, or an attack itself drove him to death," was Jo's conclusion in the foreword to her translation of Vincent's letters. The real truth, however, may have been more than she could accept. Vincent had not suffered an attack in a long time, not since leaving the asylum over two months earlier, and though he was anxious to relieve Theo of financial stress, it's possible that, for one last time, he wanted to play the knight in shining armor by making the ultimate sacrifice for a woman he admired: his courageous and intelligent sister-in-law.

From the beginning of their acquaintance, Jo had bolstered Vincent's confidence. In his darkest days at the asylum, she had lifted his spirits. With admiration and optimism, she had named her son after him—a heartfelt gesture that had inspired Vincent to leave the asylum in order to visit his godson. Jo genuinely understood the genius of Vincent's work, and she had wanted him "to love her a little." Now he may have felt responsible for her unhappiness. Maybe, too, he thought that by relieving Theo of some of his financial worries, he could defuse some of Theo's abusiveness and establish some of the domestic bliss he had tried so hard to offer to his cousin Kee and to provide for the prostitute Sien: the mother and child secure once more in the peaceful nest of their household.

Noble though that scenario might be, with Vincent as a knight and martyr, it does not take into account his predictable pattern of behavior under stress. His previous incidents of self-mutilation—burning his hand to prove his love for Kee, cutting off his ear after threatening Gauguin's life, trying to poison himself with turpentine when Signac had to leave—occurred as a result of his perceptions of emotional rejection. While it is true that Jo had rejected him, Theo had not, and Jo had since apologized. So is it possible that at that moment in his life, someone *else* caused him to feel intolerable rejection? Was there another person whose rejection of Vincent might have been strong enough to cause him to harm himself?

Indeed there was: Marguerite Gachet, who had just celebrated her twenty-first birthday on June 22, was infatuated with Vincent. In appearance, she bore a striking resemblance to Vincent's favorite peasant model, Stien, whose pregnancy had driven Vincent from Nuenen. They could have been sisters, as they had the same doe-like eyes, dark hair, chubby cheeks, and plump lips. Vincent and Marguerite had found kindred spirits in each other. Coincidentally, she shared her birthday with her brother, as Vincent shared his birthday with his deceased older brother. Just as he had been starved of his mother's love as a child, Marguerite felt unloved by a father who she believed loved her younger brother more. Marguerite's twenty-first birthday party was an event she shared as usual with her younger brother, and Vincent attended the party. His presence made Marguerite feel special, particularly since her brother garnered most of their father's attention. She felt special, too, because Vincent was selective in choosing models and had asked her to model for him. Sitting for him had further bolstered her self-esteem, especially since she knew how much her father admired Vincent's artistic skills.

It was common knowledge in the village that Vincent valued his friendship with Marguerite. Furthermore, her desire for an intimate relationship with Vincent was suspected by Gachet's housekeeper, Mme. Louise Chevalier. Gachet's own suspicion of a sexual relationship could have been aroused when he discovered that Marguerite had modeled for Vincent without his permission, posing in her garden, dressed like a bride, the garden awash with white roses and pale lemon marigolds, like a wedding garden. The painting is entitled *Marguerite Gachet in the Garden.* Her father's apprehensions could have intensified when Vincent followed this with a painting of her playing the piano in an ankle-length romantic pink gown. This painting is entitled *Marguerite Gachet at the Piano.* Another symbolic painting by Vincent during this period is of a grove of trees riotous with wildflowers. A man and a woman are walking through the woods with their arms linked. The man is wearing a black top hat and black formal suit, the woman is dressed in a long, pale green gown and a white pillbox hat, unusual clothing for a walk in the woods but appropriate for a church wedding ceremony. Entitled *Undergrowth with Two Figures,* the trees have straight, smooth trunks and are pruned of their lower branches so that they resemble the vaulted columns of a church or cathedral. The yellow, orange, and white wildflowers look like confetti, and the couple is walking as if they were strolling arm in arm down an aisle. Some art historians have interpreted this intriguing painting as a premonition of death, believing that the man is dressed like an undertaker. But the painting is too colorful and bright to be a metaphor for death. More likely, Vincent painted himself and Marguerite symbolically walking together down the aisle. A top hat was considered appropriate wear for a groom. This painting might have further fueled Dr. Gachet's concern.

Soon after Vincent's burial, reports began to circulate that he had threatened Dr. Gachet with a gun at his home before he walked out to the wheat field where he shot himself. If Dr. Gachet had accused Vincent of having an affair with Marguerite, and had ordered him to stop seeing her, Vincent might have become outraged, especially if he had avoided a sexual relationship with Marguerite out of respect for the family. This could be the reason Vincent angrily referred to Gachet as a "blind man" in his letter to Theo. Vincent had experienced the same kind of blindness in the two pious priests who accused him of impregnating Stien. He had also once envisioned the Rev. Stricker, Kee's father, as a father with "a very terrible weapon"— the key to the front door. If Dr. Gachet confronted Vincent with the same terrible weapon, it could have produced a violent reaction. An ultimatum by Gachet barring Vincent from his daughter's company, or forbidding him to use her as a model, would have been perceived by Vincent as rejection, although it would have been natural for the doctor to protect his daughter, Vincent being a mental patient. Gachet, however, makes no mention of Vincent's threatening him with a gun in his memoir, *The Seventy Days of Van Gogh in Auvers.* (Of course, it is understandable that Gachet might prefer not to discuss this incident, as this encounter could link the doctor to Vincent's death.)

Still, what remains baffling about Vincent's death is the nature of the wound itself. Why did Vincent choose to shoot himself above the stomach? A bullet to the head would have accomplished his presumed purpose with more certainty. Indeed, it could be that Vincent's intent was to shoot himself only as an act of self-mutilation, an act of penance, and that his subsequent death was in fact an accident and not a suicide attempt at all.

It could well be that the bullet he shot into his stomach was intended to end not his life but rather his keen emotional pain, for the bullet was directed at the organ where, at that time, it was believed the emotions of anguish and fear were most intensely felt. Vincent's ultimately fatal act could have been another of his attempts to perform surgery—to root out the cause of three decades of emotional pain.

Whereas Vincent's distress over Theo's financial difficulties and unhappy marriage were undoubtedly contributing factors, it seems more plausible that it was Dr. Gachet who provoked Vincent's decision to harm himself—only this time, the self-mutilation proved fatal. This, then, begs the question: Was it intentional? In a clever act of homicide, did Gachet use his skills as a psychologist to commit murder and protect his daughter from a man he considered an undesirable and unstable marriage prospect.

While Dr. Decker acknowledges that it is possible for a psychiatrist or psychologist to murder a patient by knowing the right buttons to push, he does not believe Gachet did it intentionally. "Dr. Gachet was a man of healing and his training was to preserve life, but *subconsciously* he may have wished Vincent harm because Vincent posed a threat to his daughter's welfare."

Dr. Gachet's housekeeper, Louise Chevalier, had warned the doctor of Marguerite's sexual attraction to Vincent. Mme. Chevalier was single, and it was rumored in the village that Dr. Gachet was the father of her infant daughter Elisa. Jealous of Marguerite's place in his life, Mme. Chevalier wanted more of his attention for her own daughter. When asked by the doctor for substantiation, Mme. Chevalier replied: "I have a woman's intuition."

Where did Vincent get the gun? Revolvers were available for 5 francs apiece from any hardware store, and in fact were commonly given out by hardware merchants as bonus gifts. One source says Vincent's landlord, Ravoux, was the owner of the gun, but Ravoux himself denied this claim. He did have a gun in a box of fishing tackle, but it was rusty and incapable of being fired. The most likely explanation is that the gun belonged to Gachet. Gachet had been an army captain, and a framed photograph in his house to this day shows him in full military uniform, complete with saber and pistol in a hip holster. That a doctor would provide a mental patient with a gun for any purpose would seem to be remarkably shortsighted, although it is possible that Gachet's judgment had been clouded by Vincent's threat to his daughter. As Vincent's psychiatrist, Gachet no doubt knew all about Vincent's failed relationships, so he would naturally fear for his daughter's happiness if she married him. Moreover, Vincent may have had syphilis, and, if so, Gachet would have known this; references in Vincent's letters indicate that he visited Theo's doctor, who specialized in the treatment of the disease.

When Vincent went to see Gachet for the last time, a violent discussion ensued. Gachet admitted that he and Vincent had had a falling-out, but he claimed it was over a trivial matter—a disagreement over the appropriate frame for a painting. The argument must have been far more serious, however; for, according to an eyewitness, Adeline Ravoux, at Vincent's deathbed, he refused to make eye contact with the doctor, and the two did not speak to each other. Adeline Ravoux was the thirteen-year-old daughter of the café owner and one of Vincent's models; she recalled that when Vincent was asked the reason for the suicide attempt, he replied, "It was the best for everyone." Vincent refused to say where he had obtained the gun or where it could be located, and Gachet remained tight-lipped, even to the police when they investigated the incident.

Thirty-eight years after Dr. Gachet's death in 1928, a Paris doctor, Dr. Victor Doiteau, published a book about Vincent's madness titled *La Folie de Vincent van Gogh,* in which he states that Vincent had threatened Gachet with a pistol in the doctor's house. Rebuffed by the doctor, Vincent then left, and two days later he shot himself. Dr. Doiteau claimed that the incident was witnessed by Gachet's two children, Paul, Jr. and Marguerite, and quoted Paul as saying, "We were rooted to the ground, fearful our father would be killed." This confrontation between Vincent and Gachet appears in numerous other van Gogh biographies, including one by the highly respected art historian, the late John Rewald. In his book *Post-Impressionism* (1979), he comments: "It seems utterly inconceivable that Dr. Gachet would not have tried to disarm the painter and would have left a pistol in his friend's possession." Another biographer, M. E. Tralbaut, includes the episode in *Van Gogh le Mal-Aime* (1969), stating: "Paul Gachet Jr. and his sister Marguerite . . . have told us more than once that they had been present at the scene, standing there as if rooted to the ground. They had experienced minutes of terrible anxiety they were never to forget."

Antonin Artaud, the French avant-garde writer and dramatic theorist, claimed that Vincent had died "because he had, alas, reached the end of his dismal and revolting story of a man strangled by an evil spirit," and pronounced Dr. Gachet the evil spirit. "For it is not because of himself that van Gogh abandoned life. It was under the presence of the evil influence, two days before his death, of Dr. Gachet, a so-called psychiatrist, which was the direct, effective and sufficient cause of his death." Artaud, who had himself spent time in an asylum, concluded: "When I read van Gogh's letters to his brother, I was left with the firm and sincere conviction that Dr. Gachet, 'psychiatrist,' actually detested van Gogh. . . ."

Artaud's opinion that Gachet detested Vincent may be a harsh conclusion, but perhaps the doctor at least feared him. What specifically in Vincent's letters could Artaud have interpreted as evidence of hatred directed at Vincent by the doctor? There is one sentence that spotlights it like a beacon: Vincent's claim that "I think we must not count on Dr. Gachet *at all.*" Vincent then goes on to say "He is sicker than I am. . . . Now when one blind man leads another blind man, don't they both end up in the ditch?" Vincent's *"at all"* is so definitive, so final, that it could be the red flag that aroused Artaud's suspicion. Gachet is no longer deemed a friend or a brother. For some reason, Vincent has felt betrayed. Gachet had replaced Gauguin as a brother substitute; he had bolstered Vincent's confidence and provided intellectual stimulation for his art. But no more. Could it be that in Vincent's subconscious, Gachet had been suddenly transformed into an enemy as a result of a betrayal? If so, again, the enemy had to be attacked.

Another person who spoke out vehemently against Dr. Gachet was Germaine Ravoux, an eyewitness and Adeline's younger sister. Although she was only two years old at the time of Vincent's death, she later heard reports of the incident from her parents and her older sister. In 1965, when Pierre Leprohon completed his manuscript for *Vincent van Gogh,* he sent a draft to Germaine for her review. She replied: "You will not be surprised if I tell you that I rushed to read the chapter in your book dealing with the death of poor Mr. Vincent and saw with satisfaction that you doubt the presence of Dr. Gachet and his son at his bedside during his final moments. In point of fact my father watched over Mr. Vincent with Theo. The father and son came to the burial and then to the house to take away as many paintings as possible, Dr. Gachet taking them off the walls and handing them to his son ... under the stupefied gaze of my father who thought their actions scandalous. In the end all of this happened a long time ago, and I do not wish to fight Dr. Gachet who has made a huge gift to the Louvre Museum of Vincent's work, and who *thanks to his lies* has made Vincent van Gogh known to the world, can I? Yet last night, listening to radio station Luxembourg, I couldn't contain my indignation at hearing such lies."

What lies could she have been referring to? Certainly there was Gachet's lame reason for his breakup with Vincent: an argument over the choice of a picture frame! Another lie might have been Dr. Gachet's newfound admiration for the man and his art in hyperbolic statements like the following, which was quoted by Jo in one of her memoirs: "The more I think of it, the more I think Vincent was a giant. Not a day passes that I do not think of his pictures. I always find there a new idea, something different each day ... I think again of the painter and I think of him as a colossus. Besides, he was a philosopher."

In Vincent's last letter to Theo and Jo is the likely answer to Vincent's breakup with Gachet. It *had* to be about Marguerite, and it is contained in Vincent's statement *"That desire [for marriage] has left me, though the mental suffering of it remains."* In a moment of crisis over his support payment, why would Vincent even write about marriage and relate it to his current mental anguish, *unless his hope of a marriage to Marguerite had been dashed?* Moreover, was it the love between Vincent and Marguerite that had sustained Vincent through the recent trauma with Theo and Jo? Was it the germinating force of love that helped Vincent produce his finest work in spite of the emotional whirlwind swirling around him? Love had been absent during his year at the asylum. The three paintings of Marguerite show her in romantic situations: as a bride in a wedding garden, playing the piano in a romantic pink gown, and walking down the aisle with Vincent in a cathedral of trees.

Seattle-based neurotherapist Terence Swaine agrees with this conclusion, stating: "Vincent was possibly mistaken about Gachet initially. Gachet maintained an impervious professional front until his intuition told him that Vincent was a threat to his daughter's welfare. He became sufficiently alarmed to let slip his mask of professional concern, showing his real feelings for Vincent, who was taken aback, shocked, disillusioned with a man he had thought a brother and friend.

"Gachet was an artist manqué (a wanna-be artist) and was probably jealous of Vincent's artistic genius. From Vincent's letters to Theo and Jo it is clear that Gachet lost control of his self-esteem and his fears, and hence lost his patient's trust. If Gachet warned Vincent to stop seeing Marguerite, one wonders what Marguerite's reaction might have been. She could have acquiesced to her father's command or rejected Vincent's advances at a critical moment, or both. The rejection scenario is a strong one: Jo and Theo by association; Gachet acting out of fear, dropping his defenses; and Marguerite perhaps bending to her father's will. Other cumulative pressures contributing to Vincent's dilemma could have been despair at not being able to earn a living from his career, and no further prospect of marriage, a wife and children. This anxiety could have caused self-recrimination for being 'deceived,' forcing Vincent to react in a familiar pattern of behavior—by first threatening his betrayer with violence and then turning the violence against himself."

Jan Hulsker draws the parallel in his biography: "Vincent, in first threatening violence against a perceived betrayer (against Gachet with a gun as he had against Gauguin with a razor) and then turning the violence against himself (shooting himself in the stomach, or earlier cutting off his ear), was repeating a deep-seated psychological pattern."

With Gachet the pattern of Vincent's psychological behavior certainly appears to repeat itself. While Vincent had suffered rejection from Jo, he had weathered that emotional storm, because Theo did not support her demand that he withdraw financial support, and perhaps also because Vincent felt bolstered by his love for Marguerite. Dr. Gachet's rejection was more current, though, and in light of Vincent's day-to-day involvement with the doctor's family, would have been more difficult to bear, hence Vincent's cry of anguish that he could not rely on the doctor *at all!* Judging from his paintings of Marguerite, his friendship with her was dear to him; he valued her as a model, and they had ample opportunity to spend time together whenever her father was away in Paris. Furthermore, Vincent's trust in the doctor had been implicit.

There had to be a much more serious falling-out than an argument over a picture frame. Perhaps their trivial disagreement sparked a more serious altercation. More than likely, Dr. Gachet lost his temper with Vincent over the frame, and to hurt Vincent's feelings he accused him of betraying his trust by having a sexual relationship with Marguerite. Vincent could easily have felt devastated at such an accusation, especially if he had conscientiously avoided a sexual relationship out of respect for the family. In all probability, the argument would have festered in his mind and prompted him to return to Gachet's house several days later and threaten Gachet with the pistol. Rebuffed, he left the house in a state of anger, according to the doctor's children. A clue to Vincent's anxiety stands out glaringly in his penultimate letter to Theo, declaring his complete lack of confidence in Gachet. Following on this train of thought, Vincent expresses fear of another attack: "Certainly my last attack, which was terrible, was in a large measure due to the influence of the other patients, and then the prison was crushing me. . . ."

If Vincent and Marguerite had a caring relationship, why did he not refer to it in his letters to Theo and Jo or to Wil or his mother? There could be several reasons: a concern that a relationship with his doctor's daughter might be considered controversial, a desire to wait and see how far the relationship might develop, or—most likely—that Marguerite was compliant. With Margot Begemann, who had also been a compliant partner, he wrote nothing of that relationship until she attempted suicide.

Vincent's often-painful journey to that hillside in Auvers began in an unhappy childhood darkened by his mother's chronic melancholy, as she mourned the loss of his dead older brother. The love she denied Vincent he sought in a series of eventually disastrous relationships, and his hopes of realizing a perfect love were repeatedly subverted into crushing disappointments. He was rejected by the daughter of his London landlady, a girl secretly engaged to another man. To devastating effect, he was rejected by his cousin Kee, and in a dramatic showdown with her father, he held his hand over a lantern's flame to prove his love and displace his emotional pain. His affections for the prostitute Sien rejected and his hopes of domestic bliss dashed, Vincent managed to tear himself from a heart-wrenching situation, only to soon find himself in another: Margot Bergemann attempted suicide. Then, unjustly accused by two priests for fathering an illegitimate child with one of their parishioners, he fled Holland for Antwerp and eventually Paris and Provence. Ostracism, rejection, misunderstanding, and antipathy hounded him, until he found in Gauguin a kindred spirit, a muse and mentor, a friend—or thought he had. Gauguin's departure left more than Vincent's ear mutilated, as this event sparked the seizures, blackouts, and suicidal feelings that would haunt him until he ended them nineteen months later in Auvers, in July 1890.

At the graveside, Gachet, choking back tears and barely audible, eulogized Vincent, saying: "He was an honest man and a great artist, and there were only two things important to him: humanity and art."

Gachet's graveside behavior could indeed have been prompted by a dawning realization that he had probably contributed to Vincent's death. His tears may have been more the result of profound grief and guilt over his role in Vincent's death than the expression of a genuine love for him. It is conceivable that Dr. Gachet prided himself on being "an honest man" and could no longer hide from himself his role in the death of a man he both admired and feared.

Postscript

VINCENT'S
VICTORY

A preliminary sketch for a still-ife painting with coffeepot, 1888, with notes showing color scheme, included in a letter to Theo.

> It would be really a remarkable book if one could see the way Vincent
> thought, and how much he remained himself.
>
> —*Letter from Theo to his mother, September 8, 1890*
>
> **Who will write that book about Vincent?**
>
> —*Johanna van Gogh-Bonger, in a memoir, March 6, 1891*

Since the day Vincent died, July 30, 1890, biographers have debated the nature of Vincent's mental illness. Most claim that he suffered from a form of epilepsy; others hold that he was schizophrenic. Or did his problems arise from drinking absinthe, a potent anise-flavored French liqueur? Or from his habit of licking the tips of his brushes, with their residue of poisonous lead-based oil paints? Some have suggested that Ménière's disease— a disorder of the inner ear that induces dizziness and tinnitus— caused Vincent to cut off his ear, but his letters do not refer to dizziness or distortions of sound. In his letters, Vincent complained of spells of confusion, which included sleepwalking, a feeling of emptiness in the head, a stuporous state, the ingestion of paint and turpentine. He also had hallucinations in which he saw details of his native village, Groot Zundert, with amazing clarity, and paranoid delusions in which he imagined he was being followed by an angry mob and by the police. He was afraid of being poisoned. He had nightmares. He lived in a state of anxiety that easily turned into violent behavior, and his mental and physical convulsions were strong enough to cause him to fall to the ground.

Bit by bit, the speculation over Vincent's mental disorder has been stripped away. Epilepsy would not account for his prolonged periods of highs and lows. In fact, an article published by the Van Gogh Foundation in 2003 agreed with P. H. Vesceuil, a neuroscientist, who stated that "Epilepsy as we define it today was not the most probable diagnosis in van Gogh's case" and that an accurate assessment of Vincent's psychological profile inhabited a borderline region between neurology and psychiatry. Neither lead poisoning nor absinthe abuse reasonably explains his symptoms, because his melancholy moods began before he started drinking heavily or painting. Psychiatrists disagree about schizophrenia, a psychosis characterized by withdrawal from reality and by highly variable, irrational emotional or behavioral disturbances, as Vincent enjoyed long periods of clear thinking between his devastating lows. Indeed, his letters reveal that he was well aware of his erratic behavior, keenly self-analytical about his disorder, and completely rational about his goals in life. Furthermore, Vincent's seizures were clearly connected to his intense anxiety and melancholia either over emotional rejection or from vivid memories of it; and indeed the seizures and anxiety both—i.e., the physiological ramifications of the psychological disorder—may have been rooted in the same neurological cause. (Also, while schizophrenics are known to have a distorted sense of color that heightens their color perception, Vincent's color choices were deliberate exaggerations.)

Psychiatric medicine and research in the past century has evolved a much better understanding of mental illness. The evidence in Vincent's case today would seem to indicate that he suffered from bipolar syndrome, or manic-depression, a mental illness characterized by alternating periods of euphoria and depression as well as by suicidal tendencies. Of course, in Vincent's day little was known about mental illness, and manic-depression had not yet been identified as a disease. In the end, the culmination of such intense emotional disappointment, combined with his implacable, manic depression, proved to be simply too much for Vincent to bear.

The connection between creative genius and manic-depression has been well documented by biographers of numerous artists—among them, other Impressionist painters like Pissarro, Renoir, and Cézanne, all of whom sought treatment from Dr. Gachet. Add to them such notable literary figures as Lord Byron, Edgar Allan Poe, Ernest Hemingway, Winston Churchill, F. Scott Fitzgerald, and Virginia Woolf.

Dr. Alfred J. Lubin offers insight into Vincent's psychological problems in his book *Stranger on the Earth.* He convincingly identifies Vincent's Oedipus complex (a desire to kill his father in order to marry his mother), and then traces his continuous search for a father figure in the person of his brother Theo (whom he regularly referred to as "father number two"), also "Jet" Mauve, Adolphe Monticelli, and various other teachers and companions, especially Tersteeg, Roulin, and Gachet. Dr. Lubin also was the first to describe the "Replacement Child Syndrome" resulting from his mother's using Vincent to replace a namesake stillborn exactly a year earlier. Dr. Vincent W. van Gogh, Vincent's nephew, writing a review of Lubin's book in 1973, stated: "The very strong desire to have a feminine figure care for him is an unconscious replacement of a strong bond to the mother figure, a condition which strengthens the leaning towards masochism. It is the fighting against self-damage which brings Vincent to his great activity in painting."

Significantly, Vincent's family history was rife with mental illness, and he ran a high genetic risk for manic-depression from birth. Two of his uncles were diagnosed with mental illnesses;

his mother suffered chronic depression; Wil ended her days in an asylum; and his brother Cor committed suicide ten years after Vincent's death. His mind racked by guilt over Vincent's suicide and his mental health seriously compromised by tertiary syphilis, which attacks the brain, Theo himself died within six months of his brother's passing, in an asylum for the insane, the Willem Arnstz Clinic near Utrecht. He was sent there after he tried repeatedly to attack his wife and child. Though the cause of his death was officially liver failure, he exhibited symptoms of a mental delirium similar to Vincent's. Jo had Theo's body moved to Auvers, so the two brothers could be buried side by side. The graveyard commands a hillside that to this day is still surrounded by immense fields of golden grain.

Marguerite Clementine Gachet did not attend Vincent's funeral, but she was spotted the next day, in tears, walking to Vincent's gravesite with a bunch of sunflowers in her hands. Marguerite never married. She remained in her father's house, where she lived as a recluse in later years; she died in 1949 at age seventy-nine. Dr. Gachet himself passed away in 1909 at the age of eighty-one, making him sixty-two years old at the time of Vincent's death. His son, Paul, Jr., died after Marguerite, and since neither he nor his sister ever had children, with them ended the Gachet line.

Gauguin did not attend Vincent's funeral because he was in Le Pouldu, Britanny, where he was painting and trying to scrape together enough money to purchase a ticket to Tahiti so that he could pursue Vincent's idea for a "School of the Tropics." Gauguin said he wished to end his days in Tahiti. He judged that his art was only a seedling thus far, and out in Tahiti he hoped to cultivate it for his own pleasure, its primitive and savage state. He sent a letter of condolence to Theo, which read:

> My dear Van Gogh:
>
> We have just received your sad news which greatly distresses us!
>
> In these circumstances, I don't want to write the usual phrases of condolence—you know that for me he was a sincere friend; and that he was an *artist,* a rare thing in our epoch. You will continue to see him in his works. As Vincent used often to say—Stone will perish, the word will remain.
>
> As for me, I shall see him with my eyes and with my heart in his works.
>
> > Cordially, ever yours
> >
> > P. Gauguin

In April 1891, less than a year following Vincent's death, Gauguin set sail from Marseilles by steamship. He arrived in Tahiti just in time to witness the funeral of the last native ruler, King Pomare V, and to realize that France's colonization had already begun to change the Polynesians' carefree culture and the traditions he had come to paint. In Gauguin's view, Tahiti's rich traditional culture had become, under French colonial rule, a comical copy of France. Overzealous missionaries had virtually eliminated the Tahitians' ancient religious beliefs and mythology, there had been much cross-breeding with Europeans, and the native population had been greatly depleted by European-introduced smallpox, alcoholism, and sexually transmitted diseases.

In search of native Polynesians who still clung to the old customs, and especially of the island's bare-breasted women, he borrowed a horse and rode to the wildest part of the coast, little visited by Europeans. A couple invited him to share a meal of bananas and shellfish, and asked the purpose of his visit. When he replied "To find a wife," the woman offered to bring him a likely candidate, and returned fifteen minutes later with her own daughter, a thirteen-year-old adolescent, Tehura. Gauguin described her as beautiful, and wrote in his journal:

> Through her dress of almost transparent rose-colored muslin one could see the golden skin of her shoulders and arms. Two swelling buds rose on the breasts. She was a child, slender, strong, of wonderful proportions. . . . Even her hair was exceptional, thick like a bush and a little crispy. In the sunlight it was all an orgy of chrome.
>
> I greeted her, she smiled and sat down beside me.
>
> "Aren't you afraid of me?" I asked
>
> "Aito (no)."
>
> "Do you wish to live in my hut for always?"
>
> "Eha (yes)."

Gauguin, aged forty-three, described how this child of thirteen (according to him, traditionally the marriageable age for Tahitian women) charmed him, made him timid, and almost frightened him. A simple ceremony was conducted in which a goblet of fresh water was passed around, and Gauguin agreed that Tehura could return to her mother in eight days to confirm whether she was happy; if she was, he could keep her. That night, Gauguin took her as his Polynesian bride while still married to his first wife, Mette, and corresponding affectionately with her in Denmark.

On the eighth day, he made good his promise for Tehura to return to her mother and fretted that his new bride might not return to him, for she had not been very talkative, seemed to study him suspiciously, and held back her feelings.

"The following days were full of torment," he recalled in his journal. "I was unable to fix my thought on any work." A week passed and Tehura finally returned. He wrote ecstatically, "Then life filled to the full with happiness began. Happiness and work rose up together with the sun, radiant like it. The gold of Tehura's face flooded the interior of our hut and the landscape around about with joy and light. She no longer studied me, and I no longer studied her. She no longer concealed her love from me, and I no longer spoke to her of my love. We lived, both of us in perfect simplicity." He imagined themselves as Adam and Eve in Paradise. "I was permeated with her fragrance—noa noa," he wrote. "She came into my life at the perfect hour. Earlier perhaps I might not have understood her, and later it would have been too late. Today I understand how much I love her, and through her I enter into mysteries which hitherto remained inaccessible to me. . . . By the daily telling of her life she leads me, more surely than it could have been done any other way, to a full understanding of her race."

In the fall of 1892, he announced to a friend that Tehura was pregnant and boasted, "I am sowing my seed everywhere."

Gauguin's first stay in Tahiti lasted almost two years, in which time he completed sixty-six canvases and what he described as "some ultra barbaric sculptures." After he returned to France, he took as a mistress and model another adolescent, a homeless thirteen-year-old Javanese girl named Anna, whom he found wandering the streets of Paris. Meanwhile, he had received a legacy of 13,000 francs from an uncle, and some of his Tahitian paintings were purchased at exhibition. He also negotiated a contract to supply the Paris art dealer Ambrose

Vollard with more work in return for a monthly retainer. His financial difficulties thus eased, he returned to Tahiti in September 1895 to find, to his disgust, that the capital, Papeete, had been fitted with electric lights. He complained to Mette: "Tahiti is becoming completely French. Our missionaries have already imported much hypocrisy and they are sweeping away part of the poetry." Dismayed at seeing his island Eden blighted so much by European influence, he campaigned unsuccessfully for native rights and autonomy. In September 1901, after he failed to institute a return to exoticism for the native population through newspaper articles, he sailed for the Marquesas Islands, 750 miles northeast of Tahiti, in a more remote part of French Polynesia. Confronted there with similar disrespect for Polynesian culture, he feuded with a local Roman Catholic bishop over the Church's interpretation of sin and angered the governor, who had him briefly imprisoned for libel. Gauguin died in the Marquesas of complications from syphilis at age fifty-one, on May 8, 1903, his work at the time still largely unrecognized. It was not until Vollard organized a retrospective exhibition of Gauguin's work in Paris in 1906 that Gauguin's reputation was finally assured.

Toulous-Lautrec, early in 1901, was confined to a mental institution at Neuilly, near Paris, after he collapsed in the street in a state of delirium, a consequence of drinking too much absinthe. Deprived of alcohol, he recovered and was released, but in September the same year he died of a stroke, aged thirty-seven.

The prostitute Clasina (Sien) Maria Hoornick commited suicide in 1904, by drowning.

Wilhelmina Jacoba van Gogh (Wil) began to suffer mental problems following Vincent's death. She enjoyed some brief success as a garden writer, but spent the last forty years of her life in an asylum in Holland. She twice attempted suicide, once by submerging her head in a toilet and on another occasion by trying to push knitting needles through her skull into her brain. She died in 1941 at age seventy-nine.

It was Jo who was ultimately responsible for establishing Vincent's reputation as a great artist. With Theo's death, she inherited the entire collection of paintings, drawings, and letters stored at the Paris apartment and Père Tanguy's art supply store.

Jo's brother André considered Vincent's art worthless and a burden. He suggested that she burn it. None of Vincent's surviving relatives wanted any of the paintings, and they were happy to relinquish their rights to any of his work. Vincent's art could easily have died with him. But Jo persevered: she moved from Paris to Amsterdam, where she made her living running a boardinghouse, and in her spare time she tirelessly enlisted the support of leading Dutch artists, notably Jan Steen and Isaac Israels, to keep Vincent's work in the public eye. Jo organized exhibitions, cataloged Vincent's tremendous volume of work, for the first time translated his letters from the original French into Dutch. Within ten years of his death, Jo had succeeded in making the name Vincent van Gogh synonymous with artistic genius.

In 1901, Jo remarried, her second husband being the painter and art critic Johan Cohan-Gosschalk. In 1905, a large van Gogh exhibition was held at the Stedelijk Museum. When her husband died in 1912, Jo reverted to her former married name, Jo van Gogh-Bonger. She died of Parkinson's disease in 1925 at age sixty-two. She was halfway through a translation of Vincent's letters into English.

How appropriate, too, that "the little one"—Vincent's nephew and godson Vincent Willem van Gogh—should succeed his mother as head of the Van Gogh Foundation and persuade the Dutch government to create a magnificent museum dedicated to Vincent's art in Amsterdam. The National Museum Vincent van Gogh was opened by her majesty Queen Juliana of the Netherlands on June 2, 1973. After this, he continued to steer the work of his uncle to even wider recognition by accompanying exhibitions of Vincent's paintings to other countries. Under his guidance, the work of his uncle reached even greater heights of artistic acclaim to command a reverence unparalleled by other artists, and to establish record prices at art auction houses worldwide.

What greater love could any man desire?

APPENDIX

To better understand the life of Vincent van Gogh, I followed in his tracks throughout Holland and, more extensively, in France, where he developed and perfected his unique artistic style, first in bohemian Montmartre, and then in the picturesque communities of Arles, St.-Remy, Sts. Maries-de-la-Mer, and Auvers. The villages, especially, offered Vincent an environment rich in human subjects for his portraits and natural sites for his landscapes, for he enjoyed exploring miles and miles of countryside on foot. An astute observer of nature, he would trek forth in all weather, with his canvases and paints slung over his shoulder, until some feature of the landscape would arrest his eye with a beauty that was often overlooked by others: the vigor of the ivy-girdled trees in the garden of the Asylum of St. Paul at St.-Remy, the power of a rising sun, the energy in a windswept field of ripening wheat. Understandably, the towns associated with Vincent's life and art have preserved their links with him. Here are some of the places I particularly enjoyed visiting during my research:

Arles, Provence. Many of the bookstores around the Place du Forum sell a booklet titled "Arles Van Gogh," with maps and photographs showing the locations of some of his best-known subjects, all within walking distance, including the famous *Langlois Bridge, Garden of the Poets, Night Cafe,* and *The Yellow House.* In the center of Arles, the hospital where he recuperated after cutting off his ear is now a crafts center; its courtyard garden has been restored to emulate his famous painting of it.

St.-Remy, Provence. Both the office of tourism and local bookstores offer maps that show the location of Vincent's subjects, most of which are within an easy walk of the Asylum of Saint Paul on the edge of town. The asylum itself is still a facility for the treatment of the mentally ill, so parts of it are closed to the public. However, a replica of Vincent's room and a hydrotherapy room can be visited, and marked trails outside the asylum walls direct visitors to the sites where he painted *The Alpilles Mountains, The Roman Quarry, The Olive Orchard,* and *The Poppy Field.* A road runs from the asylum through a mountain pass to a beautiful vineyard, the Mas de la Dam, which Vincent painted in resplendent autumn colors.

Sts. Maries-de-la-Mer, Camargue. Vincent visited this charming resort town on the Mediterranean coast for a long weekend during the time he was living in Arles. The office of tourism provides directions to locations within walking distance where Vincent painted *The Fishing Boats, The Street of Thatched Cottages,* and *The Lavender Field.* Some of the quaint thatched cottages he painted still survive and can be rented for holiday stays. The town is famous for its wildlife preserve and marshes, with their colonies of nesting flamingoes and herds of wild horses.

Auvers-sur-Oise, near Paris. A map from the tourist office in the Manoire des Colombiers, located in the center of town, shows the route to Vincent's grave, in a walled cemetery that is surrounded by wheat fields where he shot himself. Visitors climb the steep hill to leave flowers on the ivy-covered grave, which lies next to that of his brother Theo. Open to the public are sites where Vincent painted, among others, *Dr. Gachet's House, The Chateau at Auvers,* and *The Church at Auvers.*

Gauguin Museum, Tahiti, French Polynesia. At Vincent's urging, Gauguin left France within a year of Vincent's death to paint in Tahiti, where he produced his finest work. Gauguin's house and garden in Tahiti still survive, in private ownership. The Gauguin Museum, at a separate location, stands in a coconut grove beside a magnificent sandy beach where Gauguin briefly occupied a hut. The property has beautiful tropical plantings and exhibit areas featuring reproductions of every one of Gauguin's known paintings, some original carvings, and a great many artifacts, including his writings, ceramics, drawings, archive photographs, and biographical information.

CHRONOLOGY

1853   Born March 30 at Groot Zundert, Holland. Named Vincent after an earlier child who had been stillborn on the same date one year earlier.

1857   Birth of Theo, Vincent's brother, with whom Vincent developed a close bond that endured until his death.

1869   Employed as a clerk at The Hague branch of Goupil & Company, an art dealership, where he established a close friendship with H. G. Tersteeg, the youthful manager, and his close-knit family.

1873   Promoted to London branch of Goupil & Company. Made a promising start as a sales dealer, but after the rejection of his affections by his landlady's daughter, Eugenie Loyer, he suffered a personality change and became sullen and argumentative with customers.

1875   Transferred to Paris branch of Goupil & Company, where it was hoped that he would improve his demeanor. Formed a close friendship with a fellow employee, Harry Gladwell, an Englishman.

1876   Dismissed from Goupil & Company for his increasingly argumentative ways and distracting religious fervor. Returned to England, where he accepted an unpaid position as a teacher at a boys' school in Ramsgate and then at a school in Isleworth with an emphasis on religious education.

1877   Worked in a bookstore in Dordrecht, Holland. Criticized customers for their choice of reading material, became fanatically religious, and was dismissed. Moved to Amsterdam to study theology.

1878   Failed his theology exams, but accepted an evangelical position in a community of coal miners in the Borinage district of Belgium.

1879   Dismissed from evangelical duties for eccentric behavior and for possibly inciting the miners to strike for better working conditions.

1880   Began sketching and painting, mostly in somber tones. Enrolled in art classes in Brussels.

1881   Lived with his parents at Etten. Continued his painting. Fell in love with his cousin Kee, who rejected him. Found solace in the arms of an unknown prostitute.

1882   Moved to The Hague, where he took pity on a destitute, pregnant, alcoholic prostitute, Clasina "Sien" Hoornick.

1883   Ended relationship with Sien and moved to Drenthe, then moved again to live with his parents, who had moved to Nuenen.

1885   Painted one of his most important canvases, *The Potato Eaters*, but a love affair with an older woman, Margot Begemann, ended again in rejection after her attempted suicide. Falsely accused of fathering the illegitimate child of one of his young models, Gordina (Stien) de Groot (second from left in *The Potato Eaters*). He left Nuenen following the death of his father.

1886   Enrolled in art classes in Antwerp, but argued with his tutors over artistic merit and was expelled. Moved to

Paris, where he lived in Montmartre with Theo, an art dealer, and continued his art training. Befriended numerous Impressionist and Post-Impressionist painters, especially Paul Gauguin. Under the influence of Impressionism, he lightened his palette.

1888   Moved to Arles, in the south of France, where he was joined by Gauguin. Their friendship often declined into violent arguments about artistic technique. When Gauguin stormed out of the house on December 23, Vincent threatened Gauguin with a razor, and then cut off his own ear, which he presented to a prostitute at a local brothel. He suffered a total mental breakdown.

1889   Admitted himself to the Asylum of St. Paul at St.-Remy; the seizures he had experienced on Gauguin's departure continued. Received news from Theo's wife Jo that she was pregnant and wished to name the child after him if it was a boy.

1890   Left the asylum against his doctor's advice, went to Paris to see his godson and meet Jo, then moved to Auvers, where he placed himself in the care of Dr. Paul Gachet. After a falling-out with the doctor, most likely over his relationship with the doctor's daughter, Marguerite, and feeling that he had become a financial burden to his brother, in the late afternoon of July 27 he shot himself in the wheat fields above Auvers. He died before dawn on July 30, aged thirty-seven.

WHERE TO VIEW VINCENT'S ART

Though numerous museums in the United States feature Vincent's paintings, notably the Getty Museum in Los Angeles, and the Barnes Foundation in Philadelphia, the two best places to see the bulk of his work are in Holland:

Kroller-Muller State Museum, Apeldoornseweg 250, 7351 TA, Otterlo. Tel: 08382 1041. This modern art facility, in a park setting, features a large collection of Vincent's work, notably his *Sunflower* series.

Van Gogh Museum, Stadhouderskade 42, 1071 ZD, Amsterdam. Tel: 020 67 32 121. The most popular tourist attraction in Amsterdam, the special building houses the largest collection of Vincent's work, including the famous *Wheat Fields* series.

COPYRIGHTS

Today, Vincent's letters are archived at the Van Gogh Museum in Amsterdam. The copyright on these letters, originally translated by Johanna van Gogh-Bonger, has long since expired, and so Vincent's letters are now in the public domain.

However, for many portions of this book I chose to use a new translation by Robert G. Harrison of Montreal, who granted permission for their use. Harrison rendered all 874 letters in PDF format so they could be downloaded from the Internet, at www.vangoghgallery.com. This Web site includes all 2,200 of Vincent's works, including oils, watercolors, and sketches.

With respect to copyright on the paintings, a recent decision by a U.S. copyright court confirmed that Vincent's paintings are also in the public domain. The basis for this decision was the court's view that a photograph of a painting in the public domain is insufficiently distinct from the original to be protected by copyright. That applies to all the paintings and sketches used in this book. The same is true of the archival photography.

Photographs by Derek Fell of locations such as Vincent's gravesite at Auvers, the Asylum of Saint Paul, and Arles Hospital are the exclusive copyright of Derek Fell, and their reproduction is prohibited without his permission.

BIBLIOGRAPHY

Sources

The letters of Vincent van Gogh are deposited in the archives of the Van Gogh Foundation, Amsterdam, adjacent to the Van Gogh Museum. These include letters to Theo, to the women in his life, and to miscellaneous friends. Mostly written in French, they were first published in Dutch by Johanna van Gogh-Bonger in 1914, and then translated into English. Several independent translations have also been made, the most recent by Robert G. Harrison of Montreal, whose translation can be freely read on the Internet at www.vangoghgallery.com.

Books and Documents Consulted

Artaud, Antonin, *Van Gogh le Suicide de la Societe,* Paris, Editions Gallimard, 1974.

Collins, Bradley, *Van Gogh and Gauguin,* Boulder, Westview Press, 2001.

Couffy, Annick, *La Maison du Doctor Gachet,* Pontois, Conseil General du Val d'Oise, 2003.

Bonafoux, Pascal, *Van Gogh the Passionate Eye,* London, Thames & Hudson, 1992.

Boulon, Jean-Marc, *Vincent van Gogh a Saint-Paul de-Mausole,* Saint-Remy-de-Provence, Association Saint-Paul-de-Mausole, 2003.

Brooks, David, *www.vangoghgallery.com,* Vincent van Gogh: The Complete Works World Wide Web site.

Danielsson, Bengt, *Gauguin in the South Seas,* New York, Doubleday, 1966.

Dennvir, Bernard, *Encyclopaedia of Impressionism,* London, Thames & Hudson, 1990.

Doiteau, Victor, and Edgar Leroy, *La Folie de Vincent van Gogh,* Paris, Aesculape, 1928.

Emery, Edward, *The Ghost in the Mother: Strange Attractors and Impossible Mourning,* Posted to Psyche Matters, May 31, 2001.

Gauguin, Paul, *Noa Noa,* New York, Nicholas L. Brown, 1919.

Harrison, Robert G., *Dear Theo ... Dear Vincent ...* A CD-ROM containing the complete correspondence of Vincent van Gogh, *www.vangoghgallery.com.*

Hulsker, Jan, *Vincent & Theo van Gogh: A Dual Biography,* Ann Arbor, Fuller Publications, 1990.

Lambert, Craig, "Van Gogh's Malady," *Harvard Magazine,* May 2, 2002.

Leprohon, Pierre, *Vincent van Gogh,* Paris, Editions du Valhermeil, 2001.

Lubin, Dr. Albert J., *Stranger on Earth,* New York, Holt, Rienhart and Winston, 1972.

Maurer, Naomi Marguiles, *The Pursuit of Spiritual Wisdom,* London, Associated University Press, 1998.

Millon, Claude, *Vincent van Gogh et Auvers sur Oise,* Saint-Thonan, Editions Cloitre, 1989.

Rewald, John, *Post-Impressionism: From van Gogh to Gauguin,* New York, Museum of Modern Art, 1956.

Sheon, Aaron, *Monticelli, His Contempories, His Influence,* Pittsburgh, Museum of Art, Carnegie Institute, 1978.

Stolwijk, Chris, and Richard Thompson, *Theo van Gogh,* Holland, Waanders, 1999.

Thompson, Belinda, *Gauguin,* London, Thames & Hudson, 1987.

Tralbaut, Marc Edo, V*incent van Gogh,* New York, Viking, 1969.

van Gogh, Johanna, *The Complete Letters of Vincent van Gogh,* Volumes I, II, III, Boston, Bulfinch, first edition 1958, reprinted 2000.

Vincent, 1970, Bulletin of the Rijksmuseum Vincent van Gogh, #1, volume 1 (Roulin's letters).

Vincent, 1973, Bulletin of the Rijksmuseum Vincent van Gogh, #2, volume 2 (Opening of the Museum, Vincent's time in The Hague).

Vincent, 1973, Bulletin of the Rijksmuseum Vincent van Gogh, #4, volume 2 (Vos family, Psychoanalysis of Vincent).

Vincent, 1974, Bulletin of the Rijksmuseum Vincent van Gogh, #1, volume 3 (Anthon van Rappard).

Vincent, 1974, Bulletin of the Rijksmuseum Vincent van Gogh, #2, volume 3 (Vincent in Paris).

Vincent, 1974, Bulletin of the Rijksmuseum Vincent van Gogh, #3, volume 3 (Family relationships).

Vincent, 1974, Bulletin of the Rijksmuseum Vincent van Gogh, #4, volume 3 (Reverend Stricker).

Vincent, 1975, Bulletin of the Rijksmuseum Vincent van Gogh, #2, volume 4 (Replacement child dynamics, the Loyers, Harry Gladwell).

Vincent, 1975, Bulletin of the Rijksmuseum Vincent van Gogh, #3, volume 4 (Michelet, Zola, and The Lady in Black).

Vincent, 1976, Bulletin of the Rijksmuseum Vincent van Gogh, #4, volume 4 (Gauguin, Emile Bernard).

Walther, F. Ingo, and Rainer Metzger, *Van Gogh: The Complete Paintings,* Cologne, Taschen, 1990.

Weisberg, Gabriel P., *Montmartre and the Making of Mass Culture*, New Brunswick, Rutgers University Press, 2003.

Wylie, Anne Styles, *Vincent's Childhood and Adolescence*, Amsterdam, Van Gogh Foundation, 1975.

INDEX

ABOUT THE AUTHOR

Derek Fell was born and educated in England. After time spent as an investigative reporter and illustrator with the Shrewsbury Chronicle newspaper group, and as an account executive at a public relations agency in London, he emigrated to the USA to become a U.S. citizen.

Following a period spent as catalog manager for Burpee Seeds, Fell began creating an extensive stock photo library of plants and gardens for publication worldwide. A regular contributor of garden features to *Architectural Digest* magazine, his reputation as a leading nature photographer was enhanced by a series of award-winning books, including *Renoir's Garden* (Frances Lincoln), *The Impressionist Garden* (Frances Lincoln), *Secrets of Monet's Garden* (Friedman/Fairfax), *Van Gogh's Gardens* (Simon & Schuster), and *Cézanne's Garden* (Simon & Schuster). His wall calendar *Monet's Garden* is sold at the Monet Museum, Giverny, in addition to a photographic art poster titled *Monet's Bridge*. He worked as a garden consultant to the White House during the Ford administration and has lectured on the impressionist painters at the Smithsonian Institution, the Barnes Foundation, and the Philadelphia Museum of Art. His work was also profiled in *Nature's Best Photography*, by the Natural History television channel.

Fell's books and calendars now total more than a hundred publications. Married with three children, he lives with his wife Carolyn at historic Cedaridge Farm in Bucks County, Pennsylvania.

For more information about the author's books and awards, visit *www.derekfell.net*.